HARRIS
LEBUS

HARRIS LEBUS

A Romance with the Furniture Trade

PAUL COLLIER

First published in 2020 by Green Frigate Books

Green Frigate Books is an imprint of Libri Publishing.

Copyright © Paul Collier

The right of Paul Collier to be identified as the author of this work has been asserted in accordance with the Copyright, Designs and Patents Act, 1988.

ISBN 978-1-911451-06-8

A CIP catalogue record for this book is available from The British Library

Cover and book design by Carnegie Book Prouction

Printed in the UK by Severn, Gloucester

Libri Publishing
Brunel House
Volunteer Way
Faringdon
Oxfordshire
SN7 7YR
Tel: +44 (0)845 873 3837

www.libripublishing.co.uk

Dedication

*This book is dedicated to the memory of
Oliver Hart Herman Lebus*

1918–2009

Acknowledgements

I have numerous individuals to acknowledge and thank for their assistance with this work – far too many to name.

I was fortunate enough to be afforded the enormous privilege of meeting with the closest descendants of Harris Lebus amongst the now-large Lebus family.

I have mentioned Oliver fondly, and with his son Tim, along with John and Peter, sons of LS; all have been most accommodating, truly kind and greatly supportive.

There are staff at the Geffrye Museum of the Home, Vestry House Museum (Waltham Forest Archives and Local Studies Library) and the Victoria and Albert Museum, as well as Deborah Hedgecock and the staff team at Bruce Castle Museum (Haringey Archive and Museum Service), and Rebecca Lack (whilst working at Furniture Trades Benevolent Association).

I would like to thank sponsors: Argent (Property Development) Services LLP; Lee Valley Estates; and the London School of Furniture Making.

And finally, to editor Meg Humphries.

Paul Collier, 2019

A Word from Our Sponsors…

London School of Furniture Making

I still remember the spicy plywood scent of my grandparents' walnut-veneered Harris Lebus bedroom suite: a bit of inexpensive but good, post-war furniture for the aspiring middle classes.

As a small child, I was obsessed with playing inside grandad's wardrobe. Over time, my attentions made their mark: the pull-out trays permanently askew, the hanging rail bent out of shape and the door catch broken. I'm sure my grandad was delighted with me; being a furniture salesman, he probably got it at a discount… but still.

I've no doubt the many hours spent inside that wardrobe were what drew me to making furniture for a living and, ultimately, running a furniture school. By happy coincidence, the school is just down the road from the old factory gates.

My grandparents, the suite and Harris Lebus are long gone. However, thanks to this book, the remarkable story of the world's biggest furniture factory will live on.

Helen Welch
Founder, London School of Furniture Making

Argent (Property Development) Services LLP

We are proud to sponsor this book which documents the Harris Lebus history – an important part of Tottenham Hale's industrial heritage. It is important to pay homage to an area's past, especially as it starts to change through development.

Our plans for Tottenham Hale will bring new amenities, homes and work spaces, and our ambition is that they also bring joy. Success to us will be seeing lots of different types of people break into a smile when they walk into the big new square, or look relaxed as they read a book on a bench, or bring their family to one of the restaurants.

The communities of people who already live in Tottenham are the first audience we need to impress and we want them to feel connected to the new spaces and proud of the improvements we will be making to the area. We can't build in isolation and expect them to feel engaged in what we are collectively trying to achieve for our great city or indeed understand why; we need to involve them, every step of the way.

The Argent Team

Lee Valley Estates

It is a welcomed privilege to write a few words to preface this book that recalls the extraordinary growth in the furniture industry in Tottenham in the early 1900s. The Lea Valley has a great heritage of innovation that has evolved over time through thriving small and medium-sized businesses which have established national recognition.

Harris Lebus opened his new factory at Tottenham Hale in 1901. His vision extended beyond manufacturing to the wider development of the area: he encouraged the building of homes and promoted housing growth in South Tottenham. With a regular workforce of around 3,000, doubling during the war years, many local people have memories of working at the Harris Lebus furniture factory.

Lee Valley Estates (LVE) is a family owned company that has supported regeneration in the Lea Valley for over 30 years. In 2005, the company embarked on a project to transform the former Lebus warehouse into a new urban village. Looking at Hale Village today, we share with our development partners considerable pride in creating a successful mixed community in terms of housing tenure, community facilities and employment use.

New visitors to Hale Village enter through Lebus Street and are guided by information totem posts that provide historic information about the industrial heritage of the site. The archaeological history, including surveys and artefacts, has been donated by LVE to the Bruce Castle Museum.

Lee Valley Estates is delighted to support this book and will continue to invest in facilities that support innovation and enterprise pioneered at Tottenham Hale by Harris Lebus.

Michael Polledri MBE FCA

Anthology Hale Works

Anthology is proud to sponsor this book which helps preserve the rich history of the Lebus Factory, as part of our ongoing commitment to creating a lasting legacy in the communities where we build.

Hale Works architecture has drawn inspiration from the site's previous use by the Harris Lebus Factory, built in 1900, a company famous for its Arts and Crafts style of furniture. If you look closely, you will discover motifs from these furniture designs referenced in the building's architectural detailing.

It's important to Anthology to get to know, explore and work with the community in the areas we are developing in and we are excited to be part of this project.

Contents

Foreword

Did you know that the 'largest furniture factory in the world' that employed thousands once stood in Tottenham Hale? Although long since gone, mention the world-class name of 'Lebus' today and many will recall fond memories of the furniture made there and their own personal association with it. It was Harris Lebus furniture that people often turned to when furnishing their first home or when coveting a prize piece for the best room in the house, the 'front room'

(often bought on the 'HP'). Many locals started their first jobs working in one of the many departments at Lebus, with a good proportion working through to retirement.

At Bruce Castle Museum we have been fortunate to work on exhibitions and

An advertisement for the Link range of Lebus furniture, launched in 1957 and designed to appeal to the fifties housewife

An advertisement for Lebus furniture in 'The Cabinet Maker Furniture Guide' in 1949

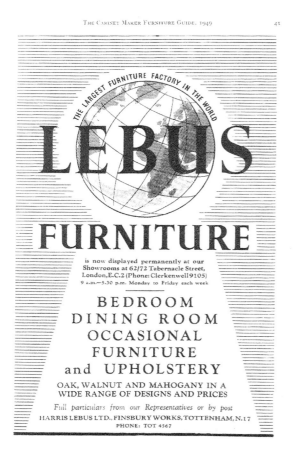

Ron Turton, polisher, is but one example from a band of loyal Lebus employees

reminiscence projects with lots of former employees who have kindly shared recollections and memories as well as donated objects, photographs and documents to the museum. The Lebus family have also generously donated to Bruce Castle Museum their very important archive and historical collections of the factory – not only a family archive but an invaluable business archive as well.

With stories from new-starters in the factory working in photography or design, to skilled workers on the factory floor including sprayers, craftsmen and cabinet-makers, often bringing their woodworking skills from Eastern Europe to Tottenham to start a new life in the UK, one thing is for sure – Lebus's is a not forgotten factory. With the wonderful collections, photographs and memories of the factory collected and cared for over many years by the Lebus family and now Bruce Castle Museum, the written history of the factory has been waiting to be researched and to inspire future generations, revealing more about its past.

Now, with the publication of this very welcome complete written history of the Harris Lebus factory, we need wait no longer. It is on one level a book of local history about a local factory, telling the story of local workers; but this history is not just of local interest. This is a story of a factory of national significance and resonance. It is the story of its founder Harris Lebus – the son of an immigrant – whose ideas, products and factory workers tell part of our national history, contributing to changing the course of furniture design, its manufacture and interior design 'taste' in this country. For the author, Paul Collier, writing this history has been a journey of discovery and love for piecing together the past – from finding remnants of the Lebus factory on his doorstep, to taking the first steps into research through his local museum and archive at Bruce Castle, and getting first-hand accounts of the factory's history from Oliver Lebus, his family and local people.

Bruce Castle Museum is grateful to many in the writing of this new work about Harris Lebus – Hazel Whitehouse (former Reminiscence Officer at Bruce Castle Museum), the Friends of Bruce Castle, Ferry Lane Action Group, Dr. Jim Lewis and the Lebus family. But most of all, our thanks go to Paul Collier for his dedication and insight in bringing this new history of the Lebus factory to life.

Deborah Hedgecock

Curator, Bruce Castle Museum (Haringey Archive and Museum Service)
October 2019

Preface

'In each of our lives occur mysterious coincidences – sudden,
synchronistic events that, once interpreted, lead us into our new
destiny… we notice those chance events that occur at just the right
moment, and bring forth just the right individuals, to suddenly send our
lives in a new and important direction.'

– James Redfield, author's note in *The Celestine Prophecy:
An Adventure*, 1993

Saturday 22 September 2007

The white Transit van carrying all my
worldly goods and chattels – and my loyal
four-legged companion Buster – spins round
the Tottenham Hale gyratory system, on to
Ferry Lane and over the humpback bridge. On
the approach to the estate, I glance to my left
at the 1950s-looking warehouse building set
well back from the road and I wonder about
its origins. As I look to my right as we pass
the end of a Victorian wall and solitary iron
gatepost with the hint of the top of a set of
descending steps, now filled in with a grassed
verge, my curiosity is again aroused. It is the
day I move to the property (where I currently
still live) on Ferry Lane Estate, Tottenham Hale
N17, and I'm happy to be moving to my new
flat.

After my move, I walk from Armadale Close
(northwards along a pathway now known as
Montrose Walk) to the estate corner shop,
which takes me through a brick-built tunnel:
a bridge carrying the rail tracks of the North
London Railway. I look up at the ironwork
bridge, the faded, peeling grey paint and the
rivets that hold it together, and wonder about
its past. A rusted, metal 'shelf' inside the tunnel
suggests to me that it once carried electric
cables through it in some distant past. Was this
the case, I wonder? And if so, when was this
and for what purpose? Several weeks pass, and
I receive a newsletter from the local residents'
association, the Ferry Lane Action Group. An
article on the inside page immediately grabs my
attention, advising that a recent council survey
concludes there is no cause to worry about any
land contamination issues… from *the former
Harris Lebus furniture factory that once stood on
our estate*.

This was my introduction to a story I knew
I wanted to learn more about. As I searched,
it appeared, to begin with, that accessible
information was scant. I learned, seemingly by

The original gatepost to the factory entrance can
still be seen at the northern end of Ferry Lane
Estate

(© Copyright Paul Collier private collection)

some hand of fate, that Haringey Local History Archives were planning an exhibition dedicated to the Harris Lebus furniture factory. Shortly after, I spotted a furniture catalogue of Harris Lebus from September 1934 for sale at a vintage bookstore. Without hesitation I purchased it online. I was bringing it *home*.

Thoughts turned to writing a book – Harris Lebus, the family furniture business. I rationalised that it was a fantasy. I had not previously attempted to write a book or felt a compulsion to do so. Sometimes I think I seldom read enough of them. But this unravelling story was a fascination and one that continues to draw me further in. I did some detective work and contacted Peter and John Lebus, who both worked for the company in its later years. They put me in touch with Oliver Lebus, grandson of company founder, Harris Lebus, who ran the company for many years. During several enjoyable afternoon meetings I spent with Oliver in the final year of his life, so much more archive material came to light that he had personally preserved. A presentation at Bruce Castle Museum to unveil the discovery of preserved World War Two air-raid shelters on Lea Valley Estates' Hale Village construction site made Oliver the guest of honour along with Peter and John. Through this acquaintance, Oliver and members of the Lebus family offered to donate the archive materials for the benefit of historians of the future; these archives were on their way *home*.

Throughout my journey into the Lebus story, I was conscious of a 'Celestine prophecy' effect (one of the few books I have read) – a phenomenon of coincidences that are somehow connected, however loosely. I met Nancy Hiller on a visit from the United States to write an article for *American Bungalow* magazine on Harris Lebus and we spent an enjoyable day together looking around the area where the factory had been. Then at an organised talk on Ferry Lane Estate by the original architect on 8 May 2011, I recognised Jack Lambert as someone I had previously been in contact with as a resident who attended neighbourhood meetings when I worked for Islington Council. Throughout the process the effect seemed to intensify; whether of significance or not, I would later discover the day when I moved to my new home was 100 years and 1 day since the death of Harris Lebus on 21 September 1907 and 100 years to the day when he was laid to rest…

Paul Collier, 2019

Introduction

'The rise of the house of Lebus is one of the romances of the furniture trade.'

– Tottenham and Edmonton Weekly Herald, 30 April 1926

Some 44 years later, on Friday 27 February 1970, the same local paper's headline read 'Lebus Shut Down – So 1,000 Will Lose Jobs'. 'Oh, it was dreadful,' recalled former employee Sissy Lewis. 'Fellas were coming along the lines shouting out, "we're finished, we're finished; we're closing down!" We all cried.

It was a terrible time because we'd spent so many years there. Me, right from a young girl and my husband from fourteen – and he was fifty-eight.' Sissy's loyal, long service and family involvement was typical of many employees of Harris Lebus, who, just as successive generations of the Lebus family had done,

Headline from the *Tottenham and Edmonton Weekly Herald*, Friday 27 February 1970

followed in their parents' footsteps. Sissy's mother had worked there during the 1914 war, filling trucks on the railway sidings.

Surely a simple, straightforward history?

When the thought to write a book about Harris Lebus and 'the largest furniture factory in the world', which stood in Tottenham Hale, North London, for a definable period of 70 years, planted itself in my mind, it would surely be a simple, but nonetheless interesting story with a clear, distinct beginning, a middle that flowed logically, and an ending that was straightforward and explicable. A man who established and developed a family-run business bearing his name, operating largely from the same, purpose-built factory (perhaps a little tweaked over time), producing trademark furniture, almost exclusively in wood, mostly to the same design influences throughout, branded, well known in its day, distinct and distinguishable to this. And whilst I was aware this romance was not destined for a happy ending, at least the indication was there as to what and when that ending would be. It proved to be anything but that simple.

Foresight to record the history of the family partnership (in part)

Five years before the firm closed its doors at Tottenham Hale, Louis Sol Lebus (nephew to Harris and referred to hereafter as 'LS') had the foresight to commit to writing a superbly detailed account of the development of the family partnership of Harris Lebus: *History of Harris Lebus 1840–1947*. Dated November 1965 and acknowledging the contribution of his cousin Louis Harris (hereafter known simply as 'Louis'), he wrote in his foreword: 'The following pages set down the story of the origin and growth of Harris Lebus until it became a public limited company in July 1947.'

Unpublished, with a limited distribution

Aside from the fact that a limited number of copies were produced, it was never published. The format and materials used – hardback cover with pages of 'typewriter' printed pages (as opposed to professional typeset print),

with whole separate pages for reproduced photographic illustrations – suggest it was produced 'in house'. In addition, it is not known what the eventual distribution list was and whether it was confined internally or distributed to any key associates outside and beyond the family and the company. Several copies exist amongst Lebus family members, with a copy now archived with Haringey Local History Archives at Bruce Castle Museum.

A question of timing

Of intrigue to this author is the question of LS's timing: what prompted him to write at that precise moment in time? Certainly, LS was well placed to record the firm's history – he had recently retired after a 52-year career with the company (the last three of which were as a director on the management board). Perhaps it was simply to occupy his days following retirement. Perhaps there was something intuitive in his timing. Presumably, LS did not know or could not foresee what further chapters lay ahead (and which had the potential to be exciting), how they might shape up, and what, if or when the ending of the story might be. What is now known, however, is that within a matter of a few short years, 'the largest furniture factory in the world' was in financial difficulty and by 1970 the Tottenham Hale site was closed and vacated completely.

The missing years from *LS's History*

And why choose to end his account at the point the firm ceased to be a family partnership? LS was all too aware that his 'history' was incomplete – he took it up to 1947 – and that at the time of writing there was more work that could be done to document the first eighteen years of the public company. Why had he chosen not to include it, despite his intimate knowledge and experience of this period? Perhaps he simply wanted to focus on the Lebus family's input and achievements during the years the business was exclusively family owned and run. It might also be that family loyalty played a part since, at the time he was writing, family members were still in senior positions in the public company.

It was the piecing together of the public company years, spanning the period from 1947 to 1970, that proved to be the hardest work as I tried to answer the overriding question as to why the Tottenham Hale factory closed down so dramatically. This era of the firm's history produced surprises – serving as an example of a clear and straightforward appearance that in fact reveals itself to be something a little different.

A chance to ask Oliver Lebus all I needed to know

At the start of my research in 2008 I learned that Oliver Lebus, Harris's grandson and chairman at the time of the firm's departure from Tottenham Hale, was living in Kensington and was contactable. This was exciting but at the same time troubling: the factory folded under his watch and I was about to meet the man who could give me the answer I needed.

Did meeting with Oliver yield the answer?

In short, he didn't say; and I don't recall asking. I have fond memories of my meetings with Oliver and, in this respect, I am glad we didn't confront this issue. It was a purely magical experience to be able to delve into filing cabinets, sideboards and cupboards with Oliver in his private study at home and to talk with him about the subject that had brought us together. It is hard to quantify which one of us enjoyed the experience more. His memory was vivid, his mind was sharp, his patience endless and his enthusiasm abounding. I shall be forever grateful for the time we had – he welcomed me on several occasions, usually for several hours at a time. His death in 2009 was indeed a sad loss.

That left me, however, with a *Titanic*-esque conundrum, in as much as the ending was clear but causal factors remained ambiguous. I continued to benefit from privileged access to original documents and information sources through Oliver's son, Tim. Oliver was a hoarder – which, from an historian's perspective, is to pay a compliment. He may well have inherited a major part of his eventual collection from his father, Herman (or perhaps his uncle Louis).

The fact that Oliver had a copy of the last ever updated internal telephone extension list with names and numbers – which I imagine he unpinned from his notice board on his last day at Tottenham Hale – epitomises the extent of the archive he had saved.

To see, read, feel and touch archive documents from the time when the Harris Lebus factory was in full production, a thriving, buzzing entity whose influence spread far beyond this local community, was both a bonus and a pleasure. Special items of once-cherished personal paraphernalia and ad hoc pages of intently written words between sender and recipient that become locked away with the passing of time – their meaning and significance undiminished – were there to be rediscovered.

Research pays dividends

As author of this work, I have happily spent many hours physically going through piles of documents, articles, in-house booklets, trade directories, letters, leases – even Harris's original death certificate. Through recourse to the Lebus archive complimented with additional sources, such as *The Times* online – every annual report giving a company 'health check' with overview of profit and loss from the inception of the public limited company in 1947 was available – I believe that I have answered that crucial question as to why Harris Lebus PLC went under.

Having researched this aspect of the story, in some ways, from a blank sheet, my view is this: no-one could have tried harder to revitalise and secure the future of Harris Lebus than Oliver. Further, my view is that Oliver was fiercely loyal to the memory of his father and Sir Herman's achievements.

Just as the passing of time (and much research and discovery) revealed the answer to the question as to why the 'unsinkable' ship sank, this book answers the question of why the largest furniture factory in the world – a claim to which there is little evidence for any challenge – was forced to cease production.

Before Tottenham Hale

A significant part of the story precedes the period during which the 'Finsbury Cabinet Works' was at Tottenham Hale: 1901 to 1970. It can begin with the furniture making of Louis Lebus in Hull in the 1840s where he arrived as a Jewish immigrant from what is now Wroclaw in Poland, where Harris was born. Louis moved his large family to London in 1857, where he continued to make furniture in the East End.

An inferred link between his furniture business and that of his son Harris (which is first recorded in his name in 1873) is tenuous, ambiguous and unproven since this was six years before Louis died, leaving the question as to whether the business was one and the same, or two *different* businesses technically unanswered.

The enigma that was Harris Lebus

The name of the business, and the man himself, are one and the same. I can't help but wonder how often or indeed whether thoughts immediately turn to Harris Lebus, the *man*, when the name is mentioned. Does an image of him easily come to mind? Can his face be readily pictured? Is there an appetite to learn more about his life and what, if anything, is generally known about him? What was he like in character? What was he like to work with and for? Where did he live? What was his home life like? Does a memorial exist?

To understand the business, we need an insight into the enigma that is Harris Lebus. There is no doubting his business acumen, but Harris was also a devoted family man. After almost 20 years as a sole entrepreneur, Harris invited his youngest brother Solomon (generally known as Sol) into partnership from September 1892.

What made the partnership of Harris and Sol work so well?

Different in character and temperament, together, Harris and Sol built up a business at Tabernacle Street in the City of London before establishing a new factory at Tottenham Hale, six miles to the north. At this juncture, Harris continued to manage the showroom, sales and administrative aspects at Tabernacle Street whilst Sol managed the manufacturing and warehousing of furniture at Tottenham Hale. Harris died in September 1907, just six years after the factory was opened.

The Finsbury Cabinet Works dwarfs the landscape at Tottenham Hale

With other locations considered and rejected, what impact would the construction of a factory cause to both the landscape – rural, with longstanding market gardening activities – and to the community in Tottenham Hale? Indeed, would this bold move into the Lea Valley set a precedent for other furniture manufacturers to follow this lead?

The original land purchase, layout and building design resulted from the vision and energy of a relatively young city architect – Samuel Clifford Tee – and sat, as if floating, in a relatively rural, marshy landscape. Built to brief and meticulously planned to enable the delivery and unloading of wood from the River Lea in the south-east corner through the processes of manufacture to warehousing and distribution by rail in the north-west corner at Ferry Lane, the Finsbury Cabinet Works, though sizeable for its day, was originally but a quarter of its eventual size.

The course of time brings adaption and expansion

The factory the Duke of Edinburgh visited in November 1955 was a conglomeration of original brick buildings squeezed between brick and concrete additions, with concreted floor and virtually all under one continuous roof, spanning 43 acres. The expansion and adaptation of the factory site at Tottenham Hale was an integral feature as the business managed demands placed on it over time, with shifts in both the products made and the methods of manufacture. The complexities of split-site working and the eventual transfer of administrative functions from Tabernacle Street to Tottenham Hale – a site initially without office accommodation – and the impact on the factory infrastructure is one issue detailed in LS's account.

The Finsbury Cabinet Works at Tottenham Hale as pictured in the 1913 catalogue
(Paul Collier private collection)

In 1954, Sir Herman Lebus announced major expansion plans in the form of a huge warehouse extension to be designed by Clifford Tee and Gale – the firm established by Samuel Clifford Tee. The warehouse was subsequently erected between the sports pavilion and the factory, covering over the extensive network of underground war shelters north of Ferry Lane, and was linked to the main factory by an automated conveyor running through a bridge under the road. The factory complex was at its largest and most complex production-wise when the new warehouse was in operation between 1956 and 1966.

Would the largest furniture factory in the world really consider relocating?

In 1966 (the year following the completion of LS's *History*) the firm was committed to selling its landholdings in Tottenham. This was to be part of an ambitious, six-year strategic plan toward the year 1973 to modernise the business and fully mechanise production, away from the then current labour-intensive methods. A brand new, purpose-built manufacturing unit was to be constructed in a yet-to-be-agreed location outside London that in the short term would run alongside Tottenham, which was also to be fully mechanised. When a second royal visitor, Princess Margaret, viewed the restructured factory in April 1968, the production plant

had been reduced to such an extent that it was smaller than that of Clifford Tee's original Finsbury Cabinet Works. By then, the whole manufacturing operation with brand new machinery, along with the warehousing and administration functions, was conducted in the new warehouse, some 250,000 square feet of covered space and with some space for storage of raw materials retained on the original site. The royal visit was during the early stage – the remainder of the long-term strategic plan sadly never happened.

I live where the veneer shop used to be

The first photograph I saw of the factory in its heyday was the one at the back of the 1934 Harris Lebus catalogue that I had purchased in an online auction. The shapes and patterns of the land on which the factory stood were all quite familiar; they match the shape of Ferry Lane Estate. To see it was simply quite magical. Inevitably, I wanted to place my flat within the picture – what part of the factory was here, in the place I call my home, back in those bygone days? I found the answer: it was the end of number 11 shop, which was subsequently extended as number 32 shop, where wood-veneer panels were machine-cut. Some reminders of the factory remain: the iron rings on the towpath where barges were tied up as wood was unloaded in the south-west corner, porcelain telephone wire plugs under

Inside cover of the 1934 furniture catalogue showing how the Lebus furniture factory once covered what is now Ferry Lane Estate

(Paul Collier private collection)

The veneer shop being extended to form 32 shop in 1954: Armadale Green occupies the spot today

(Reproduced with special permission from Walthamstow Local History Archives, Vestry House Museum)

Ferry Lane bridge in the north east corner… and one iron gatepost that once formed the main entrance.

A driving force with each successive generation of Lebus brothers

The dynamics of a business run as a family partnership make for interesting study. Why would ownership, management, remuneration and control matter? It is not uncommon for families to have moments of drama, disagreement and conflict – even if kept private and behind closed doors. And it is evident that in each successive generation a 'driving force' emerged. Knowing who the driver is, the driving force at any period of time, helps give an insight into what's driving them and what they are driving to, or for.

Harris was evidently the driving force in his partnership with Sol. They were not equal partners in terms of financial remuneration, ownership of 'goodwill' and controlling interests (as well as potential loss bearing).

After Harris's death, under a trust set out in his will, his widow, Sarah Harris Lebus, received one-quarter of the profits (along with repayment of capital share in quarterly instalments, plus interest) whilst being a silent partner. This arrangement stood until Sarah died in March 1942. (Her charity work warrants recognition.) There were agreed formulae for allocating profits, capital shares and responsibility for losses between family partners throughout the duration of the family business.

A tale of two brothers and each has two sons…

In turn, and destined to join the business, were born two sons of Harris and two sons of Sol – one of which they each named touchingly after their own father Louis, giving their own first names as middle names. Harris and Sarah's two sons, Louis Harris (known as Louis) and Herman Andrew, were born in 1883 and 1884. Sol and Esther's sons, Louis Sol (known as LS) and Simon Henry (known as Bob), were born in 1894 and 1897. Louis and Herman were officially made partners in 1907 when their father died (though both had been working in the business since before the Tottenham Hale era); LS joined the partnership in January 1922 and Bob at the time of his father's death in April 1926.

In 1946, a few years after Sarah Lebus died, her two grandsons Anthony Hart Herman and Oliver Hart Herman followed in their father

Far left: Harris in his younger years

Left: Sol Lebus, Harris's younger brother

Far left: Louis Harris (known as Louis), Harris's son

Left: Herman, Harris's son

Below left: Louis Sol (known as LS), Sol's son

Centre: Anthony, Herman's son

Below: Oliver, Herman's son

Herman's footsteps and joined the partnership, having served in the forces: Anthony in the Royal Marines, Oliver in the Royal Signals.

The following year, 1947, the partnership was dissolved and replaced by a public limited company. The family as a whole continued to hold a controlling interest. Louis and Bob retired at this point. In time two more brothers, John and Peter, joined their father LS, having completed their National Service in 1956 and 1958 respectively.

They were their father's sons

Over successive generations of the Harris Lebus business, Harris, Herman and Oliver emerge as those drivers: Harris was fourteen years Sol's senior; Herman was a year younger than Louis; and Oliver was four years younger than Anthony.

Sir Herman – wedded to his work

Sir Herman Lebus devoted 60 years of his life to the firm, from 1898 to 1957. Nearly all of these overlapped with the Tottenham years: the first nine under his father Harris's management, twenty-eight of them alongside his uncle Sol, and the last eleven spent with his sons Oliver and Anthony. And he didn't retire: when he died in 1957, at the age of 73, he was still tightly holding the reigns. This was shortly after the completion of the new warehouse north of Ferry Lane. Sir Herman Lebus had witnessed the fruition of plans for the 'largest furniture factory in the world', its subsequent phases of expansion and had steered the family partnership through two world wars and the first decade of the public limited company.

A tough act to follow

Inevitably, Sir Herman was a hard act for his sons Anthony and Oliver to follow. The late 1950s and 1960s proved a tough period with both external and internal challenges, with expectations on both set high. As fortunes waned, questions inevitably were asked. Did something of the heart and soul of the business die with Sir Herman, destined never to be the same again? Or, alternatively, was there something around the way Sir Herman steered

the company, in the same direction, in the same style and for so long? Did he somehow fail to keep abreast of developments and changes in the furniture industry, despite his distinguished record as an innovator, a leader not a follower? Whatever the truth of this, it fell to Anthony and Oliver to pull Harris Lebus into the modern age of manufacture and, in so doing, acknowledge both the blessing and the shackles of the company's history.

Cabinet furniture, three-piece suites, beds, thousands of broom handles and… war planes

What is a typical Lebus furniture piece? Were these branded? How can vintage items be confidently attributed to Lebus? A detailed audit of every Harris Lebus furniture design range and individual items produced during the operation of the business is simply not possible and was never the author's intention to attempt. However, from available sources, including recourse to original Lebus catalogues, a comprehensive account is presented in the production of both Harris Lebus cabinet furniture and upholstery. (Production of the latter was accommodated in Tabernacle Street before transferring to Tottenham Hale for a period, and subsequently, in 1950, to Woodley, Reading.)

Three distinct periods of furniture manufacture are identifiable. Commercially successful, Art Nouveau styled Arts and Craft pieces, handmade from wood with limited machine assistance and for the upper end of the market, continued until the advent of World War One. At the end of the war, a radical shift to simplified, Art Deco styled pieces took place. Mass production with increased reliance on machinery from wood and plywood for the lower-income end of the market characterised the interwar years. This fed a burgeoning market and brought continued commercial success until World War Two. After the war, in a similar vein, the company continued to mass produce modern-styled pieces, using wood, plywood, and flirting with the use of laminates and plastics, with varying commercial success. The mid-1960s saw a further significant shift to contemporary styled, light teak veneered

Bedroom furniture in the Arts and Craft style pictured in the 1913 catalogue

(Paul Collier private collection)

A typical dining room suite from the interwar years

Advertisement for the Link furniture range launched in 1957

(Paul Collier private collection)

chipboard pieces for the mass market, with initial commercial success.

How did the war years affect the business? What is striking in LS's *History* is the significant contribution that Harris Lebus made in both world wars in the manufacture of aircraft and other supplies, whilst the production of furniture was halted completely. This book explores Harris Lebus's achievements in both wars, including the manufacture in wood of the Handley Page 0/400 and V1500 and Vickers Vimy monoplane of the First World War and the Albermarle, Hotspur and Horsa gliders, and Mosquito fighter bomber during the Second World War. A miscellany of other items was also manufactured, including shell cases, landing craft, collapsible canoes and a replica Sherman tank.

And was there ever conflict between designer and management? This work explores this and other questions and offers up surprises. Harris Lebus built up a reputation for delivery to contract: from towel rails for the Initial Towel Company to ocean-liner interiors, from record-player cabinets for HMV to hospital refurbishments. Which hotel commissioned a replica of *Titanic*'s smoking lounge? And do you know what the company's mill in Lancashire produced? What the company's African factory supplied? Which bedding company Lebus bought out? Lebus also ran Merchandise Credit, Merchandise Transport and owned a set of maintenance garages in Tottenham.

Marketing, sales and distribution

A characteristic of the business throughout was the production of annual furniture catalogues, both to the trade and to households. A band of salesmen (exclusively male, it would appear) worked their patch for sales, both home and abroad. As sales targets rose and patches became smaller, this band of 'travellers', as they were known in the early years, grew ever larger, until a radical re-think of marketing strategy took place as sales dwindled in the mid-1960s. Increasingly, the company's marketing became more targeted and sophisticated, with a successful household-name marketing company engaged and a number of towns and cities up and down the land boasting their own Lebus showroom.

A proud team of employees standing in front of a Mosquito aircraft made at Harris Lebus

How we did it

Using detail from LS's *History* and with reference to a 14-part series titled 'How we do it…' contained within the complete set of the *Lebus Log*, the in-house staff magazine that spanned the period from the mid-1950s to the late 1960s, plus numerous personal testimonies, a detailed account of manufacturing processes is offered, from 'sticking up' in the timber field to placing labels on finished furniture items in the warehouse and showrooms. With the radical re-fit in the mid-1960s, the shift in production methods was from machine-assisted workers to worker-assisted machines.

Life as a Lebus worker

Who worked there? What were they like? What did they do? Were they happy? What was the factory like to work in? Were there many industrial accidents and were there any fatalities? This book gives a detailed insight into life as a 'Lebus boy' or 'Lebus girl'.

Most of those employees who left the factory gates for the last time in (or before) 1970 are no longer likely to be with us. Fortunately, in 2007, staff at Haringey Local History Archives conducted a reminiscence project in preparation for a dedicated Harris Lebus factory exhibition at its base, Bruce Castle Museum. Held the following year, the exhibition proved highly popular. A significant number of people were interviewed in the reminiscence project. I have endeavoured to make their personal contributions, accounts, experiences and anecdotal tales an integral part of this work, and as far as possible I have reproduced them in the contributors' own words, incorporating them into the text. This is because I think no-one is able to tell it better.

I have also been able to draw on contributions and personal experiences from a range of individuals made in the *Lebus Log*, including 'Woodley Whispers', which contained news from the upholstery arm. Whilst one would not expect a complete list of personnel to be found, from these resources and copies of a few early apprenticeship indentures, a valuable insight

Lebus Log, the in-house staff magazine, celebrates 10 years

into the working lives of the workforce – which reached a peak of 6,000 employees (over two shifts) during World War Two – is made possible.

Women were a key component of the Harris Lebus workforce throughout the duration at

Above: Posing mischievously, a group of women during World War One

Centre: A young man poses for the camera during World War One

Right: Staff medical facilities

Tottenham Hale, not just through wartime. There were women polishers from the outset, albeit they 'worked on the cheaper products', through to Shop Steward Sissy Lewis, who was made redundant as the firm closed in 1970. One would expect a large contingent of female office staff – imagine rows of (both male and female) sales ledger clerks.

Although health and safety legislation was pretty much non-existent, Harris Lebus took workers' welfare seriously. A business that constructs an underground complex of war shelters large enough to accommodate the entire workforce surely has a commitment to employee welfare. And employees did their bit too – during both world wars they mobilised into teams such that there was a fully trained-up fire brigade and Lebus had its own Dad's Army.

The company made provision for a practising doctor and nursing staff, with separate nursing rooms for men and women, and full X-ray facilities. There was also an in-house barber, tobacco kiosk and canteen serving hot meals. If

you want to know how it felt to do the morning and afternoon tea runs in the largest furniture factory in the world, you can read on and find out.

Restructuring in 1966 as part of the firm's six-year strategic development and relocation plan saw total redundancies of somewhere between one-half and two-thirds of the entire Tottenham Hale workforce. With just 1,000 workers remaining, staffing was down to a level akin to the early years of the Finsbury Cabinet Works.

Reflection and celebration

There is plenty to indicate that working at Harris Lebus engendered some happy times. There was naturally a patriotic draw to participate in national celebrations such as the coronation of a monarch or VE and Armistice days, when a day off work was not countenanced but neither was a proper day's work expected. There is evidence that some of the workforce were invited to Lebus family celebrations, such as the 'coming of age' parties for Herman and Louis, though it seems these were reserved for white-collar office, rather than works, staff. This rule was relaxed by the time of Sir Herman's celebration of 50 years of service to the firm, when every employee who had already passed this milestone was invited. In fact, long-service awards – inscribed watches – were regularly presented and a combined annual reunion became a tradition. For Sir Herman Lebus, hosting the royal visit in 1955 at Tottenham from the Duke of Edinburgh must have been one of the proudest moments of his life. His knighthood six years earlier was in recognition of his personal contribution, and that of the family business, to the war effort. The year before, 1954, he celebrated his 70th birthday in style: a portrait was commissioned by esteemed artist Simon Elwes as a gift from his workforce; a cake was made in the shape of the factory; and he presented a new sports pavilion named in his honour to the workforce.

There were plenty of smaller parties for weddings and birthdays as well as Christmas daytime parties for children of employees held

Staff enjoy a huge party in one of the workshops to celebrate the Queen's coronation in 1953

in the sports pavilion. The workers in each section organised a modest annual 'beano' – coach trip – and there is even a record of celebrities-versus-employees charity football matches being held on the Lebus sports field. There were clubs for every kind of sport from bowls to football, cricket to boxing – the Lebus football team in the local league was known as PandO (polishers and offices). There was a thriving array of clubs and societies ranging from photography to drama.

An honest attempt to put on record material

LS wrote in his foreword: 'It will be abundantly clear to those who read it that the writer is no journalist. *However, it is an honest attempt to put on record material from which a gifted writer can produce a history worthy of the subject.*'

LS made clear his rationale for taking the considerable time and effort (which is clearly evidenced in the produced work) to compile his detailed history of the family business, complimented with a dossier of supplementary information and appendices: he expressed passionately his desire for his work to be taken, re-shaped, supplemented and placed in the public domain. To this day, it is the author's perception that the Harris Lebus story continues to generate interest. I take issue with LS on one key point – he proved he was a brilliant journalist and achieved his aim commendably. I, however, am reluctant to claim to be 'a gifted writer'. This is, after all, my first foray into the club of book authorship. Furthermore, without his work, *A History of Harris Lebus 1840–1947*, this writer would not have been able to produce this book.

Almost fifty years have elapsed since the factory closed its gates for the final time in 1970. Although that was not necessarily the final chapter in the story, the scale of the closure and its impact on, not least, all those who were actively engaged in the company when it ceased operations surely make it difficult to see it as anything other than the natural end of the narrative. And yet, even then, there was a further period to chart: in 1975, Lebus Upholstery celebrated 25 years at Woodley. Recorded in a four-page pull-out special in the *Reading Evening Post*, several notable employees once associated with the Tottenham Hale years were evidently happily employed. The message conveyed was that the future looked bright. Sadly, within a few more years the same fate that robbed Tottenham Hale of Lebus robbed Woodley too. (Though the name Lebus Upholstery still lives on, the company is not associated with the family.)

Lebus family support

I was fortunate enough to be afforded the enormous privilege of meeting with the closest descendants of Harris Lebus amongst the extended Lebus family. Through this book I have endeavoured to answer questions that I imagine others have presumed to ask. From the wealth of information that has survived – there is much of it – themes have been examined and conclusions drawn about Harris Lebus within a wider context; the factors and influences on the furniture industry itself.

This book should be of interest to those who now live or work on what was the site of the factory; the Ferry Lane Estate designed and built within the decade following the closure of the factory in 1970 and subsequently Hale Village, the design and construction of which was beginning just as I moved in. It will also be of local historical interest and value to those who live in the immediate area and beyond. The book will, I believe, be of interest to those who do not live anywhere near Tottenham Hale or indeed do not know the area; the story,

with a beginning, a middle and an end, will appeal to anyone who has an interest in the development of a business during a particular period of history. The lives and experiences of all Lebus family members engaged in the business, their employees and other individuals associated with Harris Lebus, such as the Tottenham factory's architect, Samuel Clifford Tee, are of equal interest and have been explored in this work. With recourse to the evolution of the business, an overview of both the methods of manufacture and furniture produced is offered.

I have chosen a selection of the most exquisitely grained raw materials available, which in preference to some others, I felt could be harmonised to an envisioned design; I have cut and shaped the essential parts, assembled them with a golden adhesive of logic, carefully smoothed away any rougher edges, added a generous border of carved analysis, and delicately polished and finished with a sheen of subjective intuition. And just as any crafted piece, the book you now hold in your hand has taken a while to make – a good while longer than I anticipated at the outset.

This is *my honest attempt* to put on record material that may or may not be generally known or publicly accessible, in one place – a book that can be a point of reference for those who wish to research and develop aspects of this fascinating story still further in a continued quest to preserve history.

PART A

BUILDING A BUSINESS:
THE ROAD TO TOTTENHAM HALE

'Further from the 1870s the term "furniture manufacturer" was often used instead of "cabinet maker", "chair maker", "upholsterer"… production was being increasingly concentrated in larger works…'

– J. L. Oliver, *The Development and Structure of the Furniture Industry*, Volume 7 of the Furniture and Timber series

CHAPTER ONE

From Wheelbarrow to Emporium: Harris Lebus – The Man behind the Name

24 May 1852 – 21 September 1907

'Harris Lebus, the founder of the modern firm, was a man of outstanding character and personality, with a business genius second to none.'

Mr. C. H. Robinson, employee, quoted in LS's *History*

Paying Respects and Tributes

'A simple notice in the advertisement column of yesterday's newspapers notifying the death of Harris Lebus, aged 55 years, marks the close of a career of more than usual interest' was the opening sentence of an article in the *Daily Mail* on 24 September 1907. 'He took a keen interest in the welfare of his workmen, one of whom remarked to a *Daily Mail* Representative yesterday', stated the same article.

Obituaries, as public statements to commemorate the life and achievements of the deceased, are by their very nature intentionally prepared to focus on the positive characteristics and to perhaps overlook any flaws. An obituary in the *Jewish Chronicle*, September 1907, reads as a very personal tribute (by a writer identified only by the initials A.A.G.): 'The present writer, who knew him intimately, can say without hesitation that he owed his success and position to nothing but his own force of character, his indomitable energy and perseverance, his giant mind, and the wise counsel and devoted attachment of his wife.'

Harris Lebus pictured in his later years

Mr. C. H. Robinson, who had been with the firm for eight years at that time (he rose in the ranks to become chief buyer of factored goods), recalling events some years later, is quoted by LS as giving this balanced view: 'He was a man of violent temper which it was as well to keep away from, but he was held in the highest esteem by us all. He was a wonderful judge of character and has a genius for finding the right man for the job, and those of us who knew him well attributed a large portion of his success to this quality.' He also expressed, with some affection: 'Short, heavily built… he was about 48 when I first knew him, and to see a man of his weight taking the steep stairs at Tabernacle Street as he did was a sight to be remembered.'

'Harris Lebus was in the habit of wheeling his barrow once a week into the back yard of Lawes, Randall and Company, which was approached in those days from Tabernacle Street, and it was my father's duty to inspect the products of his week's work, assess their value, and, if possible, make a deal' wrote Sir Ernest Benn in *The Cabinet Maker and Complete House Furnisher*, 24 April 1926. He added, 'when I came on the scene, Harris Lebus was to be found in the spacious front hall of the big block of buildings that he had erected on the other side of Tabernacle Street, where, surrounded by a crowd of salesmen and other callers, he could survey the scene of minor operations twenty years before.'

The rise of Harris Lebus was meteoric. The fact that Harris had, in 1885, purchased an 80-year lease on 70 and 72 Tabernacle Street, offering sizeable workspace housed on several floors, is an indication that the business bearing his name was thriving. It was also a demonstration of his ambition, optimism and vision.

And within another two years, as business continued to flourish, staged expansions into adjacent premises in both Paradise Place (numbers 2, 3, 4, 19, 20, 21 and 22) and Whitfield Street (numbers 13, 14, 15 and 21) followed between 1887 and 1890. This accommodation served adequately until 1899 when thoughts would turn to establishing a dedicated manufacturing hub.

A headstrong character

Robinson chose to expose Harris's temperament in his testimony after the event. Alongside this must be considered the note by LS about a particular argument between a 21-year-old Harris and his father, Louis, in 1873, the outcome of which was that Harris left and went to work for an antiques dealer, D. I. Isaacs, for a whole year. Of course, all family members argue; however, it seems reasonable to assume this was no mere altercation but a serious falling out. This suggests Harris was, in the least, strong willed. LS does not expand on what their differences were or what, if any, were the terms on which he returned, or if their father–son relationship ever fully recovered – either on a personal or business level.

Despite the incident, assumptions around the transfer of a business from father to son prevail. J. L. Oliver indicates that Harris, who left the Jews' Free School in 1863 at the age of 11 to join his father at the bench, took over his father's business on his retirement around 1875; this would suggest a smooth transfer. Jim Lewis, meanwhile, writing an account of the firm in *London's Lea Valley: Britain's Best Kept Secret*, takes the view that Harris simply took over at the point Louis died in 1879. William I. Massil, in his book *Immigrant Furniture Workers in London 1881–1939*, concurs: 'When Harris Lebus took over the running of the business on the death of his father, as the older son, he inherited a small firm spread over a few workshops in the East End.' The contemporaneous *Daily Mail* article also infers a logical progression of the business from father to son (without being specific about the circumstances), expressing the spectacular rise of Harris thus: 'A little more than thirty-five years ago Mr. Lebus was an apprentice in his father's cabinet-making shop in Wellclose Square in the East End' and that 'it was then part of his duty to cart on a little barrow, for sale to the trade, small cylinder desks made in his father's workshop'. This, however, raises a question surrounding the name of the business, Harris Lebus; one wonders why it was not Louis Lebus and Son(s) or even Lebus and Company.

Harris Lebus opened a business bank account in his name

A curious note tucked away in LS's *History* (as much about the evolution of the Midland Bank as the partnership) states: 'An account was opened in the sole name of Harris Lebus on September 25, 1873'. This appears to cast doubts over the assumed transfer of a business from father to son. This is the same year that, according to LS, Harris is said to have returned to the family business after a year's absence following an argument with his father. Since LS offers no explanation on the reasoning behind Harris setting up the bank account and is somewhat ambiguous as to the whole continuity question, this only serves to add to the intrigue. Such a move seems curiously at odds with a generally assumed, logical progression that sees Harris simply taking over an already established business his father had built up, complete with name, reputation, goodwill and a customer base at either the point Louis retired or on his death on 12 June 1879. By establishing his bank account six years before his father's death and two years before the suggested retirement date put forward by J. L. Oliver, can we be sure when, or even *if*, Harris simply acquired a business from his father?

The obituary to Harris in the *Jewish Chronicle* fails to mention his father or his family origins and heritage, whilst at the same time emphasising that he was a family man and 'proud of being an *English* Jew'. The obituary in the September 1907 *Cabinet Maker* interestingly has no reference to his father either and does not mention the word 'Jew' at all. Neither mentions Harris's father by name and nor does an article in the *Tottenham and Edmonton Weekly Herald* of 27 September 1907, which appears to be an amalgam of the *Daily Mail* and the *Jewish Chronicle* obituaries.

Ancestry, Heritage and Judaism

According to LS, the story goes that Louis Lebus[1] arrived in Hull from Germany sometime

1 Research undertaken by the Lebus family in compiling their family tree indicates the original family name was 'Leibes'.

Louis Lebus, Harris's father

during the 1840s (J. L. Oliver specifically stated it was 1838). He had left Breslau (now known as Wroclaw in Poland), the historical capital of Silesia, which straddles the borders of Germany, Poland, the Czech Republic and Slovakia. Breslau has a complicated history, having been part of the Kingdom of Poland, Bohemia, the Austrian Empire, Prussia and Germany at various stages.

Louis left behind his father, Solomon (then in his fifties), his mother, Babejettel (in her forties), and four siblings – Lazarus, Samuel, Herman and Helene. It may have been that instability in the region and tensions between orthodox and liberal Judaism prompted Louis Lebus, a single man in his twenties, to come to England alone and settle in Hull. After London, Hull was the next biggest port in England. Many immigrants arrived there from continental Europe in the early-to-mid-nineteenth century and at that time there were extensive mills, most of them wind powered, for sawing timber and cutting veneers. The marriage of Louis, by then a cabinet-maker in his thirties, to Helena Pflichter, a dressmaker in her early twenties, took place at the end of the decade and they settled in Duncan Street in The Groves, an area of Hull on the north bank of the River Humber. Harris was born on 24 May 1852. Isaac was born the following year, followed by Phillip two years later.

Move to London's East End

Sometime in the mid-1850s (J. L. Oliver suggests it was 1855), the family moved down to London and settled at 12 White Church Lane, Whitechapel. (J. L. Oliver suggests Louis was based in Leman Street E1 initially.) The area of East London was then evolving both as a furniture-making hub and a place of settlement for the Jewish community; it was by no means uncommon for cabinet-makers, Gentiles or Jews, to work from home with just a room or garret either making goods to order or for hawking. Rachel was born in 1857 and Benjamin four years later. In 1862 they moved a few doors along the same road to number 24. Eliza was born in 1865. A further move followed in 1866, the short distance to 37 Wellclose Square E1 where Sol was born that year, followed by Louisa two years later. In 1877 the family also occupied next door, number 38. On 12 June 1879, Louis died. Rachel registered the death with the cause being ulceration of the pylorus (stomach) and exhaustion, which does not sit well with the notion of a life in retirement. Louis was 62 and left Helena, a widow, and eight children. A note in the *Jewish Chronicle* on 20 June 1879 reads: 'Mrs. Lebus, Mr. H. Lebus and family return their sincere thanks for the numerous visits and letters of condolences during their week of mourning for their late lamented husband and father, 91 Cannon Street Road, Commercial Road E18.' A subsequent note in the *Jewish Chronicle* on 29 August 1879 informed of a ceremony on Sunday 31 August at 4 p.m. to set a tombstone for Louis at West Ham (Jewish) Cemetery. Helena died the following year at the age of just 50.

Harris has young siblings to care for

Harris, as the eldest surviving family member, had responsibility towards his two youngest siblings now that both their mother and father

had died, especially given the age gap: Louisa was only 11 and Sol was still only 13. The older siblings, Isaac (27), Phillip (25), Rachel (23), Benjamin (19– he left the Jews' Free School on 21 September 1874 at the age of 13, though it is not known where he worked after) and Eliza (18) were likely to be able to look after themselves. (According to LS, all of Louis and Helena's children emigrated to California except Harris, Sol and one daughter.)

Family Man – Sadness and Joy

'In his own home he was a veritable king. He was idolised by his wife and children and a better husband and father or friend or a happier man it would have been impossible to find' stated the obituary in the *Jewish Chronicle*, September 1907. Harris was a married man and father himself by 1880 – he had married Sarah Myers in 1878 and they quickly had two children. Their first child, Maud, was born in June 1879 and Lena followed the next year. That same year they moved to larger properties in the same road, numbers 5 and 9 Wellclose Square. This was largely a residential area with its charming Georgian houses occupied by merchant sea captains, a Scandinavian timber merchant, the Danish Embassy, a theatre and the infamous Mahogany Bar.

The 1881 census shows Harris and his family living nearby at 70 Campbell Road, E3, which may indicate, for the first time, a separation between business premises and living accommodation. Another daughter, Elizabeth, was born in 1882 followed by their first son, Louis Harris, the following year and their second son, Herman Andrew Harris, in 1884. Harris and Sarah had three more children at this address: Ethel in 1886, Phyllis in 1887 and Marjorie in 1891. That same year produced a family tragedy – the death of Maud at the age of just 13.

In 1894, Harris, Sarah and family move to 'Sarita', 11 Netherhall Gardens, Hampstead NW3 and on 5 January 1895 baby twin girls – Gladys Muriel and Winifred Amy – were born. However, a report in the *Jewish Chronicle* on 1 March tells of their tragic news – the death of

11 Netherhall Gardens pictured in 2008; recently, development of the property has returned the exterior to its original red brick and divided the building into nine high end apartments

(© Copyright Paul Collier private collection)

one of the twins, Winifred Amy, who was just seven weeks old, on 27 March (Gladys Muriel survived and lived to be 83). The birth of the twins would be the last for Harris and Sarah.

The 1901 census noted that eight live-in servants shared the grand Victorian villa: a cook/housekeeper, domestic maid, parlour maid, two under-parlour maids, two housemaids and a nurse.

His family at his bedside

There is a touching insight into Harris's family life recorded in the September 1907 *Jewish Chronicle* obituary. Harris had not been well for almost a year and during a bout of flu-like illness had, shortly before his death, gathered his eight children – whose ages ranged from 27 to 12 – together and 'exhorted them to remain faithful to his example and teaching'. Chronic interstitial nephritis (kidney disease) of ten months' duration, general oedema (fluid retention and swelling) and heart failure were recorded as the cause on the death certificate of Harris Lebus. His 'rank or profession' is recorded as furniture manufacturer (not cabinet-maker).

Resting place of Harris Lebus

On Sunday 22 September 1907, the day following his death, Harris was interred at Willesden Cemetery, plot number 29, section N, row G.

After Harris…

His charitable work…

Harris's *Jewish Chronicle* obituary tells of the work he did for his local community: he had been instrumental in bringing about the extension to his local synagogue since he moved to Hampstead 13 years ago; and the *Daily Mail* referred to the donation Harris made for furnishing new residential accommodation for nursing staff at the Prince of Wales General Hospital in Tottenham in 1906.

The Prince of Wales General Hospital originated in the nineteenth century on the south-east side of Tottenham Green. Avenue House was converted and opened, with a new hospital block, in 1868; the old house was replaced in 1881 and further extensions included the John Morley Wing, opened in 1887. From 1899 it was the general hospital for the district and further additions were made. After adjacent property had been bought in 1917, additions included a building for outpatients, opened in 1932, and a new home for 55 nurses. It had 200 beds and dealt with acute cases. It would become the Tottenham District Hospital. The committee was supported by Mrs. Sarah Lebus, Louis Lebus and, in turn, Oliver Lebus.

Arguably, the greatest charitable legacy of Harris was the work he undertook with the Furniture Trades Benevolent Association (FTBA). Harris was one of the original founders of the FTBA, the first general meeting of which was on 8 July 1903 at the Inns of Court Hotel, Holborn. Harris was elected Honorary Treasurer – a post he held until his death. It is said that he and a close friend, Samuel J. Waring Jnr. (later Lord Waring), pledged one thousand pounds each. The story goes when the committee asked Harris for his contribution, he said he would give it when they showed him Waring had given his cheque; they did and Harris duly gave his. That said, minutes of the inaugural meeting state Waring gave £1,000 and Harris £262 (annual subscriptions were £105).

The original aims of the FTBA were threefold: to provide cottage homes for the aged poor and their widows; to provide orphanages where their children could be educated; and to provide convalescent homes for rest and restoration of health. The orphanage was established at Radlett, Hertfordshire in 1905. According to the list of donors in the minutes of the inaugural meeting, Harris gave the orphanage two writing tables and an oak one; Sarah pledged all the children's clothes needed for the next five years. Many meetings of the FTBA committee were held at Tabernacle Street. A home for older people who had retired from the furniture trade was established at Sleaford, Sussex; Harris made one of the first nominations, of a retiring Lebus employee. Sarah continued to work with the organisation after Harris's death – she pledged to provide all the children's clothes for the orphanage for another five years in 1908.

A memorial

In 1914 the FTBA extended the orphanage. In honour of Harris, the new hall – opened on 18 July 1914 – was named the Harris Lebus Memorial Hall. Mardi Jeens of Radlett Historical Society, in a letter to the author on 14 October 2008, wrote that behind 1 Rose Walk is a building 'now known as The Masonic Hall, and the Freemasons meet there… [but] over the main entrance remains the plaque stating that it is the Harris Lebus Memorial Hall'.

The orphanage subsequently moved location from Radlett to Southward Lane, Highgate N6 in 1920 because the original location was considered somewhat isolated from schools. The new location was a house called The Limes (later renamed Radlett House), which had a big lake in the garden; it was previously owned by Samuel Price, the solicitor to the Harris Lebus partnership. The final

Artist's impression of the extension to the orphanage in which sits the Harris Lebus Memorial Hall
(Courtesy of Radlett Local History Society)

THE THIRD NEW HOME AT RADLETT, OPENED JULY, 1914.

location for the orphanage was Apsley Guise, Bedfordshire. A convalescent home, Edenfield, for sick or injured employees in the trade, was subsequently established on the Fylde coast of Lancashire, next to the River Ribble.

His family…

Harris had made his will just a couple of years before his death; it is dated 18 April 1905 and was proved on 20 March 1908 (his death certificate record, held by district of Hampstead, is dated 5 May 1908). The *Daily Mail*'s 24 September 1907 article suggested his estate was estimated at 'several hundred thousand pounds', a phenomenal sum at that time.

Harris left his wife Sarah a widow at a relatively young age: she was 51 and they had been married 29 years. Sarah was financially provided for in Harris's will under the provision of his partnership in the business – in essence, she was a silent partner with a quarter of the profits until her death. In addition, in accordance with her late husband's

Sarah Lebus pictured in her later years

will, Sarah received repayment of her share of capital, valued at £318,358, payable in 100 equal quarterly instalments (over 25 years), with interest at 4% per year, from 29 September 1910.

Mrs. Sarah Harris Lebus (as she was officially known) enjoyed life as a socialite. Sarah was, however, generous and supportive to charitable causes – not only the FTBA that Harris had helped set up as well as causes in the locality of the Tottenham Hale factory; she was also supportive of Jewish refugees. Sarah's social engagements and charitable support often went together. On 8 July 1935, Sarah attended *The Call of the Wild* at the London Pavilion in aid of the fund for German Jewish women and children and, on 12 January 1939, she was at the first showing of the film *Stolen Life* at the Plaza Theatre – this was a Lord Baldwin fund in aid of refugees – and the women's appeal committee for German and Austrian Jewish women and children. Later that year, a different cause: on 17 April 1939, Sarah attended the premiere of A. E. Mason's *The Four Feathers* at the Odeon, Leicester Square, a United Artists Corporation film in aid of the research department for the National Hospital for Nervous Diseases.

Death of Mrs. Sarah Harris Lebus in 1942

Sarah Harris Lebus, of 29 Belgrave Square, London SW1 and Lakeside Road, Poole, Dorset, died 17 March 1942 (*London Gazette*, 26 November 1943). She was laid to rest next to Harris. An obituary in the Minutes of the Annual General Meeting of the FTBA in April 1943 read:

> It is with the deepest regret the Executive Committee have to record that during the period under review the association sustained a great loss by the death of Mrs. Harris Lebus. The late Mrs. Harris Lebus had always taken the greatest interest in the well-being of the association from its foundation in 1903 and up to the date of her decease had been a Lady Warden of the Children's Home. She had been a generous contributor to its funds and her loss will be deeply felt.

The Times (online) reported that in auctions of Sarah's possessions at Christie's in 1943 and 1944, Maple and Company paid £3,360 for a set of seven large panels of Brussels tapestry titled 'The Hunts of Diana', signed Guillaume Van Leefdael in December 1943. That same month, her diamond necklace of 52 circular-cut graduated stones mounted in separate collets with an additional row of 19 diamonds mounted in similar style and detachable sold for £5,400 and, in February 1944, Sarah's green paste and diamond corsage brooch sold for £1,000.

Vision, achievement and legacy

I can say with some degree of confidence that Harris Lebus, the man, had unbounded vision. He did live to see his vision, a shared vision even, evolve and come to fruition, if only in part. To attempt, however, to analyse further what Harris himself felt about his achievements – whether he himself felt he reached, surpassed or fell short of his own personal vision – would be to delve into the realms of pure speculation.

What is beyond mere speculation today is the fact he left his mark: Harris Lebus, the inimitable, unmatched, entrepreneurial, spiritual, philanthropic family man, who lived, breathed, toiled, dreamed, designed, created, crafted, employed and managed – whose name is forever synonymous not only with the said specific enterprise and its legacy but arguably of the furniture industry itself. The evidence, in undeniable abundance, demonstrates that he achieved, and monumentally so. Harris could justifiably be immensely proud of his own personal achievement.

His sons, Louis (who registered his father's death) and Herman, had been working with their father in the family business since the end of the last century. His desire that they would continue his work was also fulfilled: they were made official partners in the Harris Lebus family business on his death, in accordance with his will.

There are many subsequent chapters in this story that Harris Lebus sadly did not live to see. He would not see what was to become of the business enterprise and the achievements attained by his brother, Sol. He would not see the impact his sons Louis and Herman made, or Herman go on to be awarded both a CBE for his contribution to World War One and one of the highest accolades of the land – a knighthood in 1947 for his contribution to World War Two. He would not see his grandsons, Anthony and Oliver (Herman's sons), his nephews LS and Bob (Sol's two sons), and in turn LS's sons, John and Peter, join the family business and its evolution into a public limited company in 1947.

And the lingering question surrounding the firm's origins…

An article in the *Cabinet Maker and Complete House Furnisher*, 1 July 1950, stated: 'the extraordinary growth of Harris Lebus Ltd. over the years is a monumental tribute to the sound foundation on which the company was laid nearly a century ago by Mr. Harris Lebus'. Whatever the reason, the Harris Lebus bank account is synonymous with the start of the Harris Lebus 'Empire' – and the goodwill of the firm belonged exclusively to Harris.

CHAPTER TWO

Leading the Way in Manufacturing: Harris and Sol – A Perfect Partnership

'Harris was the central figure in the picture but there was always the suggestion of the faithful brother Sol behind, and there was never any certainty as to which of the two could claim the greater credit for the enormous achievement of the partnership.'

– Sir Ernest Benn, *The Cabinet Maker and Complete House Furnisher*, 24 April 1926

19 September 1892 – The Partnership is Made Official

Harris made his younger brother Sol his business partner on 19 September 1892. The bank account was changed to Harris and Sol Lebus. Profit and loss sharing was set at192/240 with Harris and 48/240 with Sol (based on an old pound of 240 pennies), and Harris retained the 'goodwill' exclusively. At the age of 26, Sol was 14 years Harris's junior. In less than ten years they would have a factory at Tottenham Hale and the partnership had 15 years until the untimely death of Harris. There was evidently a close bond between the siblings: at the time of the 1891 census, Sol had been living with Harris and Sarah at their family home, 28 City Road, EC1. In the same year that saw Sol made a partner, he married Esther Wharman; they set up home at 45 Petherton Road, Canonbury, N5, and Harris, Sarah and family moved to Hampstead. In 1894, Sol and Esther had their first baby, Louis Solomon (LS), followed by Bob in 1897 and Helene Pearl the following year. They then moved to a bigger home, 171 Highbury New Park, N5.

1894: A 'great fire in London' and an ingenious recovery plan

According to *The Times*, 21 June 1894, a 'great fire in London' with '20 businesses destroyed' including the Tabernacle Street premises had 'started in either Angus's or Lebus's'. Not even this would deter Harris and Sol. The two partners devised an ingenious plan whereby tools purchased at the expense of the firm were hired out over a set period to cabinet-makers who had the responsibility of safeguarding them, which created an opportunity to manufacture elsewhere, such as in makers' homes. This helps give some insight into employees, their origins, where they were living and, by inference, the diversity of the workforce. LS's *History* included a photocopy of an 'Agreement for hiring of Tools: H. Lebus Esq., Saul Lebus Esq. *and the several persons mentioned in schedule*' dated 14 September 1894. The address on the schedule is 391 Paul Street. Those 'several persons', 36 in all, were paying weekly hire charges of one or two shillings, and in some cases sixpence, for tools valued at two or three pounds. When paid in full, the tools were then the property of the 'hirers'. Although

Buildings, including Tabernacle Street, gutted by fire

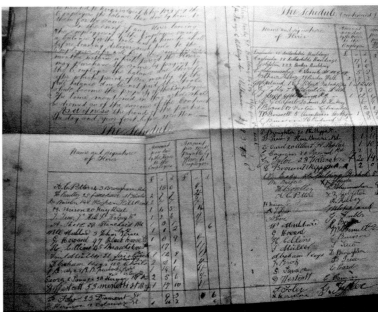

Original 1894 tool hire agreement

this is not an exact science, from the surnames of the 36 employees listed in the 1894 tool hire agreement at Lebus, around a third might suggest either Jewish origins or immigrant status: Saul Mullar, Abraham Keys, K. Krasy, H. Herman, E. Buisson, Mr. Englanda, Mr. Goldstein, E. Schumacher, A. Goldfast, E. Bousins and Mr. E. Broiventi. Most of these cabinet-makers lived in the East End – Shoreditch, Hoxton, Hackney, Whitechapel, Moorgate, Stepney, Islington and Bethnal Green. Mr. G. Howard of 97 Blackhorse Road, Walthamstow hired just over one pound's worth of tools for one shilling a week, his home being about six miles north of the City (and incidentally just a mile further from where the factory would subsequently be developed).

Tabernacle Street Rises from the Ashes

Following the fire, the partners secured temporary premises at nearby Paul Street to continue business. After the refurbishment of Tabernacle Street, in addition to moving back into 70 and 72, Harris and Sol also took numbers 62 through to 68 (even numbers); they had virtually the whole block, spread over five floors including the basement. A corner

unit, which bed manufacturer Mr. Marriner took, was the only exception.

With the accommodation in Paul Street retained, permission was granted to erect a bridge to connect the second floor of

Tabernacle Street

Covered walkway connecting Paradise Place with Tabernacle Street premises

Tabernacle Street with Paradise Place – there was now a total of 121,000 square feet (over 11,240 square metres) to accommodate the burgeoning business.

A multi-use building: steam works, salesroom and offices

Harris Lebus had already been an employer of some 30 men during the Wellclose Square era and had built a reputation for quality 'Arts and Crafts'. The processes of cabinet-making, polishing, finishing and fitting (handles etc.) were completed by craftsmen working on a piece from start to finish, collectively producing a variety of hand-made solid-wood furniture. Where special treatments were required, wooden parts were contracted out to be machined at nearby mills. Machine-assisted crafting in-house was an enviable prospect for Harris and, collectively, the buildings in the Tabernacle Street complex had, by the closing years of the nineteenth century, facilitated this – but only to a limited extent.

A stationary steam engine by Marshall, Sons and Company of Gainsborough, Lincolnshire drove a range of machines; the Marshall driver

was Mr. Edward Daughters. Two steam boilers heated by coal made by Thomas Robinson and Son Limited of Rochdale – who had forged a reputation for manufacturing woodworking machines using line shafting and belts – assisted with some parts of the cabinet-making process. Machines for carving, traditionally a hand-crafting process, were amongst the first to be installed, according to LS. Alfred William Perrin was in charge of the carvers. Repairs were contracted out to a firm in Hoxton. Two chamber kilns were heated by steam for drying and seasoning wood, as were the tanks of glue made from animal derivatives. According to *Furnishing the World: The East London Furniture Trade, 1830–1980* by Pat Kirkham, Rodney Mace and Julia Porter, 'the small number of *larger* firms noted in the Booth survey… were distinguished by the fact that they utilised… machines on their own premises'.

In the days before electricity, gas provided the lighting – some it of the incandescent mantle type but much of it from hazardous naked-flame fishtail burners. After joining as a new apprentice on 24 March 1898, it was the job of Albert Church to light them in the mornings.

Tabernacle Street was a multi-use building: alongside cabinet-making, there was a sales showroom for both Lebus-made and factored (bought-in) furniture items, a warehouse and offices for the partners, designer, draughtsman and administrative functions for sales and distribution. An upholstery factory of moderate proportions was established at the rear; made-up frames were mostly bought from nearby manufacturers to be upholstered in-house to traditional methods and in line with fashion trends. All finished goods were stored in the large basement area awaiting sale or despatch. A variety of furniture items were also bought in large quantities at wholesale prices for the purpose of retail; these served to compliment the range on offer in the ground-floor showroom and to cater for practically all of a potential customer's furniture requirements.

All purchasing was done by Harris and Sol, the list including bookcases, writing tables, flat-top

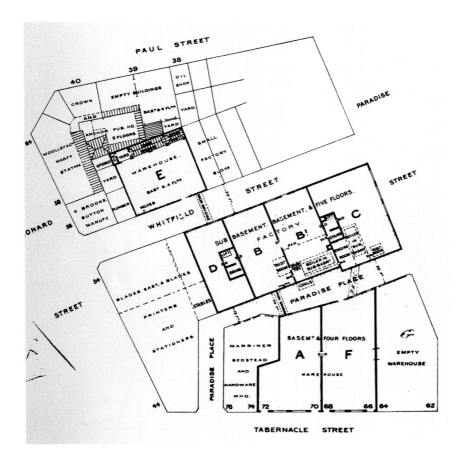

desks, bureaus, assorted worktables and office chairs suitable for home or offices. In addition, there were occasional tables, palm stands, hallstands and hall seats, fire screens and over-mantles, music stools, cake stands, shaving stands, display cabinets for china, chesterfield sofas and drop-end sofas (chaise longues), heavy Jacobean dining suites with court cupboards and other assorted dining room and bedroom furniture. Some of these purchased items may be described as products from a process known as 'fancy cabinet-making', usually smaller, lighter and more intricately detailed – such as jewellery boxes – and more often than not designed for the specific use of 'ladies'.

There was private office space for the partners and, even before the fire, Tabernacle Street was connected to the telephone – its number was 262 and the address for telegrams was 'Bedroom, London'. There was office space for the one designer, Basil Archer, and his one draughtsman, Mr. S. D. Porch (known as Dickie). Immediately adjacent was a designated Sales Ledger department to undertake the daily

record-keeping for orders and despatches. There were around 45 clerks employed in conditions of a 'rather Dickensian manner', according to LS, all seated at high desks and stools. Sitting within shouting distance, Mr. Tapley ran the department and was frequently called to the partners' office to answer queries about an order or despatch. Ledgers for accounts were meticulously kept by hand with ink pens in copperplate-style writing (round handwriting using a sharp pointed nib instead of a flat nib) in heavy leather-covered volumes with brass locks (most of the Lebus Ledgers relating to this period still exist today). In the absence of typewriters or office machinery, letters were copied through the use of a letter press (in which lead letters of the alphabet were assembled in a block accordingly) and ink pads.

A need for a new dedicated manufacturing hub alongside Tabernacle Street

The first record of turnover is for 1887: £34,100. In the five years that followed, recorded turnover increased almost threefold to £105,200 by the end of 1892. Despite the fire, turnover recorded at the end of 1894 was a healthy £86,300, 30% down on the previous year, when it had reached £120,000. Within a couple of years, turnover was back to pre-fire levels, exceeding £210,400 in 1897 and reaching £249,100 by the end of the century.

The first payroll is for 1892: £32,967, which increased to £37,010 in 1893. In the year of the fire, payroll was reduced to £28,446. By 1897 the payroll figure exceeded pre-fire levels at £46,469 and by the end of the century had reached £59,622 when, according to LS, there were 1,000-plus employees.

Harris's intention from the outset appears to have been to retain Tabernacle Street – it was strategically advantageous for sales to the West End and had good rail connections nearby. And Harris loved being there – to move in appropriate circles, to generate business deals. Conversely, Sol's 'predilection was for country rather than town life' according to the *Tottenham and Edmonton Weekly Herald*, 30 April 1926, and so, with increased sales, a burgeoning business and limited space for cabinet-making, there was only one option… to search for a new site large enough to accommodate the processes of furniture manufacture. This site was most likely to be further away from the city.

Samuel Clifford Tee engaged as architect

Architect Samuel Clifford Tee, who set up in business at 50 Moorgate Street, EC1 in January 1895, was engaged to design and supervise the construction of a new factory building, once he had identified a suitable site and concluded all land conveyance and associated issues. According to LS, all this was performed for a fee of £3,000. A copy of Clifford Tee's invoice of June 1900 (*A History of Harris Lebus, 1840–1947*, Appendix 11) detailing work undertaken month by month over the preceding year showed that securing land suitable to build a factory for his client was indeed a complex affair.

The search begins

Old Ford: After visiting a site at Old Ford with Harris in June 1899, Clifford Tee undertook several more journeys to look at two adjacent sites that could be purchased as a package and had meetings with their respective owners. The following month, after detailed investigations, Clifford Tee advised his client against the suitability of the site at Old Ford because of 'bad foundations'. Had the Old Ford site ultimately been chosen, the story might have had a very different outcome.

Tottenham Hale: Clifford Tee then had to begin another search and arrange the next site visit – at Tottenham Hale – this time with Sol. However, the process towards the prospective purchase did not go smoothly and almost did not happen at all. Work was undertaken over several months: after firstly checking out the drainage issue of the land (bearing in mind the issues with the Old Ford site) and identifying Mr. Button, Stamford Hill, as the owner of some of the land in the location visited, negotiations became gridlocked when the owner would not sell for less than £2,000 per acre and was not inclined to sell less than 20 acres (Harris only wanted 10 acres at an offer of £1,200 per acre). Discussions ran on into October that year.

Meanwhile, another plot at that time occupied by Ware Nurseries was also looked into. This was owned, in part, by the New River Company but was under offer from another prospective purchaser and Clifford Tee's persistence on behalf of his client yielded no dividends. When Clifford Tee tracked down Thomas Ware to discuss the prospect, he was informed that he had already sold his interests in the land to Mr. Herrmann, a rival businessman. An entry in Tottenham Urban District Council's minutes dated 1 August 1899 (in original hand-written minute books held by Haringey Local History Archives at Bruce Castle Museum) records an application from Mr. H. Herrmann and Company of Dod Street, Limehouse, 'to erect a factory and workmen's cottages on land near Tottenham Lock on the east side of the Great Eastern Railway and engineering the nearest point at which their drains could be connected with the council's sewer'. Dutifully pursuing the interests of his client, Clifford Tee subsequently tracked down Herrmann and initially discussions looked promising as he was prepared to sell. However, when he failed to keep appointments, the outcome looked less and less promising and Clifford Tee's patience was continually tested.

Clapton: By late July, Clifford Tee turned to the possible options of various plots of land in the Clapton area. The first was on the Amhurst Estate, but after discussions with the estate surveyor, spending time drawing up plans and being encouraged with a price of £90 per acre on a lease, an eventual offer for the freehold was declined by Lord Amhurst. After similar efforts to explore lands east of the Lea Navigation in the same vicinity, Clifford Tee found they were designated Lammas land.

Edmonton: By August, Clifford Tee was looking at Edmonton, but after a promising start, in which 30 acres could be purchased for £350 per acre from a Mr. Richards, the architect decided it was inaccessible.

Stratford: Later that same month, Clifford Tee was exploring Stratford, but a relatively high rental of £150 per acre and 'bad foundations' proved prohibitive.

Somewhere between Tottenham and Edmonton: By then, it was September; the land in question turned out to be Glebe land owned by the Rector of St. Giles and, since part had already been let for rifle butts, it was deemed unsuitable.

Canning Town: Although it was suitable, the Gas Light and Coke Company would not sell.

Willesden: Land by the canal was considered, the owner contacted, but Clifford Tee decided ultimately the locality was not suitable.

Leyton: A site at £750 an acre from Mr. Savill and Sons looked promising, but again there were drainage issues, and discussions with both Leyton District Council and the Great Eastern Railway proved complex and remained unresolved.

Lea Bridge Road Station: In October, a plot of 10 acres at a price of £1,000 per acre came to

Clifford Tee's attention and looked promising – so much so that Harris himself visited with Clifford Tee on several occasions. But once again, drainage was an issue. Clifford Tee was engaged in trying to resolve this with the District Council when…

The Tottenham Hale site comes back on the market

On Saturday 4 November 1899, a call was made by Mr. Elwell at the Great Eastern Railway informing Clifford Tee of a site in Tottenham Hale that was on the market. He immediately recognised this as the same one Mr. Herrmann was thought previously to have purchased. Clifford Tee was at once on the case, meeting Mr. Hicks, the owner, on the following Monday. The asking price was £9,200.

The reason that dissuaded Mr. Herrmann from developing the site was, once again, the issue of drainage. According to Clifford Tee's invoice, Tottenham Urban District Council had given notice to Mr. Herrmann and Company that the surface of the whole of the ground must be raised by two feet before the authority could drain the land.

Over the course of the next six weeks or so, Clifford Tee set out to go 'minutely' (his word) into this issue in an attempt to prove the council's surveyor wrong. As a back-up plan, he also negotiated a joint agreement with the Great Eastern Railway Company to enable the laying of a sewer pipe under their land in the event the council were unable to provide drainage.

Tottenham Hale Site Procured

From January to the beginning of June 1900, Clifford Tee undertook conveyance work, which involved visits to the site to stake out land, take measurements, verify details of the deeds, produce plans and resolve issues for the preparation of the contracts. He reveals his sense of relief when he records the phrase 'on hearing that the purchase was finally completed on this date' in his invoice of 1900 – from expression of interest to purchase had taken a whole year. (One assumes that the fee agreed between Harris Lebus and Clifford Tee at the outset was regardless of the amount of work involved.)

According to LS's *History*, the agreed price at the point of sale was £6,963 and adds 'original figure inserted in the indenture £8,823 deleted in ink and initialled'.

The complexity of the process to secure an expanse of land suitable for the construction of a sizeable factory involved purchasing further patches to connect various plots together as one usable site. On 1 June 1900, a further 2.4 acres (described as 2 acres, 1 rod and 23.5 perches in the deed) were purchased collectively from the New River Company and the General Land Company Limited for a sum of £2,065. Even with this done, the usable site of 13.5 acres – an upside-down, slightly misshapen, elongated triangle, bounded by Ferry Lane in the north, the Lea Navigation in the east and the Great Eastern Railway to the west – did not directly adjoin these boundaries; rather it 'floated' as if an island, separated from these potentially useful transportation resources by land belonging to other landowners, over which it was necessary to cross to access them. That said, Clifford Tee had the foresight to negotiate a small plot measuring a quarter of an acre (1 rood) just south of Ferry Lane and to the east to secure direct access to the Lea Navigation. An additional plot of similar size, 0.21 acres (34 perches), again south of Ferry Lane though not abutting, brought the possibility of road connection closer.

Furthermore, the land had the obstacle of another railway – the Tottenham and Forest Gate Railway – running right through the middle of it, in effect cutting it in two. And if all that were not enough to contend with, Pymmes Brook ran in a south-to-south-westerly direction. Whilst being a natural boundary on the eastern side, the brook would prove to be an obstacle in itself over time, as would the small pumping station just south of Ferry Lane in the centre of a plot of land belonging to the New River Company.

The Architect's design challenge

The challenge for the architect was immense: to design a factory fit for purpose, in a predominantly rural setting, on an awkwardly shaped and inaccessible plot, around inherent geographical features, on marshy land prone to flooding, making maximum use of available space. Clifford Tee's arrangement with Harris was also to oversee the building works, which started soon after leases were signed. With the plot south of the Tottenham and Forest Gate Railway designated entirely as a timber field for unloading and storage of raw materials, construction was north of this railway and south of Ferry Lane, with the western boundary being the railway sidings and the eastern boundary being Pymmes Brook.

While construction of the factory was underway, various entries in Tottenham Urban District Council minutes confirm Clifford Tee's quest to improve accessibility of the site to transport links: 18 September, 2 October and 18 December in 1900; and 22 January, 5 February and 7 May in 1901.

The timber field at the southern extreme of the original plot and the bank of the Lea Navigation in the south-west corner was accessed along a 'cart track', running in parallel with the Great Eastern Railway and through a narrow arch under the Tottenham and Forest Gate Railway, for which the firm initially only had a 'right of way'. Clifford Tee successfully secured a further strip of land to the southern corner of the site to connect directly to the bank of the Lea Navigation, which went through on 21 May 1901. The lease extended the original access land strip to a width of 30 feet; subsequently, it was conveyed to the firm for the sum of £125 by Tottenham Urban District Council.

With reference to Clifford Tee's invoice, authorisation was made for the firm to 'set down and keep in repair tram, or rails, or lines and run, draw or convey trucks, carriages or other vehicles'.

Interestingly, the firm had designs on an unloading crane from the outset, as on the

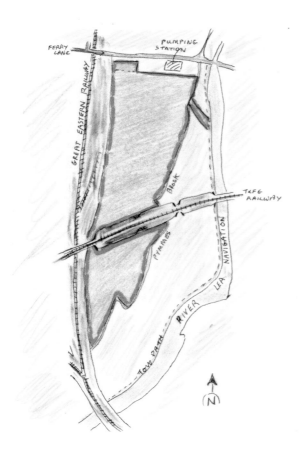

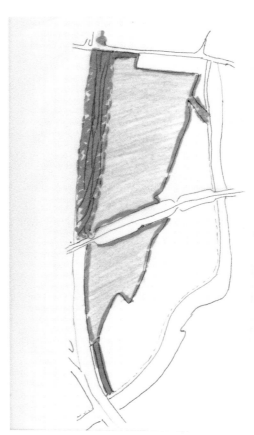

Land purchased initially at Tottenham Hale in 1900

Land purchased subsequently at Tottenham Hale in 1901

same indenture appeared the word 'crane' on the southernmost extremity of the plot adjacent to the river. However, the ambition to install the crane would not be realised until much later.

In September that year, a further parcel of land in the north-west corner just south of Ferry Lane was secured and, whilst not abutting Ferry Lane directly, it served to ensure that some of the frontage of the factory was at least visibly 'opened up' to the road. Crucially, in the same month, a successful negotiation with the Great Eastern Railway Company yielded an agreement to lease private railway sidings, connected to the rail network and running alongside the entire eastern boundary of the purchased lands.

Alfred James Bateman engaged as builder

The contracted builders were not a London-based firm: the offices of Alfred James Bateman were in Ramsey High Street, Huntingdonshire. Little is known about Bateman's building

works. The Huntingdonshire Local History Archives Service could only find a single record of his work in the locality (his company built an extension to the Ramsey High Street police station in 1875) despite a hand-written note on company-headed paper containing the printed phrase 'established for 100 years' (*A History of Harris Lebus, 1840–1947*, Appendix 23).

The date of the hand-written 'private and confidential' letter from Bateman to Harris requesting funds is dated 16 March 1903, suggesting the building work in the initial phase spanned several years. The tone of the builder's letter appears to be hesitant, tentative and apologetic: Bateman is requesting a cheque for £1,000 (of the £1,340 agreed). This was a sizeable sum in those days and it is presumed Bateman's letter was necessary to keep his bank manager at bay.

> Nothing but pressing necessity should induce me to bother you – from whom I have received more consideration than

from anyone else in my life – about money matters, but I enclose a letter just received from my bank which will speak for itself and with all my resources hung up, I really do not know where to turn. Will you therefore kindly forward me a cheque for £1,000 and the remaining £340 can stand over as long as you wish. Thanking you in anticipation and for all past favours, yours respectfully, Alfred. J. Bateman.

A possible explanation as to why there is little information in local archives about Bateman's firm might be that much of his work was done in London where he may have made himself a reputation, rather than in Huntingdon. At the time his company was awarded the Lebus factory contract, he was a member of his Urban District Council, but he gave up this position in 1901 – perhaps to focus on the Lebus build. In fact, Bateman went on to build the Palace Theatre, High Road, Tottenham, which opened on 31 August 1908 – a foundation stone at the front entrance confirms this.

Building work spanned a number of years on and off, with the initial building phase and further extensions, thereafter, as suggested by a mention in the *Tottenham and Edmonton Weekly Herald*, 8 July 1910, reporting on the Tottenham Urban District Council meeting held on 5 July 1910: 'With regard to the labour that would be employed in putting up the building… the builder was generally a brick maker as well. He came from outside the district – Huntingdon… brought his own men and paid 7d or 8d an hour'.

The 'Harris Lebus – Finsbury Cabinet Works'

Through a single wrought-iron gate from Ferry Lane, a flight of concrete steps led down to a cobbled pathway. Located in the north-west corner of the site, running parallel with Ferry Lane, the first building approached was building A, the general office – a relatively understated one-storey brick building, its roof not much higher than the raised humpback bridge. The north-facing windows of the general office looked out over the marshes through a series of brick-built arches under Ferry Lane, which became shorter in height as the bridge descended; an elaborate raised mosaic incorporated in the design above the windows at the front in deep blue and white glazed pottery tiles announced 'HARRIS LEBUS – FINSBURY CABINET WORKS'.

LS stated the factory opened in 1901, although no evidence of a fanfare opening ceremony can be found. A five-year contract with the National Telephone Company Limited for an exchange line (plus private lines to Tabernacle Street and Maple and Company) at a cost of £12 15s per annum dated 19 March 1901 indicates

Workers standing at the front entrance to the factory on Ferry Lane in 1905

Staff in building A – On the left is Mr. W. H. Wright, chief cashier; on the right is Mr. Gillingham, with the Accounts department under the windows on the right. Mr. Flatau's timber purchase was later squeezed in further back. Beyond the screens at the furthest end were the designers, Basil Archer and Dickie Porch.

when construction of the general office was completed and operational.

With private office space for the partners, the general office accommodated Mr. Frank Geary, the works manager (and subsequently Mr. A. C. Harris, his assistant), a design/drawing section for Basil Archer and Dickie Porch, the administration associated with timber purchase for Mr. Flatau and an accounting section for both Mr. Gillingham, who was in charge of the works accounts, and Mr. W. H. Wright, chief cashier.

The ground plan, building design and construction process for the 'Finsbury Cabinet Works' was meticulously thought through and executed by Clifford Tee. The brief specified

the creation of a dedicated hub containing a collection of buildings (some incorporating Clifford Tee's desired 'saw tooth' roof design) to accommodate specific, designated processes in furniture-making, warehouse storage and distribution, and to operate alongside 'Tab. Street' (as it was affectionately known). Consequently, there was limited provision of office space. The general office *was* that office space.

Getting to work

'Ferry Lane… was a proper lane… there were no pavements or street lamps down there,' recalled Elsie Lambert, one of the first workers, employed between 1902 and 1905, as noted in *How Things Were: Growing Up in Tottenham 1890–1920* (a Tottenham Workshop publication, c.1980). She continued, 'In the middle of the road at Tottenham Hale – I believe there is a roundabout there now – there used to be a big shelter where they used to put stray horses. They called it the "pound". Horses used to stray and get lost and they was put in there 'til they was claimed, 'cos it was all marshland out there then.'

Tottenham Hale in the early 1900s was an isolated spot: road transport and infrastructure were not, as yet, well developed. The site could only be approached from the west via a dirt-track Ferry Lane (at one time called Mill Marsh Lane), which narrowed over the humpback bridge spanning the Great Eastern Railway and descended steeply, with the site on the right. This track then ended abruptly at the Lea Navigation by Tottenham Lock – there was no connecting bridge over the river or Dagenham Brook beyond. It is hard to imagine a journey to work on a cold, dark winter's morning with little, if any, street lighting.

Public transport at the time was also limited – a train journey from Liverpool Street station to Tottenham Hale was an option. For employees arriving from surrounding areas, such as Manor House or Seven Sisters, a horse tram service ran along Tottenham High Road, the nearest stop being at High Cross; the onward journey to the factory necessitated a slog by foot. That said, at some point, according to Fred Fisk, Mr. Willan, who lived in a farmhouse on the Walthamstow side of the water, ran a service of omnibuses from the Hale along Seven Sisters Road to the West End.

From Walthamstow and beyond, horse trams started east of Dagenham Brook. Much later, when the River Lea and Dagenham Brook were bridged, the connection by road between Tottenham and Walthamstow was from the Hale through Ferry Lane, making this a busy thoroughfare: four trolley-bus traction stanchions survived until removed by Hale Village contractors in early 2016.

From Tabernacle Street to Tottenham Hale

According to LS in 1899, at Tabernacle Street, there were 1,000 manual workers and 45 office staff. As well as transfers to the new works, fresh workers were recruited. Joseph Ashmele, a 15-year-old Polish immigrant who worked with Lebus in Tabernacle Street between 1899 and 1901, chose not to transfer. He left Lebus employ and, after 12 years' employment with Messrs. Rubery and Stockwell in Curtain Road, went on to establish his own business as a manufacturing upholsterer in 1911, with showrooms at 17–19 Pancras Street. There is evidence that loyal Harris Lebus employees transferred to the factory in the roles they had at Tabernacle Street, such as sole designer, Basil Archer, and his draughtsman, Dickie Porch.

There is every indication that some employees resettled and moved to Tottenham Hale to live. Alfred William Perrin, manager of the carvers' workshop, is one such example; according to apprenticeship indentures in 1898, he signs as a witness and gives his address as 17 Rockmead

Mr. and Mrs. Albert Church pictured in 1910; Albert moved over from Tabernacle Street to work in the new factory

Road, South Hackney, but by 1908 he is living at 23 Talbot Road, South Tottenham, in an area of small Edwardian villas within walking distance of the factory. Albert Church, who lit the gas lights first thing in the morning as a new apprentice carver in Tabernacle Street in 1898, moved to 44 Woodland Park Road, N15. From various articles in the *Lebus Log*, he was still living there in 1955.

Mr. Edward Daughters, the Marshall-engine driver, transferred to the factory when the engine was relocated. His story as a loyal employee is worthy of special mention. Edward joined the firm in 1875 when the business was at 37 Wellclose Square. He subsequently witnessed the extension into the adjacent number 38 and was part of the relocation to numbers 5 and 9 in the same road. He was then at 70 and 72 Tabernacle Street, remained with the firm through the recovery period following the fire and moved to the new works. Edward was by then living at 113 Higham Hill Road,

Edward Daughters, who started work with Harris Lebus in 1875, moved his place of work to Tottenham Hale along with the Marshall steam engine he drove to power the machines; he lived nearby in Walthamstow

Walthamstow, as was his son George, also an employee. George's apprentice indenture, signed by his father on 28 January 1906, gives this address. Edward was still working when he subsequently died in 1915.

At the time of Harris Lebus's death in September 1907, the obituaries in national publications, such as the *Daily Mail* and the *Cabinet Maker and Complete House Furnisher*, were quoting employment figures of 3,000 and of 3,000 to 4,000 respectively. However, that same year, a less-inflated figure was suggested in the *Michigan Artisan* (27th year, No. 16, 25 February 1907), which quoted Louis as saying: 'We have about 2,500 hands'.

Just a few years later, Clifford Tee reported to the meeting of the Tottenham Urban District Council, according to the *Tottenham and Edmonton Weekly Herald*, 7 January 1910, that 'the factory employed 2,000 hands'.

The Changing Face of Tottenham Hale

'Tottenham Hale was within the memory of many residents still living, a quaint old-fashioned district, with old cottages – some of which are still standing – with long gardens in front, some of them reached by narrow wooden bridges across a running stream. The Hale, once a picturesque district, has recently become thickly populated with the poorer classes, many of whom are foreigners. Factories are rapidly being built...'

– Fred Fisk, *The History of the Ancient Parish of Tottenham*, 1923

The location at Tottenham Hale, six miles north of the city, could not have been in starker contrast to the dense, congested, bustling urban location of Tabernacle Street, EC1.

On site maps of the factory, a small shed sat at a strange slantwise layout in relation to surrounding buildings because it was built on the site's periphery in 1905, right on the bank of Pymmes Brook. William Thear (known as Bill), who joined the firm in 1907, recalled looking out from V2 shed over Pymmes Brook – a bathing haunt for 'tramps of both sexes, whose language at the invasion of their privacy was quite unprintable!' (*Lebus Log*, No. 6, November 1955) Bill's choice of the word 'tramp' demonstrates prejudice; many people of the 'poorer classes' would not have had access to running water in their homes. At that time, given the rural nature of the location and before the impact of industry and road surface water pollution, the brook water was probably quite spring-like and crystal clear. The choice to bathe had always been afforded; the factory in a rural landscape was in fact the 'invasion'. Some of the first workers enjoyed a swim: Charlie Holland remembered swimming in the Lea Navigation as a young apprentice in 1908 (*Lebus Log*, No. 13, December 1958) and being fearful he might be caught.

A precedent set – plant nurseries give way to industrial development

In establishing a manufacturing base at Tottenham Hale, Harris Lebus set a precedent for others to follow. The process of change to an industrial landscape was now well underway.

During the previous half-century, Thomas Softly Ware owned a sizeable amount of the land in Tottenham Hale, which he used to nurture his exotic bulbs and specialist flowering plants. By 1890, he had already sold off some of his land interests but, according to the rates book of that year, he still had an eleven-acre nursery south of Ferry Lane, west of the Great Eastern Railway, another six acres between the railway and the canal, as well as 140 acres of marsh and meadow grazing land. Hale Farm Nurseries moved to Feltham, Middlesex in 1899, retaining the name. In the first product catalogue of 1900 (archived at Bruce Castle Museum) an explanation is offered to explain the move: 'the very extensive building operations and railway developments'. Fred Fisk suggests that, after Ware Nurseries, the site was sold and it was announced in 1899 that a factory for making ginger beer was about to be erected – but the negotiation fell through.

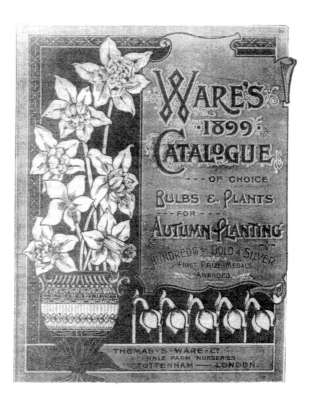

Ware's plant nursery catalogue of 1899

The first sizeable factory in the area was indeed that of Harris Lebus; its presence would shape the future landscape of Tottenham Hale, and this happened rapidly. Within a few short years there was a convergence of several more factories to the west of the Lebus factory, between the London and the Great Eastern Railway and Broad Lane, and along Fountayne Road and Fawley Road (where Tottenham Hale Retail Park is now), as well as Ashley Road.

Millington & Sons (whose origins may be traced back to Bishopsgate in 1824) established their Crown Works manufacturing stationery in Fountayne Road in 1903. Bought out by Dickinson in 1918, they produced the Basildon Bond stationery brand – a form of high-quality watermarked writing paper. They also became a major manufacturer of envelopes: their 'outlook' envelope being the earliest window envelope, first made in 1905.

Clifford Tee designs another local factory

Samuel Clifford Tee was instrumental in the industrial growth of the area. He designed the Eagle Pencil Company works (now known as Berol House) in Ashley Road, no doubt having secured this project after his success with Harris Lebus, whom he continued to retain as a client. The Eagle Pencil Company works were completed and operational by 1907. The founder, Daniel Berolzheimer, was Bavarian and had been trading in the United States from 1894, before setting up a London office at the turn of the century.

Tottenham's Jewish community and perceptions of the Lebus workforce

The presence of Tottenham Jewish Home and Hospital – offering care and religious facilities to poor immigrant Jews – in Tottenham High Road at the turn of the twentieth century suggests the presence of a Jewish community. There were other factories with owners of Jewish origin. In 1906, the Gestetner Cyclograph Company established a works on Broad Lane, having transferred from Cross Street, Islington, N1. The firm patented a copying machine and produced duplicating machines, stencils, styli, ink rollers and other related products. The founder, David Gestetner, who came to London from Hungary in 1859, was of Jewish origin, as were the founders of A. W. Flateau and Company, a wholesale boot and shoe manufacturers who moved their manufacturing base from Hackney Road to Tottenham Hale.

The authors of *Furnishing the World* claimed that 'one firm which absorbed a huge number of unskilled Jewish workers was Lebus… [I]n the late nineteenth century it was estimated that 90 percent of the Lebus workforce were "greeners" employed on very low wages'. If that were the case, it would be reasonable to assume that a number of workers who transferred and moved into the area were Jewish. 'It's part of Tottenham folklore that a notice hung outside the factory stating that "No Englishman Need Apply", and a "riot" in High Cross between Jewish and Gentile cabinet-makers in the early 1900s is well remembered, too' is the claim made in a Tottenham History Workshop publication: *How Things Were – Growing Up in Tottenham 1890–1920*.

The book, based on reminiscences and memories of local people who lived through the end of the nineteenth century and the early years of the twentieth century (along with interpretation arising from the necessary editing process), records some anecdotal stories and provides some insight into the make-up of the Lebus workforce in its early years. *How Things Were* states that many of the workers in the early days at Tottenham were Jewish, or immigrants from Eastern Europe, and that 'Yiddish was spoken as much as English'. It goes on to state that there was a question mark as to 'whether the notice actually existed or not' and further that, if it did, rather than it being official, 'it's as likely to have been put there by an anti-Semitic troublemaker'. There is no evidence to suggest that such practices of exclusion ever existed or that, in reality, the workforce was anything other than a healthy, diverse representation of the local community. Perhaps the issue is more about perceptions and prejudice than anything else.

The excerpt from *How Things Were* continues, 'There were certainly many non-Jewish Tottenham people who found work there' and the book cites examples of local residents who found work with Lebus. James Ferguson, the son of a Tilbury docker, lived with his sister in Colsterworth Road, High Cross. He joined in 1910 when he was 14 and a couple of years later began working as an apprentice engineer, alongside a fitter repairing varied machinery, Harry Downham, the son of an engineering worker who lived in Welbourne Road, High Cross. The latter was taken on in 1910, when he was around 16, carrying planks on a special protective cap on his head to mitigate against the coarse-cut machine, which would cut it into rough sizes for the finer working. He would also stock it up when it came off the saw. Wally Scott, of Stanley Road, found his first job there in 1920, when he was 14.

Extracts of a meeting of Tottenham Urban District Council, 5 July 1910

These extracts of a meeting of Tottenham Urban District Council, 5 July 1910 (*Tottenham and Edmonton Weekly Herald*, 8 July 1910) demonstrated current views, perceptions… and prejudices:

Mr. A. E. Beales: Had Messrs Lebus introduced a class of people that kept up the rateable value of the adjoining roads? The mansion in which he (the speaker) lived had twice been reduced in rateable value, and so had nearly all the houses in that road, while it was the same in High Cross Road and Chestnut Road. This was due to the class of people that had been brought there. That locality used to be a pleasant part of Tottenham, but now it has been created practically into a slum…

Mr. I. Akker: … Mr. Beales had cast a slur upon the work people employed by Messrs Lebus… Mr. Beales said that Messrs Lebus employed a set of men that degraded the parish. But the parish is no worse today than it was twenty-three years ago, when he had come there. Mr. Beales spoke of the slumdom of the High Cross and Welbourne Roads… It was because they were a Jewish firm and employed a number of Jews that Mr. Beales had spoken as he had done.

Mr. A. E. Beales: No, no… he had never been to Messrs. Lebus.

Finally, the record was set straight when Mr. C. E. Brown spoke.

Mr. C. E. Brown: … said that if Mr. Beales did not go himself, some of his associates went… Messrs Lebus had only ten percent of foreigners employed, and any member of the Council had the consent of the manager to inspect their books, and to go through the factory in order to see whether that was a fact or otherwise.

Business rates and local economy

At a meeting of Tottenham Urban District Council (*Tottenham and Edmonton Weekly Herald*, 7 January 1910), Clifford Tee, who was present at a meeting to discuss the purchase of additional lands, said that Harris Lebus was currently paying an annual business rate of £2,500. This, of course, was when the factory was in its infancy and sat on around 13 or so acres of land. The thrust of Clifford Tee's argument was that the presence of the Lebus manufacturing operation and its employees boosted the local economy. The presence of the first sizeable factory in the locality would have stimulated the local building trade and, with more factories paying business rates, workers moving to the area to rent or buy property, spending in the local economy and stimulating house-building, public transport ultimately improved.

Harris and Sol – Complementary Characteristics

In the month before he died, Harris and his family were on holiday at the Hôtel des Roches Noires, Trouville-sur-Mer, a fashionable French seaside resort. The hotel was immortalised in a Claude Monet painting in 1870 when he stayed there with his young bride. Dated 13 August 1907, a letter to Sol (the content of which is business-oriented, though not directly to do with the firm) ends with: 'I am pleased to say we are all well, hope you found all at Herne Bay the same, with love to family… from all here, your brother Harris.' It was most probably the last letter he sent to Sol.

Quoted in LS's *History*, reflecting on the partnership some years later, C. H. Robinson commented:

> It is evident that the siblings were as different in character as each other, and yet this proved to be their strength. The partnership of the two brothers was, in many ways, an ideal combination for the building up of a very large business. Harris had unbounded energy and driving power, which he used relentlessly on himself as well as others. His partner, his younger brother Sol, many years his junior, was himself an outstanding character. Sol had dynamic energy… a great capacity for getting things done and was a tower of strength to the partnership. Sol was chased by Harris, and in turn chased the staff. Whilst working at great pressure and expecting others to do likewise, he had a happy knack of getting on well with people and was most popular. He was intensely practical and spent most of his time in

the factory where he would think nothing of taking the tools out of a man's hand and showing him personally how to do the job. Harris's determination and wide vision and aptitude for taking risks, used to sometimes scare his brother. Sol's flair for obtaining factory output, his grasp of detail, his shrewdness and ability, made a splendid team… like most partners, they had tremendous quarrels, but that was natural with two such strong personalities. Against outside attack they were intensely loyal to each other.

Louis and Herman join the partnership

Louis and Herman began working in the family business around 1898, in the time when the Finsbury Cabinet Works was still only a vision and all operations were conducted at Tabernacle Street. Once they started work, Louis shadowed Sol, and Herman shadowed his father to receive their training. LS suggests that the business account with the bank was changed to Harris, Sol, Louis and Herman on 27 July 1904, though a later letter from the firm's solicitor stated they were officially made partners on the death of Harris in September 1907. Upon Harris's death, each of the four remaining partners (including Sarah Lebus, the silent partner) were due a quarter share of all profits (60/240), with losses split equally among the three working partners at a third (80/240). For the best part of twenty years, between 1907 and 1926, Sol worked with his nephews running what was probably the world's largest wholesale furniture manufacturers employing a sizeable workforce.

Sol Lebus: 21 January 1866 – 20 April 1926

'I suppose the riddle will never be solved as to which of the two brothers was the greatest genius in the phenomenal rise of our first great big furniture factory on mass production lines.'

– Sir Ernest Benn, *The Cabinet Maker and Complete House Furnisher*, 24 April 1926

'The death of Mr. Sol Lebus – loss to the furniture trade' was the headline of the *Tottenham and Edmonton Weekly Herald*, 30 April 1926. The article reads:

The sudden death took place, from heart failure on Tuesday of last week, of Mr. Sol Lebus, at his home in Portman Square, London. Mr. Lebus was at all times greatly engrossed in his business and to the end of his life visited almost daily both the huge furniture manufacturing works of Harris Lebus at Tottenham Hale and the firm's extensive showrooms at Tabernacle Street. When on the previous Friday he followed his usual custom, nothing was noted in his appearance suggesting illness. On the Monday Mr. Lebus was at home, suffering from a slight cold, but it was confidently anticipated he would be returning to the works in a day or two, a hope which was unfortunately not destined to be realised. On the following day came the almost incredible news that his death had occurred, following a heart attack.

Mr. Lebus was a man of simple taste… Unobtrusive in his methods, but thorough in everything he did, Mr. Sol Lebus exerted a wide influence. To say that he was liked and respected by his employees would scarcely do justice to the good relationship between employers and employees, which has, in the long run, always prevailed at the Lebus works. According to the 'Cabinet Maker', Mr. Sol Lebus was regarded by his employees as a friend, rather than 'the governor'.

Resting place of Sol

Sol Lebus was buried in Willesden Cemetery on Friday 23 April 1926 in Section MX, Row 21, Number 20. Next to him, in Number 21, is his wife Esther, who was buried on Sunday 6 November 1949, having died on Friday 4 November 1949.

PART B

ACHIEVEMENT:
THROUGH THE TOTTENHAM HALE YEARS

'The furniture industry looks to pioneering as well as entrepreneurial foresight in location. Lebus chose the strategic site at Ferry Lane, Tottenham… the whole procession of migrants from East End to Lea valley followed this lead.'

– J. L. Oliver, *The Development and Structure of the Furniture Industry*

46

CHAPTER THREE

Around 'the Works' in Less than Eighty Years: Adapting and Expanding the Tottenham Hale Factory Site

'Yes, we have a large factory. Americans who have visited us say it is the largest in the world. It is surely larger than any other furniture factory in Europe and if there is anything larger on this side [America] you ought to know about it.'

– Louis Lebus, *Michigan Artisan*, 25 February 1907

Drama: Thursday 10 November 1955 – visiting royalty to 'Harris Lebus Ltd. Furniture' factory

As the flags fluttered restlessly in the winter breeze atop regimented poles aligned along the north-facing factory frontage, promptly at 10.30 a.m. the royal car – a large, black Austin Princess saloon – appeared over the crest of the humpback bridge of Ferry Lane. A few moments later and much to the delight of large crowds, including relatives of the 4,000 employees, His Royal Highness the Duke of Edinburgh stepped from his car at the main entrance; a neon sign (which covered over the original elaborate, raised mosaic of deep blue and white glazed pottery tiles) proudly announced his destination: 'HARRIS LEBUS LTD FURNITURE'.

The Duke took a brief walk down the steps and over the original cobblestone way, witnessed a proud salute from concierge Bill Ferris and received a warm greeting from the public limited company's chairman and

managing director, Herman Lebus. Now in his seventies and knighted for his and the firm's contributions to two world wars, Sir Herman invited the entourage – a select party of V.I.P.s and press, including reporter Robert Hawes of the *Tottenham and Edmonton Weekly Herald* – through the front entrance and into what was originally the small general office, now his exclusive private office.

Flags welcome the Duke of Edinburgh to Harris Lebus Furniture

Clifford Tee's Vision and the Factory of the Fifties – A Comparison

At the time of the Duke's visit, Harris Lebus was a dense, adapted, sprawling mass of mechanised manufacturing infrastructure, walled like a fortress, virtually under one roof and clamped assertively on the edges of an urbanised, mixed cluster of industrial businesses and homes. It was starkly different to and three times the size of the facility that had been designed and built originally. At half a mile long and one-sixth of a mile wide, all purchased and available land, some 45 acres in total, had been put to maximum use. There were plans afoot for a brand-new warehousing and distribution facility north of Ferry Lane and south of the firm's sports field and pavilion. Clifford Tee's original Finsbury Cabinet Works, covering thirteen-and-a-half acres, was a compact array of individual, purpose-built hand-crafting and, to some extent, semi-mechanised workshops on a damp, mud-flatted plain nestling incongruously in a rural shroud connected inherently by a grand design. Even then, a twenty-four-year-old Louis could claim the factory to be 'the largest in the world'.

'Tab. Street' and 'the works' – split-site working

During the half-century preceding the Duke's visit, there had been extensive alteration, adaption and additions to the original factory site in response to requirements placed on the infrastructure through changing demands – increased volume of throughput and types of products made during progressive phases in the firm's evolution. It must be remembered that it had been designed to a given brief – a dedicated hub for making, storing and distributing furniture on a large scale and in an order of convenient progression (even if that progression was, in practice, in batches). Giving up Tabernacle Street was simply not an option, with Harris fulfilling his wish to continue holding court and Sol overseeing manufacture at the factory; the extra space created by moving cabinet-making out of these premises in the heart of East London was utilised primarily for sales, as well as the upholstery side of the business. As a consequence of this, a distinct line of separation was drawn from the outset between operations (cabinet-making) and strategic development and sales. Running a business from split sites required considerable assimilation and coordination between the two locations and their functions. Within a few years of operating, the factory infrastructure was already proving to be unsuitable for the increasing demands that would subsequently be placed upon it.

The site map seen by the Duke of Edinburgh before his tour, inclusive of land both north and south of Ferry Lane, might be described, south to north and schematically, as long, rectangular in shape and almost entirely surrounded by transport – river, road and rail; the River Lea Navigation down the eastern long side and the over-ground railway from Tottenham Hale station to East End London's Liverpool Street station down the western long side. The northern boundary of Harris Lebus was the Keith Blackman factory.

1966–1978 – Contraction, Closure and Construction

Three consecutive 'islands' – A, B and C

For ease of identification in the landscape, south to north, there were (and still are) in effect, three consecutive 'islands' – A, B and C – each of around fifteen or so acres. Between islands A and B is the Barking to Gospel Oak over-ground railway; between islands B and C runs Ferry Lane.

> 'One day people will live where furniture is now being manufactured, as the whole area is expected to be redeveloped with new homes and parkland.'
>
> – *News from Lebus*, No. 1, February 1968

1966 – major restructuring and relocation strategy for the company

A little over a decade after the Duke's visit with Sir Herman, his son Oliver, now chairman, embarked on a seven-year strategic development plan. Key to this 1966 plan was

Aerial photograph taken in the interwar years showing the complete Lebus site, within which (south to north) islands A, B and C can clearly be seen, separated by rail and road

a major restructuring and reinvention of the company that would see a phased withdrawal from Tottenham Hale over a number of years in favour of relocation to one of Britain's expanding towns, which had yet to be agreed with the government. The sale of the entire factory site was *planned*. This is a crucial, but easy to overlook, point.

It was agreed to sell the site in three progressive stages – islands A, B and C – to fund reinvestment and the Greater London Council (GLC) was keen to buy land to satisfy a demand for local social housing. Homelessness in the borough was at 'astronomic level', according to the headline of an article by Kevin Kavanagh in the *Tottenham and Edmonton Weekly Herald*, 12 January 1973. 'On 31 December there were 256 homeless families on the books of the council's homeless families unit,' stated the article. Island A was sold on 8 December 1967 and vacated immediately. Island B was sold for £1.5 million on 1 April 1968, with about half leased back to the firm for two years to continue with manufacture of solid components; this arrangement would expire on 31 March 1970. Island C was under contract to be sold and vacated by 31 December 1973.

The 'new look' Lebus of 1966, in many ways, bore striking similarities to the company's position at the turn of the century. It was as if it had come full circle – the company owned a mere 15 acres of land, had made large-scale recent investment in new 'robot' machinery and reduced the workforce through redundancies to 1,000. In addition, Lebus was also looking to set up a larger manufacture base in a dedicated, purpose-designed and built factory complex and facing the prospect of split-site working.

With a twist of fate, the strategic plan dramatically went awry. The final stage sale happened sooner than planned; this aspect of the story is explored later in the book.

Flat and virtually featureless; ideal for residential use

The planning document for Ferry Lane Estate, to comprise some 750 houses and flats, was submitted to Haringey Council's planning committee on 27 November 1972. It described the site south of Ferry Lane, islands A and B as: 'Having been cleared of its industrial buildings the site is flat and virtually featureless lying approximately two to three feet above the towpath'. The planning document explained that 'British Rail is considering alternative routes for the new rail connection to the proposed third London airport at Maplin Sands. These routes could follow either the Cambridge or the new South Tottenham to Barking line and land has been reserved along the latter route until a firm decision can be reached by British Rail.' (Stansted was later served by the Cambridge line. In 2018, Network Rail began a project to reinstate rail track to expand the Stansted Express service from Liverpool Street on reserved land that had once contained the Lebus private sidings.)

By the beginning of the next decade, the Pevsner Architectural Guides state, 'east of the railway, off Jarrow Road… the Ferry Lane Estate of the 1970s, a rare appearance of GLC work in this area; pleasantly laid out low rise housing on former industrial land'. (*London 4: North*, Bridget Cherry and Nikolaus Pevsner). Construction brought the process of change south of Ferry Lane full circle – from mixed rural and residential with market gardening and small houses in 1900 through industry and manufacture and back to residential once more.

"It was such a big place… when I think about it, you could get lost in there, nobody would know you was lost, it was so big. It was like a little town wasn't it? If you go on to the Ferry Lane Estate and see what they've built from there up to Stamford Hill near enough isn't it, you know".

Phyllis Roberts, canteen assistant during the 1950s

Retracing Steps – Industrial Expansion and Remodelling

Using today's landscape for anchorage, south of Ferry Lane occupying islands A and B sits the housing estate of the same name and to

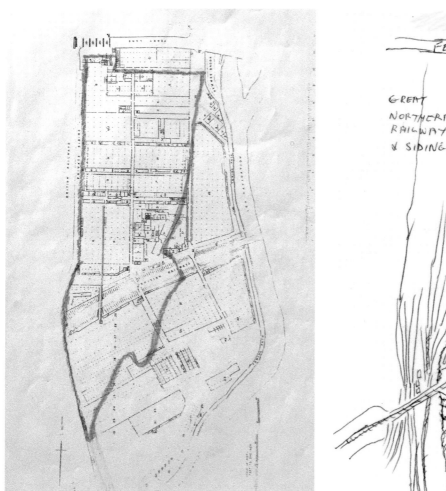
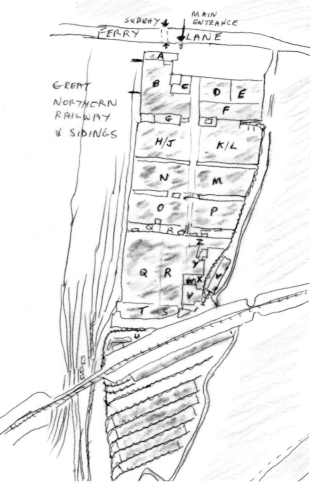

The original land shown on a full site map and Samuel Clifford Tee's original factory plan

the north, occupying island C, is Hale Village and Lockwood industrial estate. During the Lebus years, for the sake of simplicity, island A contained a timber field, the raw materials store; island B was the main production area; and island C contained a colossal warehouse, built in 1956, and the sports field.

The factory of Clifford Tee's design maximised use of the 'upside-down, slightly misshapen, elongated triangle' – an amalgam of four adjoining plots that had previously been with separate owners – 'floating' somewhere in the middle of islands A and B. With reference to today's street map and Ferry Lane Estate accommodation blocks, the original Finsbury Cabinet Works stretched from Jarrow Road (where it runs parallel with Ferry Lane) in the north (island B) to the other end of this road, just south of where it divides into Yarmouth

Crescent (island A). The part of island A utilised was largely set out as the timber field; where Queensferry Walk residents now live, stood the original timber sheds. Across the front gardens of Yarmouth Crescent, trucks with flanged wheels ran along iron rails following the route the road now takes. The bulk of Clifford Tee's original factory was on the western part of island B from Erskine Crescent to Jarrow Road. Pymmes Brook marked the eastern boundaries of the original Finsbury Cabinet Works. Montrose Walk, the main pedestrian thoroughfare, roughly follows the original flow of the brook from what is the top of Reedham Close, diagonally through the school buildings and under the Barking to Gospel Oak railway.

The progression of furniture manufacture was northwards from the unloading of wood delivered by river in the south-west corner of the timber field through buildings labelled Z to A. The first buildings north of the Tottenham and Forest Gate Railway were the steam factory's powerhouse, occupying buildings W, X, Y and Z. With the Marshall engine moved over from Tabernacle Street, it would have been impossible to miss the new tall brick-built chimney and its smoke emissions, at 140 feet high (just under 43 metres) with the word 'LEBUS' in light-coloured bricks. The drying kilns were V, the stables and truck storage U, the carvers were accommodated in T and cutters in S. Q/R was the saw mill, parts were stored in P, the makers worked in M/N, using glue cramps for jointing in O. Polishing and the school of polishers was accommodated in K/L, fitters were supplied from stores in G, with final touching up in H/J. Warehousing and packing was undertaken across C, D, E and F. Despatch to private sidings took place at B.

The general office, building A, was just at the point where Jarrow Road turns south; it faced northwards towards the arches under Ferry Lane. Most of these are now filled in (presumably with factory demolition rubble) creating a grassy slope between Ferry Lane and Jarrow Road. (An original gatepost and the top step sit at the lower end of the iron railings as the Ferry Lane bridge slopes towards what was once the main entrance.)

Outmoded and out of room

'The Parks and Open Spaces Committee reported that on 24 May 1910 the council referred to them a letter from Messrs Lebus, asking for a definite reply to their offer to purchase the Lammas Land near their works, and stating that, since their letter of January 24 last they had prepared a rough plan of their factory extensions…'

– *Tottenham and Edmonton Weekly Herald*, 8 July 1910, district council meeting held on 5 July 1910

'The plant in those days, although very large, was becoming outdated in many ways; it had suffered considerably as a result of the tremendous load put upon it during World War One'. This is the assessment given by LS in his *History*. There were competing pressures for accommodation in an expanding plant, not least from the need to house an Engineers' department to service an increasing amount of machinery. Even before the war, with a burgeoning export trade, a lack of space was particularly acute in the storage, packing, distribution and shipping warehouses. Allocation of office space proved to be woefully inadequate and Harris Lebus was perennially hampered by shortage of space. The inconvenience of regular flooding and various issues in establishing a reliable and extensive power supply posed additional challenges. Alongside the strategy to utilise more land, longer-term solutions to benefit production arrived as two key factors came in to play – flood prevention work by the Lea Conservancy Board (as it was then known) and the rolling out of the national electricity grid between 1927 and 1934.

Completing the jigsaw puzzle of land

From the outset, the strategy to acquire additional surrounding land occupied Clifford Tee for some years, alongside his other commitments. Among the archived items found amongst Oliver's possessions is a handwritten letter from Clifford Tee to Harris Lebus dated 2 July 1902. It concerned the purchase of additional land adjacent to the original Finsbury Cabinet Works and the price that should be offered – Clifford Tee wanted to take a calculated risk in his proposed offer price to the council. After discussing with Sol, Clifford Tee had written to Harris, who was away: 'hoping you are all having this lovely weather that we are all getting just now and enjoying your holiday,' Clifford Tee closes his letter.

The process to secure the additional land needed to construct the proposed C2 building took a good while. It was not until April, May and August of 1909 that Clifford Tee secured three plots of land to the east of the general office – two years after Harris's death. One was from the Great Eastern Railway Company, one from a freeholder, with a further 1,670 square yards on a 999-year lease from the Metropolitan Water Board on which sat a water

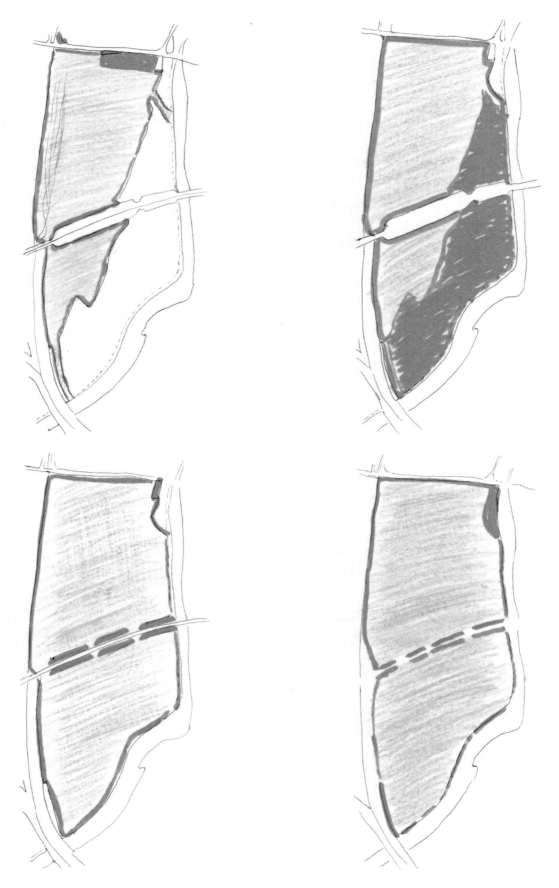

Land acquired progressively between 1909 and 1934 south of Ferry Lane sees Harris Lebus occupy all available land in islands A and B

An interwar image from the 1924 Lebus catalogue shows how islands A and B are utilised

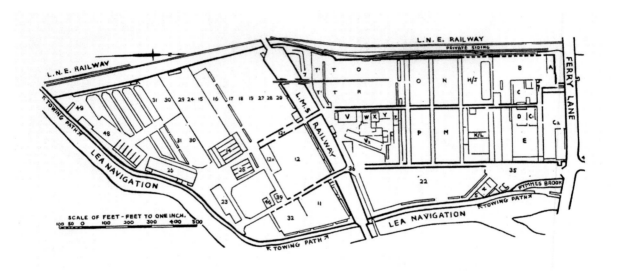

A drawing taken from the 'Train for your career' in-house staff manual from around 1950 shows that, when letters of the alphabet were used up, additional workshops built were assigned a figure from 1 onwards. In some instances where buildings were further extended or merged, some of the original allocated numbers disappear.

pumping station. These purchases brought the factory frontage up to Ferry Lane.

After a long battle over ancient Lammas land and access rights of way, Clifford Tee had acquired the bulk of the lands south of Ferry Lane abutting the entire length of the bank of the Lea Navigation by April 1911. As part of this acquisition, a number of employees of the firm (under the supervision of a Mr.

J. Daniels, who was apparently knowledgeable on this aspect of local history) had to attend 10 a.m. Sunday worship at the Tottenham Parish Church of All Hallows on six consecutive weeks and pin a public notice to the main entrance door. To complete the jigsaw puzzle of land south of Ferry Lane seemed logical; securing the whole of the lands contained within islands A and B, in progressive stages, took 34 years.

From a rooftop vantage point looking north over the glass-roofed C3 building to island C – beyond the car park proudly sits the new sports pavilion named after Sir Herman Lebus and in the far distance on the right is the Keith Blackman factory. Dated 21 September 1955, this photograph pictures the scene a couple of months before the Duke of Edinburgh's visit.

(Reproduced with special permission from Walthamstow Local History Archives, Vestry House Museum)

In June 1937, a little over 27 acres (27 acres and 11 poles) were purchased north of Ferry Lane from the London and North East Railway Company for £25,850. Just under 11 acres (10 acres, 3 rods and 16 perches) were immediately sold to Messrs. Keith Blackman (whose firm made heating and ventilation products for the Admiralty) for a mark-up price of £16,275; an agreement was reached between the respective firms to put in Mill Mead Road. The remainder of newly purchased land constituted island C.

Flood prevention work

The factory site was prone to regular flooding; the banks of the Lea Navigation were not reinforced. With the acquisition of surrounding lands, Pymmes Brook, which once flowed alongside the east side of the factory, now ran through the middle. After heavy rains, it flowed uncontrolled at a considerable rate with a deluge of water flooding the entire site. This regularly happened a few times a year and to a

depth of several feet. In 1919, Tottenham Hale experienced one of the worst floods recorded, lasting from Tuesday 18 February to Saturday 22 February; for the first time, even rail travel was suspended. Charlie Holland remembered the floods of 1919 and described the depth of the water as 'up to five feet in places' (*Lebus Log*, No. 13, December 1958).

In cooperation with the Lea Conservancy Board, a major project to redirect Pymmes Brook was completed by 1930. From its original path (running north-east to south-west adjacent to the river Lea through the middle of the factory under the Tottenham and Forest Gate Railway) the brook was diverted with the construction of concrete walls into the Lea Navigation just south of Ferry Lane. Despite this redirection, floods in 1947 were exceptionally bad. A reminder of the height of the flood waters is etched into the bridge carrying Ferry Lane over the Lea Navigation.

Flooding in 1919; looking north, Lebus railway despatch on the right

The power house pictured around the start of the First World War: to the left is the Siemens generator; in the middle left, far distance the figure of Edward Daughters standing next to the Marshall steam engine can be made out; in the centre of the photograph is Sam Jones, Chief Engineer

Overall, this project benefitted Tottenham Hale in general, not just the Lebus site. Pymmes Brook still carries potential flood waters to this day.

National Grid reaches Tottenham Hale

With the availability of mains power from the North Metropolitan Electric Power Supply Company in December 1928, operations became more mechanised, sophisticated and extended. Before mains electricity, the issues of lighting provision and driving the machines were problematic.

Original lighting was from large arc lamps that were not entirely efficient and required continual maintenance. In 1911, the addition of a William Robinson turbine and generator made by Siemens Brothers and Company Limited, London powered metal filament electric lamps and saw the removal of the original arc lamps the following year. Fluorescent strip lighting was not introduced until 1946.

Even with the National Grid, at the time of the Duke's visit to the power house – complete with its imposing switchboard – the 'boilers were making steam from waste wood and pumping it into the generating machines', observed Robert Hawes in the *Tottenham and Edmonton Weekly Herald*, 11 November 1955. He continued: 'the two turbo-alternators are capable of producing sufficient power from

wood waste to light a fair size town'. On the generating plant, LS wrote in 1965 that 'today it is the largest and most efficient wood-fired generating equipment in the country'.

Originally designed as a steam works, Clifford Tee's factory had three huge Lancashire boilers. Heated by coal, they produced enough steam to drive the variety of machines needed in

The Parsons turbine installed in 1934

(Reproduced with special permission from Waltham Forest Local History Archives, Vestry House Museum)

Above: The powerhouse at the time of the Duke's visit

(Reproduced with special permission from Waltham Forest Local History Archives, Vestry House Museum)

Top right: Arthur Suter watches over the boilers

(Reproduced with special permission from Waltham Forest Local History Archives, Vestry House Museum)

Right: Sawdust extractors that helped provide fuel for the boilers

(Reproduced with special permission from Waltham Forest Local History Archives, Vestry House Museum)

the manufacturing process. From the outset, the prime mover was the 350-horsepower reciprocating engine of Marshall, Sons & Co in Gainsborough. This had been transferred from Tabernacle Street. The Marshall with its huge flywheel drove all the woodworking machines in the mill and machine shop at an average speed of 4,500 rpm through belts and shafts, which necessitated a labyrinth of pits running across the mill and machine shop floors. The Marshall 'engine driver', Edward Daughters, had transferred from Tabernacle Street with his beloved engine – Edward had been driving the machine for 25 years before Tottenham and continued to do so until he died in 1915. He controlled it like a bus conductor: one ring on the bell stopped the engine, two rings started it – and that was the code for all the machines connected to it. There was space to store coal, which either arrived by barge or train, and a dump for ash and detritus from the burning

process. The Marshall, which had remained in constant use since its installation, was finally taken out of service in 1934 and replaced with a 2,700 horsepower Parsons turbine.

Additional boilers of the Babcock & Wilcox water-tube type were added; by the mid-1920s there were nine. Seven Lancashire boilers were fired with slack coal or coke breeze and two water-tube boilers were fired with wood waste collected from the factory. Collection involved pneumatically conveying sawdust and wood chips to the boiler house and then placing the mix in the large chip tank and mixing with recycled waste brought in sacks from factories in the surrounding district after first passing over a conveyor to identify and remove metal objects. The two main turbines, each of 6,000 horsepower, produced two-thirds of all the energy needed to run the factory. In the winter months, excess steam produced in

Above: One of the main drive wheels

Top right: The engineers' section

Right: Part of the engineering department with blacksmith's facilities in V2 shed

the process was used to heat workshops and offices. All boilers were initially hand fired, but subsequently converted to fire automatically.

Migration of other East End furniture makers

Without doubt, it was the successful outcome of Clifford Tee's endeavours in designing the Tottenham factory for Harris Lebus that was a catalyst for other East End furniture manufacturers to see the potential advantages of the Lea Valley. Initially perhaps viewed as a brave move, migration gathered pace with the completion of the National Grid as it rolled out between 1927 and 1934: Bluestone and Elvin relocated from Shoreditch to Walthamstow in 1928; B. and I. Nathan from Curtain Road to Hackney in 1928 and later to Angel Road in Edmonton; and Beautility from Bethnal Green also to Edmonton around 1933.

Engineers' department and machine maintenance

The maintenance and efficiency of machinery, and the power behind them, was the responsibility of an evolving Engineers' department.

There were many problems with early machinery maintenance reliant on belts and shafts – enough to keep two men in full-time work. This could be anything from overheated bearings to a breakage in the main shafting belt. The belts or ropes were made of cotton and were susceptible to stretching and shrinkage as a consequence of changing temperatures and weather conditions. Mr. Dibnah, the works' carpenter, was expert at splicing these. Often the repair work was done overnight because, if a main belt broke in the Marshall, it would have to be stopped, resulting in the entire mill and machine shop becoming inoperable, and thus the entire plant having to be shut down.

Sam Jones was chief engineer in the early years. LS described him as 'endearing' and goes on to say he was 'a tubby Yorkshireman… who was the living image of Mr. Pickwick [the character in Charles Dickens' *Pickwick Papers*], even to the steel-rimmed spectacles.' Mr. Bill Downing subsequently held this post; LS described him as 'an electrician of no great knowledge but he was responsible for a huge plant and scarcely fitted such responsibility'.

The appointment in 1924, of Bernard Humphrey as assistant chief engineer proved a real asset to the firm. 'He was Surveyor, Builder, expert on matters of Land and Leases, Fire Insurance, Fire protection Safety, Timber Seasoning and the Factories Act,' described LS. Humphrey graduated with a BSc in Engineering in 1921 – his studies had been interrupted by World War One, during which he served in the Royal Flying Corps. He was previously at the Forest Products Research Laboratory at Princes Risborough and was recommended for the position by Mr. G. Gosling, who had himself already joined Harris Lebus. After two years, Humphrey succeeded to the post of chief engineer, a post he kept until retirement in 1958, and Mr. C. E. Leaman then became chief maintenance officer. Arthur Suter, who joined the firm in 1919, was, for a number of years, the boiler house chief, retiring after 45 years on 14 February 1964. Walter Hepworth, powerhouse foreman, retired in 1959, as did Arthur Ward, chief machine inspector.

The Engineers' department was extended into the V2 cooling shed when new kilns, 14 and 25, were built before being moved to a brand-new building, 63, in 1955. It is described in the *Lebus Log* (No. 6, October 1955) as 'Lofty, light in construction, roofed with ruberoid on aluminium decking'. Along the east wall of the building and above the filler drying tunnel were arranged foreman's offices and mess-rooms for the men, all reached by steps from the ground floor. Set out with benches, the development also afforded additional workspace for carpenters and electricians as well as space for the saw sharpening and steel hardening sections.

The warehouse – a need for extension from the outset

Included with Clifford Tee's July 1902 letter to Harris Lebus is a hand-drawn plan showing 'new C2 warehouse proposed', with buildings/ work areas labelled 'office (A), B, C1, C2, D, D1 and E, and an unlabelled building drawn in feint. 'I joined the firm in 1908 with the idea of learning the art of export packing,' said Harry Thornton, as quoted in the *Lebus Log*, No. 21, December 1961. 'At that time our export trade was expanding. Working space was rather cramped as we only occupied the two small workshops at the beginning of the main corridor, C1 East and C1 West. It was not long though, before the old pumping station which, together with a couple of goats and a few geese flapping around, giving us a truly rural aspect, was pulled down and a new (two-storey) building erected on its site, designated as C2 shop. Into this new building, the Shipping department was duly transferred.' A later extension was subsequently known as C3. At the junction of Jarrow Road and Ferry Lane was the East Gate and Yard.

A brand-new warehouse for the fifties

A huge new warehouse building of 250,000 square feet erected in the mid-1950s saw the complete utilisation of all Lebus landholdings. The building was several years in the making as a consequence of local planning diktat – the 15-acre site had become scheduled as an open space for public recreational use under the Abercrombie Plan. Following a public enquiry and an appeal by the company, the right to develop the site was secured – a single-storey warehouse building with both cycle and car parks and a sports ground and pavilion for employees. The new warehouse building was once again designed by Clifford Tee and Gale. The *Lebus Log*, No. 8, in April 1956, reads: 'Another 17,000 tons of hard-core have been spread, and rolled; another 3,500 tons of concrete mixed, pumped and poured into foundations… [A]long the… south frontage

The whole Lebus site, islands A, B and C, photographed around 1960 with the large new warehouse on island C

can be seen the skeleton of the two-storey block… towards the north end of the building site a mobile crane can be seen erecting the structural steelwork of the main warehouse building.' By July 1956, the *Lebus Log*, No. 9, informed readers that the building would have concrete flooring with the roof made up of steel decking, surrounded by a layer of heat-insulating board then a felt and bitumen sandwich finished with a layer of granite chippings; there would be no water downpipes showing from outside, leaving the facing brickwork and decorative stone frontage clear. The design subsequently won architecture awards.

Connecting the new warehouse to production unit

There were five arches descending west to east under Ferry Lane providing access. Building A, the general office, had the view northwards through these in the early days of the Finsbury Cabinet Works. One was the pedestrian walkway originally used to cross under Ferry Lane, later to access the underground war shelters and, later still, to access the sports ground and pavilion.

From 1956, the second-tallest arch carried the new huge furniture conveyor belt through to the new warehouse. The *Lebus Log*, No. 9, July 1956, explained:

> The line of the conveyor corridor had to be driven right through what was previously the office of our Chairman – building A. This has involved demolition of the western end – the portion so demolished will be rebuilt as a two-story block with offices for directors and other staff provided above a tunnel through which the conveyors will run. At an early stage of demolition, the western extremity of the neon sign had to be taken down. This has the appearance of depriving HARRIS LEBUS LTD of 'FURNITURE' for a while. The superstitious should pause however, before drawing any doleful conclusions, since this kind of sign fortunately is neither portent nor omen.

Above: The new warehouse (*Industrial Architecture*, Spring 1958)

Looking in a south-easterly direction from a vantage point on Ferry Lane bridge, construction work to accommodate flow production by conveyor to the new warehouse saw the demolition of part of the original warehousing and distribution facilities and the general office (buildings B and A). The original tiled letter Y of the word 'Finsbury' at the front of the general office building is just visible to the extreme left of the photograph. Of interest, in the centre of the photograph, is a later extension to the western side of the three-to-four-storey building – presumably to accommodate lifts between floors.

(Reproduced with special permission from Waltham Forest Local History Archives, Vestry House Museum)

Merged photographs taken as the framework for the new warehouse takes shape; looking east, Ferry Lane and the factory frontage is to the left

(Reproduced with special permission from Waltham Forest Local History Archives, Vestry House Museum)

Looking south and highlighted in white, the arch through which this conveyor once ran is clearly visible on the right of the photograph

(© Copyright Paul Collier private collection)

Opposite: An artist's impression of the conveyor travelling under Ferry Lane (*Lebus Log*, May 1957)

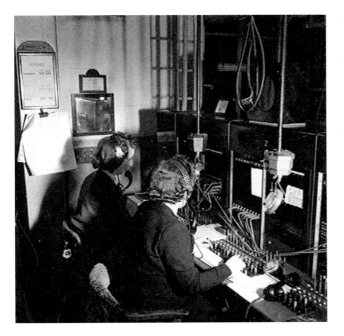

Telephone operators on the main switchboard pictured in the interwar period

The *Lebus Log* of May 1957 picks up the story of the new conveyor belts: 'As to the problem of handling to and from and inside the new warehouse, Messrs. Bagshawe of Dunstable, one of the foremost conveyor makers, with whom we have a long association has helped to make a test conveyor.' An order was placed in February 1954 and installation completed in January 1955, with four similar conveyors for offloading at the new main warehouse ordered in September 1955. These machines, each 649 feet long in the form of an endless rectangular loop, were then installed and in service in the storage area. The *Lebus Log* explained that the major item in the layout is the conveyor connecting the main factory with the new warehouse, which had to be capable of handling the entire output of the factory at the speed with which the finished product comes out of the production shops (south of Ferry Lane); and further, that this could only be achieved with a speed consistent with loading and offloading at any point in the warehouse by lateral movement, similar to the method adopted for the existing slat conveyors.

The working widths, therefore, all had to be similar to that of the main slat conveyor to enable easy transfer, also achieved through having them at the same level. Finished furniture products would thus be carried to the storage area in the new main warehouse, where they were either unloaded or transferred to a temporary resting place via one of the smaller loops, or else taken direct to the load preparation area.

The conveyor was 4 feet, 9 inches wide, 2,192 feet in length, had 274 wood pallets (which were pressed and machined completely in-house at Lebus by the mill and machine shop) and had six identical four-speed underground units that helped to keep the balance. If one motor failed, all automatically stopped.

From the transfer point in building B, the circuit wound its way under the west end of A building (which had been rebuilt for this purpose). Next, it passed under Ferry Lane, where it turned seven degrees east, then ran straight through to the warehouse, rising approximately 13 inches in this section but gradually merging to the higher floor level before turning due east across to Mill Mead Road. Here it made a 180-degree turn back to the west side, returning to building B where, in effect, a complete circuit had been done. The total time for a complete trip could be varied – anything from 60 to 100 minutes.

Today, this tunnel is not usable, although at the time of writing, all five can be seen from a vantage point in Hale Village, including the set of handrails for the pedestrian tunnel. When the conveyor was installed, a new set of pedestrian steps were built from ground level to connect with Ferry Lane humpback bridge – the steps are still used today for access by residents to Ferry Lane Estate.

Offices – a lack of purpose-built facilities

'Office work covering bought ledger, sales ledger, accounts, cash receipts and banking, cash payments to outside makers, accountancy and secretarial was still done at Tabernacle Street,' described LS in his *History*. At the same time, there was the need to audit bookkeeping in relation to distribution activities at the

Tottenham works; inevitably, there would be duplication involved in the paperwork between the firm's two sites. Not surprisingly, 'rather more work than normal auditing was undertaken,' LS added.

A permanent office had been allocated at Tabernacle Street for Mr. Gilbert Clarke of the firm's auditors, Pannell Fitzpatrick & Co. The firm subsequently employed Mr. S. E. F. Thomas as chief accountant. As an aside, according to LS, he had a curious hobby for an accountant – that of conjuring; 'this however, remained a hobby; he was never known to conjure with the books!'

This issue was addressed by the firm several years after World War One. As quoted by LS in his *History*, Thomas wrote in 1921: 'I would suggest that the conclusion drawn from this document seems to be that office duties generally can be carried out just as well at Tottenham as in London; that there may be a saving of £20 per week in so doing if the present Tottenham staff can perform *all* the work now being done by the London General Staff.' Although LS acknowledged that Thomas was 'a most shrewd person well on the ground', he pointed to a note in the concluding paragraphs of Thomas's report that gives some insight into what the latter might really have felt: 'I fear, however, that this would not work out in practice and we would find that both ends would soon require more help and so the visionary £20 would quickly disappear.' This less-than-enthusiastic endorsement is either an indication that he was not convinced or, reading between the lines, perhaps did not relish a move to the Finsbury Cabinet Works. Since the move had not been anticipated when Clifford Tee was given his brief for the original design, there was no dedicated office space for them to move into – which may be why Thomas was not keen.

Despite this warning, office functions were subsequently moved and merged at Tottenham as a way to tackle the issues of split-site working, in particular the inevitable duplication. Some of the office functions were squeezed into C, on the first floor,

amongst warehouse functions, with a specially constructed light wooden staircase providing access. Offices were also accommodated on the upper floors of the existing K/L building in space freed up from the polishing school. Other office spaces were ingeniously created: the personnel manager went in to the former 'brass room' (in which metal components such as drawer handles had been stored); the chief engineer took over the former carvers' workshop T; and the production development manager was accommodated in T1. The first telephone switchboard was installed in the general office, building A, in 1908, where it remained until 1945; Sir Herman's private office occupied another part of the building. By the start of the Second World War the firm already had dedicated, sizeable departments covering varying administrative functions.

'Operation Togetherness' – bringing office functions together

For the first time in the company's history, 'Operation Togetherness' in the spring of 1968 brought together all office and administrative staff to the central accommodation in the new warehouse building. Prior to this, offices had been as much as a quarter of a mile away from each other.

The reorganisation was reported in the first edition of the newly launched *News from Lebus*, No. 1, February 1968. A new 15,000 square foot mezzanine floor had been added to the still relatively new warehouse for an open-plan general office and separate rooms for managers and senior staff. Directors' offices were now adjacent, with a long, false ceiling of thermoluscent plastic (a heat-sensitive material which cooled temperature in summer and retained heat in winter) to cover the glass overhead windows to avoid overheating. A modern reception area was incorporated into the new development. *News from Lebus*, No. 2, May 1968, reported: 'Teams of painters, carpet layers, electricians and GPO men, worked during February and March to get the open-plan office ready in good time.' The colour scheme for the office would be Mushroom Grey and Cotswold Green. Patrick Brignell, organisation and methods manager, achieved the move of the 150 staff who survived redundancy over the course of one month – most of the moves were done during weekends to minimise disruption to work.

Welfare facilities

At the start of the Second World War, shelters to protect workers from air raids were constructed north of Ferry Lane on the southern part of the site and a sports ground established on the northern end. In Erskine Crescent, at the north end, the canteen and library were accommodated on the upper floors of the existing K/L buildings in space freed up from the polishing school. During World War One, an extended and modernised first aid and general medical facility, with a doctor's surgery, nursing station, and separate men's and women's therapy rooms, was established in a building north of R workshop. Prior to this, a basic medical facility had been running for a decade accommodated in U building, formerly the horse stables.

Laboratory, finishes and spray polishing conveyors

Just south of where Pymmes Brook now enters the river Lea, the laboratory in which cellulose polishing formulas and synthetic glues were manufactured was erected. Built at a north-west–south-east angle, it was a testament to the redirected brook. For the process of doping Handley Page and Vickers Vimy war planes, special workshops were erected in the north-east of the site – 8, 9 and 10 were somewhere in the middle of what later became shop 22. With further expansion, much of Reedham Close, south of the laboratory and down to the estate convenience shop and railway, was the huge assembly shop 22, in which furniture parts were made up. The polishing shop had 12 internal polishing lines by the end of the 1930s and roller conveyors were also installed in the maker's shop. Between polishers and the warehouse, an output conveyor was installed to carry finished items from B and D shops to warehouses C1, C2 and C3 – reducing the need to load, move and unload finished items on old platform trucks.

Upholstery production

Upholstery manufacture moved to Tottenham from Tabernacle Street between 1943 and 1950 in H/J shop and then to Woodley, outside Reading. Once established, the company's works in Headley Road, were 'probably the largest upholstery production unit in the country,' wrote Mr. A. McMillen in an article celebrating 25 years at Woodley in the *Reading Evening Post* on 23 July 1975. The upholstery production unit was on the old Woodley airfield; the office part of the factory was called 'Hawkhurst' and, according to former employee Shirley Hiscock, who sent her recollections to the author for this book, had previously been a children's home. Dave Lewis, another former employee who also sent his recollections to the author, recalled: 'Behind this old listed building was the main upholstery shop… and on the other side of the road was a modern building which housed the upholstery cutters and the machinists.' In 1960, Record Mill in Lancashire was purchased to further extend upholstery production facilities and as a manufacturing base for the new venture of mattress-making (Eventide Bedding had been acquired by the company in 1959). The mill, most recently occupied by British Celanese Limited, at 100,000 square feet, was comparable in size to the Woodley factory and four times the size of H/J shop at Tottenham. Major refurbishment to the building was required before production could begin, including brickwork repairs, removal of all the old timber floors, the laying of 7,000 yards of asphalt and conversion of the old coal-burning Lancashire boiler to oil power. There is an absence of records relating to any production and output.

New mill in the timber field and extended machine shop

From the outset, two tunnels under the Gospel Oak to Barking railway provided access: from east to west, the East Main Corridor (the bridge that first aroused my curiosity) and the original brick-built access tunnel – tall but narrow, it serves no real purpose today. In 1928, the firm secured strips of land either side of the Gospel Oak to Barking railway, and between the Ordnance Survey maps of 1915

Above: Looking north, the East Main Corridor ran through this railway arch

(© Copyright Paul Collier private collection)

Below Left: Then and now: the original (later West) Main Corridor pictured before World War One

(© Copyright Paul Collier private collection)

Below: Looking north, the railway arch through which the (West) Main Corridor corridor ran

(© Copyright Paul Collier private collection)

and 1936 a brick-built arch was constructed, which formed access under the railway for the West Main Corridor. In 1938 a new tunnel was constructed under the railway between the brick-built tunnel and the West Main Corridor Bridge to connect the new mill 28 with the extended machine shop Q and R (S and U were also subsumed in this space). A conveyor powered by mains electricity ran northwards through the tunnel from Queensferry Walk to what is now a multi-use games area.

Built in 1938, looking north this tunnel connected the new mill with the extended machine shop; the fading internal wall paint in magnolia and brick red is still visible

(© Copyright Paul Collier private collection)

Then and now: looking north, this brick arch took trucks on iron rails from the timber field to workshops on island B

The same view today

(© Copyright Paul Collier private collection)

Unloading cranes

In 1929, just over a decade after the first crane was installed (an automatic unloading conveyor mounted at the south-west corner of the timber field in 1918), a new Butters crane was installed further northwards at the Lea Navigation edge. Subsequently, unloading from the barges was accomplished by the use of this apparatus.

New buildings for planes become sub-assembly and veneer workshops

In a new workshop on Gosport Walk, south of the Gospel Oak to Barking railway, Horsa and Hotspur gliders, and later Albermarle and Mosquito aircraft, were made during World War Two; workshop 12 became the sub-assembly shop. Armadale Green housed the veneer shop 11, which was later considerably extended, and shop 32 covered a large part of Armadale Close.

Original plywood storage shed 29, pictured on 15 October 1956 a few years before it was redeveloped for additional parts storage

(Reproduced with special permission from Waltham Forest Local History Archives, Vestry House Museum)

New Drying kilns

In the area bounded by Kessock Close, Armadale Close and Yarmouth Crescent, new drying kilns were erected in 1933 – 14 and 25 on the factory plan. The original kiln complex V was now redundant; V4 shop was converted to form an extension to the Jointing department.

Extended parts store

In December 1959, a self-contained shed at Ferry Lane Wharf, on the opposite side of the River Lea, was taken on a short lease as a plywood store. At approximately 400 feet long and 40 feet wide, with ground and upper-floor storage amounting to 32,000 square feet, it was serviced by an overhead two-ton lane crane, which travelled the full length of the shed. Both barges and lorries could be handled with the facilities available. All the plywood – originally stored in 29 shed – was transferred, thus freeing space that was given over to the parts store.

The final building phase on Hale Village, fronting Ferry Lane, Spring 2019

(© Copyright Paul Collier private collection)

Lebus sports field and new warehouse redeveloped

North of Ferry Lane, on lands once occupied by the Lebus factory, the Secretary of State agreed to Haringey Council's proposal that the Harris Lebus sports ground could be used for future industrial purposes. Some campaigners who wished to see green space preserved in overall plans for the Lea Valley Regional Park were disappointed, and Lockwood Industrial Estate opened around 1982.

The story is picked up again early in the new millennium: the enormous warehouse north of Ferry Lane – which attracted my attention when I first moved to the estate in 2008 – was, that same year, in the process of demolition. In 2017, the last accommodation blocks of Hale Village were constructed and, with a tower block under construction at time of writing in 2019, the transformation is almost complete.

A short period in time, a significant amount of history

Whilst industry was met with some resentment by local residents in the early twentieth century, within the space of 80 years the Harris Lebus factory at Tottenham Hale had both come and gone – a relatively short period in the span of time and yet a significant amount of history for posterity.

CHAPTER FOUR

The Making of the Firm of Lebus: Selling and Success

'Used to wonder where it all went, who bought it?'

– Ron Turton, polisher, 1954–1967 (as recalled as part of the Coombes Croft project)

Adjudging Success

Success is not one thing but may be many things…

Aside from the events that forced the firm to close its Tottenham Hale gates in 1970, there is no doubting the commercial success of Harris Lebus (which continued through upholstery sales at Woodley for a further decade). The issue of how to measure that success is complex.

Volume of sales, level of profits, quality of furniture products, and aesthetic and commercial appeal of designs – individually they might each be yardsticks by which to measure sales and success. Taken in isolation, they would not reveal a true picture; considered collectively, however, they reveal a more accurate account. To help explain: sales figures alone would be skewed by the fact that the firm did not only sell its own manufactured furniture but dealt in 'factored' (or bought-in) goods and therefore acted as wholesaler for other smaller firms; in addition, the actual production costs of individual furniture items were not calculable until processes were set in place in 1934.

There are indications that designers at Harris Lebus were not necessarily in a position to let their creativity run loose. In essence, there were tussles between the designers' professional 'speculative predictions' as to what might satisfy a furniture-buying public and the 'evidenced patterns' of sales representatives working in the field.

In addition, other factors – ranging from restricted supplies of raw materials to changing tastes and public policies such as hire-purchase regulations – influenced the firm's commercial outcomes.

Success might be measured in terms of the firm's legacy

Often considered one step ahead, Harris Lebus influenced and shaped Britain's furniture industry as a whole. That alone might be taken as one of its legacies. And then there is its contribution during two world wars.

As furniture-making ceased, Harris Lebus focussed its efforts on manufacturing war supplies and planes. The firm's contribution to supplies in both world wars was phenomenal, for which Herman Lebus received initially a CBE and then a knighthood in 1946 for his personal achievements relating to both war work and the furniture industry in general. The pre-World War One era leaves a legacy of major contract work including hospital and hotel refurbishments and ship interiors.

So great was the impact of the two world wars, decisions taken over the design, type of products, raw materials, methods of manufacture and target market enabled furniture produced to be identifiable as falling into three distinct manufacturing periods. The first period was Art Nouveau and Arts and Crafts up to the advent of World War One in 1914; the second was Modern Classical and Art Deco between the two world wars, 1919–1939; and finally, after World War Two, from 1945 to the dissolving of the partnership and formation of the public limited company in 1947, through the regulated and controlled Utility furniture years to the idiosyncrasies of the fifties and sixties.

The firm's pre-World War One era products are most noteworthy in the antique furniture trade; despite the absence of branding on many furniture pieces, they are distinguishable as being Lebus-made.

In commercial terms alone, despite different target markets, both periods either side of World War One were lucrative. The post-World War Two period proved to be the most commercially challenging and yet design-wise had the potential to be the most exciting, free and radical. However, in reality, this period at times proved disappointing.

How to fill Harris's shoes

Up until his premature death in the autumn of 1907, Harris Lebus had always been the dominant figure in the firm, negotiating business deals, large or small, taking care of this side of the business in his own inimitable way. His death would have come as a shock and the spotlight shifted onto the next generation of Lebus brothers – Herman and Louis – at a difficult time, as the Finsbury Cabinet Works was becoming established. Although Sol was now the experienced senior partner, it would be safe to deduce he had not been at the forefront of such dealings and thoughts would

naturally have turned to 'how to fill Harris's shoes'. And, no doubt… it would have been a daunting prospect.

Consider the story of how Harris did business with Maple and Company, as outlined by LS in his *History*.

Drama: In London's West End, Harris is making a sales deal…

In an intimately lit, smoke-hazed, floral-patterned, heavily curtained popular restaurant and bar, in which the abundance of furnishings, fabrics and sombrely dressed patrons makes the room seem darker than mid-afternoon, sits Harris Lebus, holding court. The business-suited gentlemen at his table are Horace Regnart and his colleague from Maple and Company, Stanley Wharton. Harris is in a happy place, jovial even, and feeling slightly mischievous.

'Now Regnart, I have three new designs for bedroom suites I want to show you,' says Harris, as he reaches down for his leather briefcase. He pulls out three sheets of heavy cardboard and says to Regnart, somewhat facetiously, 'You can set your own price on each of them!'

Horace pulls his favourite ink pen from his inside jacket pocket and proceeds to do just that, scribbling wildly and without taking the time to think through rationally.

On seeing the figures, Harris beams boldly – he knew he had caught Horace on a good day, his defences down. The pricing was far in excess of what even Harris had anticipated; but a gentleman's bond is a gentleman's bond and Horace, Maple and Company's business manager, stuck to his bargain.

Horace Regnart appears to have been manipulated by Harris into a deal at a price inflated beyond his expectations when, by all other accounts, it was Horace Regnart as a major customer who normally dominated furniture makers. '[T]he bulk of the huge range of stock for which they were renowned was obtained by various unscrupulous means from the multitude of small makers in the vicinity (London's East End) and eastwards who prospered and perished at the hands of Horace Regnart, the office boy who became Maple's business manager'. Harris and Horace appear to have enjoyed a relaxed, personal friendship. Perhaps they had a certain affinity and a mutual respect as both had successfully worked their way up from humble beginnings in their respective businesses. In addition, both businesses claimed to be the biggest (and inferred they were the best) in their industry. 'The largest and most convenient furnishing establishment in the world,' a statement on a receipt proudly affirms, in a manner difficult to ignore. (The statement was attached to a small batch of correspondence from Maple and Company dated 1 June 1908, contained in Oliver's archives.)

Visits to Grand Rapids, Michigan, America's foremost furniture manufacturing region

Harris had visited the Grand Rapids region of Michigan in the United States during the 1890s, taking inspiration and gaining much knowledge. Earlier in the year of his death, he had encouraged his two sons to make a trip there – perhaps to prepare them for their future. Grand Rapids had emerged as the prominent place of furniture manufacture in the States, having eclipsed New York State, Cincinnati and Ohio. According to J. L. Oliver, 'Spindle shapers were introduced at Grand Rapids in 1890… between 1870 and 1890 the total number of furniture manufacturing businesses at Grand Rapids increased from 8 to 54, employees rose from 281 to 7,250 and during the 1870s an important new selling device was instituted at Grand Rapids – the semi-annual Grand Rapids Furniture Exposition at which manufacturers laid out special displays for buyers coming over increasing distances.'

Herman, 23, and Louis, a year older, clearly demonstrated their aptitude on this American platform. The lead article on the front page of the *Michigan Artisan*, 25 February 1907, described them as 'sharp, keen observers… not at all backward in the matter of asking questions'. The article, entitled 'London

Furniture Makers: Talk with two sons of Harris Lebus who are on an American pleasure trip', detailed their itinerary, their brief stop in Grand Rapids in a schedule which included Chicago, Milwaukee, St. Paul, Minneapolis and Winnipeg, and then on to the West Coast before returning east through the southern states. In reality, it was anything but a pleasure trip.

A snapshot of the firm

What the siblings are reported to have said in the *Michigan Artisan* presents both a snapshot of the firm in 1907 and an insight into their individual characters. Herman's interests appear to have revolved around business etiquette and processes; Louis, in comparison, was pragmatic in his approach, expressing concern for the minutiae of furniture manufacture and sales:

> We make all kinds and styles of furniture, from the cheapest to the most expensive and from little chairs to roll-top desks, parlour and chamber suites. We have nothing like a regular sales season on our side. It is all year with us, though we ship more in some months than in others… business has been quite good for us for several years. The people of England are quite prosperous, and business of all kinds is good and steady. We do not need an exposition to introduce new styles… designs are not changed so often as they are here. We have no organisation of manufacturers, no combinations as you have here and without united action an exposition (exhibitions) would not be successful.

Herman is reported as saying:

> We are going all over your country. That may mean a long trip, but if we keep up with your people here it will soon be over. Your people here move quickly – always rushing. Your businessmen are quick. They could not do things their way in England, but it seems to be easy here. Everyone seems to have what you call a 'cinch' on his business here while on our side it is a struggle for everybody.

It would be Herman (as the eldest of the two siblings) who would emerge as the new driving force of the next generation; he was his father's son.

Art Nouveau/Arts and Crafts – Leading Up to World War One

Harris Lebus furniture style 1873–1914: Art Nouveau/Arts and Crafts

In his *History*, LS indicated that the style of furniture produced by Harris Lebus was much the same leading into the Edwardian era as it had been during the later Victorian period. He suggested there were no new major influences, writing, 'in the 1890s and carrying over into the first ten years of the twentieth century, characteristics of design altered little.' He cites William Morris (who began his business in Queen Square, Bloomsbury, in 1865) as having a 'profound influence' on furniture (as well as fabric) design. Although his comment is made in general, it appears that his influence impacted on furniture designs produced by Harris Lebus. He also referred to Emile Galle, leader of L'École de Nancy, a specialist in glassware design who began incorporating stained glass panels into furniture designs in the 1880s, as an inspiration in the rapid spread of his ideas into Britain and as having 'influenced everything in the home'. LS added, 'in commercial furniture it developed rapidly and became exaggerated to fretwork with silk and cretonne fabrics behind'.

Designer and Draughtsman

In the early days at the Finsbury Cabinet Works, furniture designs and associated drawings were produced by just two men, Basil Archer and Dickie Porch; Archer as designer and Porch as draughtsman. They both worked through the Finsbury years having transferred from Tabernacle Street. Archer would prepare sketches, occasionally in colour, from which the partners would choose their preferred designs. LS's description of him reads, 'by nature a fussy, petulant, difficult character and if, for some reason, major alterations were suggested in the designs, or they were rejected and more called for, he would sulk for days'.

This description of the characteristics of the designer with Harris Lebus given by LS is intriguing, leaving unanswered questions: could Archer simply not take criticism or were his creative ideas being stifled?

Upholstered furniture made at Tabernacle Street

With upholstered products manufactured in premises adjacent to Tabernacle Street, most of the made-up frames were bought from nearby manufacturers to be upholstered in-house to traditional methods and in line with fashion trends; Moroccan leather and Rexine (faux leather) chairs were then in vogue.

In addition, large quantities of drawing-room suites, club-type sofa and chairs and box ottomans (blanket boxes for bedrooms) were produced.

Dining and bedroom suites

A dining room suite consisted of sideboard, dining table and chairs. Sideboards were four- to seven-feet long and had 'heavy top parts with columns and mirrors, shelves for knick-knacks and every combination of drawer, cupboard and display compartment'. Extending dining tables were of the screw expander type with loose, spare leaves. The simple drawer leaf was virtually unknown. Completing the set were four dining chairs with two additional 'carver' style chairs. In addition, 'dining trolleys' were an option.

A bedroom suite consisted of a matching wardrobe, chest of drawers and washstand. Wardrobes were three to six feet in width, sometimes even wider, with loose plinths (lowest section or base, usually plain or with decorative mouldings) and loose cornices (large section of moulding at the top that lifted off for removals). Chests of drawers' sizes ranged from three to four-and-a-half feet in width. Washstands were of a similar width to the chests of drawers with marble tops and tiled backs. In the era before bathrooms with running water were commonplace, washstands were an essential bedroom furniture piece for use with china sets consisting of water jug,

Furniture grouped and arranged in the Tabernacle Street showrooms in the first decade or so of the twentieth century

bowl and soap dish. In addition, free-standing towel rails were an option, as well as chairs (usually with cane seats).

'A large amount of mahogany and oak suites were a "derivative" of Jacobean, Sheraton and Adam periods, with inlaid or carved decoration inspired by classical tradition but reduced to commercial large quantity manufacture', according to LS's *History*; carvings – either hand-made or produced with the aid of a machine – were a prominent feature. Harris Lebus was reputed to be the first furniture manufacturer to import Sequoia (Californian Redwood) from America, which resulted from his trip to Grand Rapids in 1893. It was used for the unseen back panels of wardrobes and the bottom panels of drawers.

Writing tables and cylinder-fall desks

One specialism was beginning to emerge – writing tables and cylinder or cylinder-fall desks. These resemble a bureau with a revolving cylinder cover which rolls down to hide away paperwork and so forth. They were often called roll-top desks. A contract with Gunn Furniture Company in 1902 granted Harris Lebus permission to manufacture their roll-top desks at the Finsbury Cabinet Works. LS points to the No. 5 four-foot roll-top desk which 'sold well for many years at £3 15s'. In 1913, the oak version was £6 13s and the version in satin walnut, finished with either walnut or mahogany, was £7 6s 6d.

Sheraton bedroom suite inlaid with satinwood, including a 7-foot wardrobe, a 4-foot, 3-inch dressing table and washstand, bedside cupboard, towel rail, with four chairs – one of the most expensively priced suites in 1913 catalogue at £230

(Paul Collier private collection)

Oak bedroom suite with 5-foot wardrobe, 3-foot dressing table and washstand, pedestal bedside cupboard, with three chairs, cane seated, was one of the least expensive suites in 1913 catalogue at around £30

(Paul Collier private collection)

Arts and Crafts oak dressing table recently available on an online auction site

(Reproduced with owner's permission)

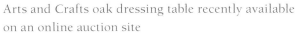

Detail of marquetry flower in Art Nouveau style

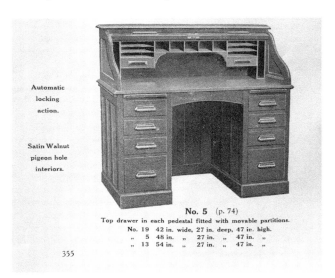

One of the most popular desks, No. 5, as pictured in the 1913 catalogue

(Paul Collier private collection)

1908 office furniture catalogue

The initials H. L. L. (Harris Lebus London) engraved on an escutcheon plate

Trademark on escutcheon plates

Roll-top desks were often trademarked with 'Lebus Desk' engraved on the escutcheon plate. Some wardrobe and chest of drawer locks displayed face plates engraved with the small initials 'H. L. L.' – Harris Lebus London.

Making sales of furniture products – home and overseas

Maple and Company continued to be the firm's largest single domestic customer after Harris's death in September 1907 and towards the end of the first decade of the Finsbury Cabinet Works accounted for an annual average of 13% of the firm's gross turnover. In summary, the firm's marketing strategy was to arm its sales force with catalogues to either make direct sales to the public in their designated area or to encourage retail outlets to buy wholesale and stock current furniture products made by the firm.

The earliest catalogues produced were printed from original line drawings, mostly black and white plus one- or two-colour drawings, bound in hard, grey covers; one catalogue

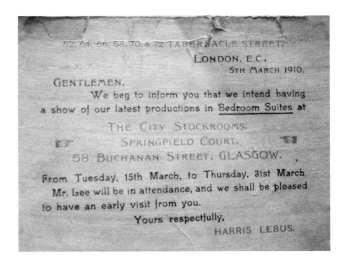

An invitation card from Ernest Lee to view furniture products at the Glasgow showroom in 1910

was produced annually in the years preceding World War One. The printing of catalogues was contracted out at a cost of five shillings each; for instance, the 1913 catalogue comprised 383 pages of products and was printed by Hanbury, Thomsett and Company, Kensal Rise, North West London. The development of photography improved the quality of catalogues; an unnamed driver with the firm with a keen interest in photography produced the early prints in a studio at Tabernacle Street.

In 1896, before telephone communication had significantly developed, the firm employed five travelling sales staff. John Measor covered Scotland, Ireland and the northern counties of England; Gardner Lewis covered the midlands; Mr. Meredith covered Wales and the west; Mr. Apted covered the south; and Fred Measor (son of John) handled sales in the south east, including the south coast. By the time the Finsbury Cabinet Works was operational, travelling sales staff charged with the responsibility to travel the length and breadth of the country to promote Harris Lebus furniture and generate sales had doubled from five to ten. Mr. A. Thompson joined in 1909 and Mr. P. Irish in 1910. When John Measor (who was still working into his 70s) retired, Ernest Lee covered Scotland, Ireland and the northern counties of England. He remained with the firm for 32 years. According to LS, 'he

The first set of travelling salesmen

was a man of jovial personality, immaculately dressed and, in the early days, often with morning coat and striped trousers, fancy vest (waistcoat) and top hat and always a flower, generally a red carnation, in his buttonhole. He was as well-known as any traveller on the road, a most popular figure who, in addition to his designs, usually had a pocketful of funny postcards'.

London, New York, Paris

The firm had one UK showroom before World War One and Charles Boryer (known by his nickname 'Jock') was the manager, supported by Frank Felce. They were the face of Tabernacle Street for the first half of the twentieth century and were well known to customers throughout the country. The showroom was generally busy most days and they would be called at the end of the day to report on direct sales made and enquiries from potential new customers. In rare slack times, they tidied up and rearranged the showrooms. Mr. Cammock first joined as the London sales representative, driving around in a pony and trap (his pony was called Satin Walnut). After developing tuberculosis and recovering in South Africa, he became sales representative there, as well as securing regular sales accounts in Australia, New Zealand, India and South America. This post necessitated long sea voyages and he returned to London once a year. LS recalled some of the more curious sales orders Mr. Cammock secured on his travels and which the firm custom-made. These included 'a fabulous carved gothic style throne for the Sultan of Zanzibar' and 'an enormous consignment of highly ornate and very large pieces destined for a Rajah's palace in India'.

Mr. Nazzari was the European sales representative; Italian by origin, LS described him as 'a fine-looking man with a well-trimmed beard, a typical Latin and a most engaging personality'. A Harris Lebus Paris showroom opened in 1909 at 21 Faubourg St. Antoine in a wholesale furniture district. LS stated that one had been opened nine years previously at 2 Rue de la Roquette. Based on his successes, Nazzari was later given South America and produced an enormous amount of business with a firm

called Thompson in Buenos Aires, as well as a small amount of business with the Wanamaker department store on New York's Broadway.

The authors of *Furnishing the World* remind us that in the eighteenth and early nineteenth centuries, Britain was the largest exporter of furniture in Europe and Harris Lebus capitalised on this market. As World War One loomed, the firm's export market almost doubled in size from just over 11% of turnover in 1908 to 20% the following year, and by 1913 the export market generated £81,641, a quarter of the firm's total turnover.

Turnover from exports to Europe when totalled were relatively small; France and Italy were the main markets. After South American trade, the biggest single export markets were South Africa, New Zealand and Australia.

Furniture prices 'made up'

Before the firm developed a method to calculate exact production and unit costs for individual furniture items which would, in turn, have informed pricing policy, furniture pricing was done weekly on Saturdays. Frank Felce and Jock Boryer, lead sales staff, would assemble with the partners at Tabernacle Street; each would scribble a suggested price for each suite on their pads, compare notes and agree a compromise. Prices would then be relayed to the factory, the sales force and any other relevant parties on the following Monday. In his *History*, LS stated, 'there was plenty of latitude in margins, and since competition was less keen, it proved a satisfactory method.'

Undoubtedly, there were some indicators to go by. A cabinet-making witness to the Select Committee on the Sweating System in 1888 described how a retailer may sell a dining table for 34s 6d, 'a common pine table with birch legs five feet by three feet six inches, with one flap to it'. What he described is what was known as a common dining table in the trade, which he goes on to state would take two days' work to make and would cost him, for materials alone, 13s (5s 6d for the top, 4s for the legs, 1s 4d for the screws, 2s for the fixings and another 2s for the polish) and that he would be lucky to get 16s for it. Sample makers hand-made very small quantities of the highest grade six-foot and seven-foot mahogany, Sheraton, satinwood and walnut bedroom suites; these retailed at between £200 and £300 each. To put these furniture prices into context, in this period an apprentice polisher's weekly pay was around 10s 6d and the basic full rate around £2 10s a week.

As World War One loomed, the 1913 Harris Lebus furniture catalogue was arguably the pinnacle of the era. The range of products offered was indexed under 'Bedroom', 'Dining Room', 'Drawing Room', 'Hall', 'Office and Library' and 'Miscellaneous' – coal boxes and cabinets, footstools, lavatory glasses (small wall-mounted mirrors), photo frames, screens (moveable room dividers or fireside), tables and nests of tables, three-piece suites and individual washstands.

A statement shows that a pricing formula was applied according to the desired finish: satin walnut bedroom furniture was supplied finished in mahogany or walnut cover at an extra charge of 7.5%; satin walnut bedroom furniture (except chairs) was supplied enamelled white at an extra charge of 20%; and oak bedroom furniture (except chairs) was supplied enamelled white at an extra charge of 25%. Soft furnishing stuffing materials were graded A through to D; the more expensive sofas and lounge furniture was stuffed with A stuffing.

Furniture ranges were identified by name, catalogue number and patent registration. The Sheraton bedroom range, for example, was 2026 and 589809 respectively. Pricewise, the suite consisting of a wardrobe in five parts, dressing table (with plate glass mirror), washstand, pedestal cupboard (bedside cabinet), towel airer and three (cane-seated) chairs was around £86 if mahogany inlaid and £126 if satin wood inlaid. The dining room suite 0150, mahogany inlaid consisting of a table, a sideboard, a mirror-backed china cabinet with plate glass shelves, dinner wagon/'hostess trolley', two armchairs with D stuffing (grade A was the best quality) covered

in morocco, and four dining chairs would have cost around £120 (and with the larger table, just under £130).

A regular provincial customer at Tabernacle Street

This regular visitor is best left for LS to describe:

> There was a curious Irishman, Mr. [Peter] Dee of Cork who came to London two or three times a year on a binge. He would visit Tabernacle Street in an intoxicated condition and place an enormous order. Since the salesmen knew within a little what he required, the order was reduced accordingly. He would then usually borrow some money to get him home which he always repaid.

Strictly speaking, this contemporaneous description of Peter Dee and Sons' showroom at 65 George Street, Cork from a local directory does not fit, except, assuming much of his products were Lebus supplied, it is so exquisite:

> A more extensive, varied, interesting, attractive, or complete stock of furniture, cabinets in marquetry, and other fashionable styles, carpets, curtains, beds, bedding and other household equipment is not to be found in Cork or the South of Ireland, and the firm under notice deserve all the substantial success they are achieving as the record of their enterprise in maintaining so perfect an emporium and placing before the residents of the district a range of choice in furniture and furnishings that could hardly be surpassed at even the largest of metropolitan or continental establishments.

Major contracts work

Harris Lebus had forged a reputation for delivering on large-scale contracts before Harris died; one such contract was the total refurbishment, after a disastrous fire in 1903, of Friern Barnet Hospital (then known as Colney Hatch Asylum) in New Southgate. Contract negotiation was an element of the business in which Herman continued to excel; this was especially the case in securing major contracts during the two world wars. Other contracts secured in the pre-war period included thousands of bookcases for the Educational Book Company and the Encyclopaedia Britannica, large numbers of gramophone cabinets for HMV and an enormous number of towel cabinets for the Initial Towel Company. Some contract work was also done for Waring and Gillow of Lancaster, who specialised in ships' furniture; one of the most prestigious contracts of this era was for fine inlaid mahogany furniture for staterooms of an entire deck of the Cunard ocean liner *Aquitania* (which was later put to military use in World War One as a hospital ship).

A replica of the First-Class Smoking Lounge of the *Titanic*?

In 1911–1912, the Midland Railway Company acquired the Adelphi Hotel, Liverpool, retaining the architect Robert Atkinson to redesign it. On its opening in 1914 it was described as 'the world's most palatial hotel'. Harris Lebus was contracted to furnish all 400 bedrooms in French walnut and the Sefton Suite was rumoured to be a replica of the First-Class Smoking Lounge of the *Titanic*.

Continuing the shipping theme, ships' bulkhead work (panelling) was undertaken by the firm on two short-lived steamships that took thousands of immigrants from Liverpool to Boston from 1912 to 1917: the *Franconia*, which was torpedoed and sunk by German Submarine UB-47 on 4 October 1916, and the *Laconia*, which was torpedoed and sunk by the German Submarine U-50 on 25 February 1917. After pre-war success with *Laconia* and *Franconia*, Harris Lebus was called upon again for bulkhead work: five identical twin-screw steam passenger liners, ordered by the Australian Commonwealth Line, were to operate between London and Australia. They were completed between 1921 and 1922 and were each named after a bay situated in one of the federal states of Australia, becoming known as the Bay ships. Three were made by Vickers Armstrong in Barrow: *Moreton Bay*, *Hobsons Bay* and *Jervis Bay*. The other two, *Largos Bay*

and *Esperance Bay*, were slightly different and constructed on Clydeside by William Beardmore & Company.

The horse-drawn wooden sleighs, of plywood construction, made by the firm for the Archangel expedition of 1918 to 1919, were featured on worldwide Pathé news.

Furniture Production Interrupted – The Products of World War One

World War One – Broom handles to Handley Page

Following the outbreak of war, Herman contacted the Ministry of Munitions, formed in 1915 under the direction of David Lloyd George, prime minister from 1916 to 1922, to discuss the manufacture of Army supplies. These were regulated to meet rigid and elaborate Woolwich Arsenal specifications. It was Herman's initiative to suggest these specifications be simplified in order that more manufacturers (such as Harris Lebus) could contribute to the production of expendable items. With Woolwich Arsenal modifications agreed, products subsequently manufactured were well constructed and fit for purpose, and crucially could be made quickly and inexpensively. The first enquiry for war-related items was for wooden reels on which cordite could be wound; it came from the Government Small Arms Factory at Enfield under the directive of Colonel Wornum. By coincidence, land next to the Enfield factory had been explored by Clifford Tee as one possible option for the Finsbury Cabinet Works. The order ran into thousands. Tent pins were one of the most frequently requested orders and some three million were produced. Orders came in for wheelbarrows and ammunition boxes, a total of one million tent shelter poles, several thousand tent bottoms, several thousand cordite boxes and 25,000 broom handles per week.

Handley Page 0/400

In 1917, the parent firm ran out of space to fulfil orders for the Handley Page 0/400 medium-sized biplane bomber, designed for military use. Through his contact with the

Ministry of Munitions, Herman seized the opportunity and obtained a contract for its production at the Finsbury Cabinet Works. With a wing span of 100 feet and equipped with a Rolls Royce 250 horsepower engine, the Handley Page 0/400 was the largest bomber used in World War One. It could carry two Admiralty personnel and six 112-pound bombs. With eight-hour endurance and a top speed of almost 100 miles per hour, the plane could climb to ten thousand feet in 45 minutes. In May 1918, Mr. A. L. Flower of the Alliance Aeroplane Company Limited in Oldham made a visit to the Finsbury Cabinet Works. The firm was also commissioned by the government to assemble American aircraft imported from the United States and to make the 0/400 – the purpose of his visit. LS proudly stated: 'After being taken round the works he said he was much impressed with what he had seen and considered that Harris Lebus held the foremost place among the factories he had visited in other parts of the United Kingdom.'

Handley Page V1500

The Handley Page V1500, a much larger aircraft than the 0/400, was also manufactured at Tottenham. It was intended to bomb Berlin, but LS explained, 'no quantity was ever delivered, and the war ended before they went into service.' It is not known how far down the line the manufacture process went or how many, if any, were fully completed.

Vickers Vimy monoplane

The Vickers Vimy, a smaller monoplane, was also manufactured by the firm. LS stated, 'this was the identical machine in which Alcock and Brown made the first transatlantic flight'. The non-stop flight of just under 16 hours' duration from St. John's, Newfoundland to Clifden, County Galway on 15 June 1919 was in a modified version of the Vickers Vimy.

Whilst Harris Lebus would not be the only firm that could lay claim to the production of Handley Page or other warplanes, the quality of their output was a key determinant in winning these contracts.

Art Deco/'Modern Traditional' – The Interwar Years

After World War One – a new direction

There were decisions to be made as to what direction the firm should take in terms of rebuilding a consumer market, both at home and worldwide: should it carry on as before or change? The partnership of Harris Lebus was demonstrably visionary, forward-thinking. What type of furniture, for whom? Were there changes to production methods that could be made following experience of engineering in wood, post-war? In addition, there were issues around duplication and inefficiency in split-site working to be addressed.

At a meeting on 23 July 1920, Sol and his nephews, Louis and Herman, reached a decision that would ultimately determine the destiny of the firm: to shift manufacturing policy fundamentally to affordable furniture for the lower ends of the market and the majority of the buying public. Mr. Gilbert Clarke, the firm's auditor, was present and party to the decision. An extract from minutes of the meeting held at the Finsbury Cabinet Works reads:

> [T]he Furniture Trade of this country was divided into five classes. Of the highest class, the firm had done but very little; of the second class the great bulk of the trade had been composed; of the third class a little had been done; but of the fourth and fifth classes nothing whatever: it was accepted that at least 70% of the British Furniture Trade consisted of kinds of goods in the fourth and fifth classes, that the firm had not hitherto attempted to manufacture. The firm is of the opinion that the classes of person that have hitherto bought its furniture are now less able than before to make purchases, but that the classes of person that hitherto bought inferior furniture have acquired additional spending power; it thus foresees a decline in the demand for furniture of the sorts it has hitherto manufactured. The firm, therefore, has decided to attempt the manufacture of, not the lowest class

of furniture, but of the fourth class; it is not its intention to make anything that is not likely to wear well, and puts forward as an analogy between the present and the proposed kinds of furniture – the motor cars of Rolls Royce and Ford.

A few short years after this decision was made, Sol died, in 1926, and his two sons, LS and Bob, joined the firm in 1923 and 1926 respectively.

Chief Designer

With the production of furniture resuming after World War One, Herbert Randles Kinsley – a former lieutenant in the army – succeeded Basil Archer as chief designer when Archer retired in 1919. Herbert was the son of landscape artist Albert Kinsley (1852–1945). He remained with the firm into the early years of the public limited company, retiring in 1951. Little is known, however, on his thoughts around furniture design and designing for Harris Lebus.

Harris Lebus furniture style, 1919–1939: Art Deco/Modern Traditional

In his *History*, LS comments on this period thus:

> This was the seed of the modern form of manufacturing and designs were based on what was called 'traditional' lines. Since a high proportion of the products were manufactured in oak, the early influence of the classical designs on which pre 1914

1934 catalogue

Advertisement for summer sale, June 1931

designs were based, began to decline… the firm pioneered and built up a name for well-constructed, inexpensive furniture, light in construction, with shallow wardrobes, much veneered plywood and larger drawer and door tolerances.

The first bedroom suite to be made after the war was the D34 four feet suite, selling at £8 10s, and a five feet oak suite of similar design for £9 10s. During this period, the sales of palm stands, shaving stands, coal boxes and such like faded out.

'One of the major new furniture products of the period were china cabinets – the pride and joy of every working class and lower middle class "best room"' stated the authors of *Furnishing the World*. Specifically citing this one example of post-World War One design, LS laments, 'China cabinets, in a "modern" form produced by Harris Lebus sold in very large quantities… its present counterpart, although somewhat vulgar in design, is restrained compared with the flamboyant cabinets of the early days.' His use of vocabulary is telling.

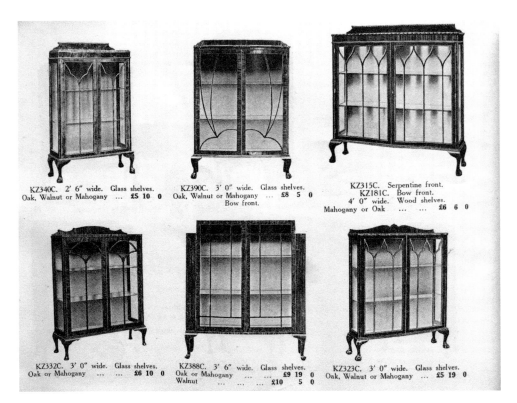

KZ340C. 2' 6" wide. Glass shelves.
Oak, Walnut or Mahogany ... **£5 10 0**

KZ390C. 3' 0" wide. Glass shelves.
Oak, Walnut or Mahogany ... **£8 5 0**
Bow front.

KZ315C. Serpentine front.
KZ181C. Bow front.
4' 0" wide. Wood shelves.
Mahogany or Oak **£6 6 0**

KZ332C. 3' 0" wide. Glass shelves.
Oak or Mahogany **£6 10 0**

KZ388C. 3' 6" wide. Glass shelves.
Oak or Mahogany **£9 19 0**
Walnut **£10 5 0**

KZ323C. 3' 0" wide. Glass shelves.
Oak, Walnut or Mahogany ... **£5 19 0**

China cabinets
of 1934 (top)
compared with
Louis style of
1913 (bottom)

(Paul Collier
private collection)

"Louis" China Cabinets.

No. 6467 (p. 51)
4 ft. wide ... £7 6 6

No. 6164 (p. 49)
4 ft. wide ... £8 5 0

No. 5942 (p. 49)
4 ft. wide ... £10 6 6

187

Kinsley's claim to fame was an exhibit at the Royal Academy and Royal Society of Arts' exhibition at Burlington House, Piccadilly. Between 28 November 1935 and 7 March 1936, Harris Lebus exhibited bedroom suite design, which consisted of wardrobe, mirrored dressing table and stool, table and chair, and an armchair, which became known as the Academy suite. This exposure proved profitable and many hundreds of the suites were subsequently sold. It represented a shift in policy to work with exhibitions as a means of marketing the firm's products.

Catalogues

The catalogues of the interwar period were updated and reissued on a monthly basis since, according to LS, 'new designs were introduced continuously throughout the year'. During the 1920s and 1930s, Harris Lebus catalogues were printed in the factory using offset printing machines. Still with grey covers, they were smaller (A5 size) so that they could be produced at the lower cost of sixpence each. There were two versions of the catalogues – wholesale and retail – for distribution to the appropriate customers, with either a 50% mark-up or a 100% mark-up. Specifically, the 1934 catalogue stated that 'prices in this catalogue are subject to a thirty-three-and-one-third percent trade discount' and that 'these prices apply to England and Wales only'.

1934 – furnishing the many between the wars

As the interwar years rolled on, a 1934 catalogue brings into sharp focus the changes at Harris Lebus – mass-produced products aimed at the lower end of the market.

For the sitting room, an upholstered three-piece suite could be purchased for as little as 15s (compared with a Chesterfield sofa at between £22 and £28 in the 1913 catalogue). The Littleport (UZ513) was covered in various shades of beige and brown check pattern at 6s a yard with hand-sprung seats stuffed with hair and fibre. The most expensive, at 40s, was the Litchfield (UZ488) in hide with velveteen feather-filled cushions.

With dining and bedroom furniture, products could be bought either as a suite or separately, allowing a household to purchase as and when budgets allowed.

The price of a dining suite ranged between 10s and 50s. At the cheaper end was the Gainford – a dark tan oak dining suite consisting of a decoratively carved sideboard (GZ625), a draw-leaf extendable table (GZ621) and four small chairs with loose seats in brown Rexine

The Monmouth three-piece suite, choices and prices offered in the 1934 catalogue

(Paul Collier private collection)

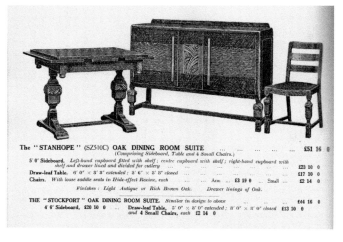

The Stanhope oak dining suite, choices and prices offered in the 1934 catalogue

(Paul Collier private collection)

(GZ627). At the relatively expensive end was the Stanhope (SZ510C) in either light antique or rich brown oak.

Aside from the bed itself, suites for bedrooms consisted of one wardrobe, a dressing table with mirror and one form of chest of drawers. Prices came in at just under £10 rising to around £30, depending on style and finish. At the cheaper end, the 'Barnard' suite could be built up from a choice of individual items finished in dark oak tan, with cupboard linings of polished whitewood, decoration of carving and Erinoid handles (trade name for an early form of plastic produced by Erinoid Ltd, Birmingham). A single wardrobe (BZ8704) fitted with two nickel-plated rods and six sliding hooks was £4, a dressing table with two drawers lined with whitewood (BZ8740) was £2 (or £3 with a frameless mirror with polished edges, BZ8766).

A range of bedsteads could be purchased separately to mix and match. For example, there were several decorative styles of bedstead offered that would match the BZ8700 catalogue ranges, including the 'Barnard' above in five sizes, priced between £1 10s and £2 5s respectively.

'Secret culture' gives way to shared information around production costs

Before the 1930s, wrote LS, 'management down the line had little knowledge of costs but it was evident that in the modern production unit, if people were to manage successfully, they needed yardsticks to measure their efficiency; the old idea of everything of this nature remaining "secrets" of the partnership had to go by the board.'

Budgetary Control introduced in 1934

LS explained that 'a major tool of management was the inauguration of Budgetary Control; this system emanated from the United States of America and Harris Lebus was the first firm

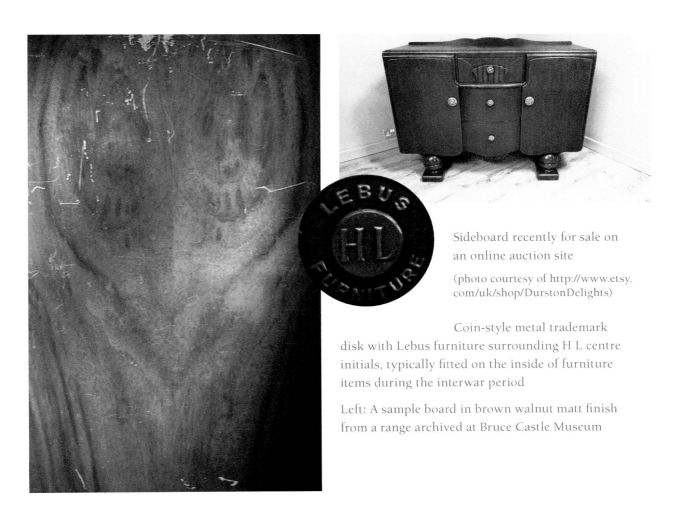

Sideboard recently for sale on an online auction site

(photo courtesy of http://www.etsy. com/uk/shop/DurstonDelights)

Coin-style metal trademark disk with Lebus furniture surrounding H L centre initials, typically fitted on the inside of furniture items during the interwar period

Left: A sample board in brown walnut matt finish from a range archived at Bruce Castle Museum

in the (furniture) industry to install such a system.'

The factory budget was to be based on the sales budget; the number of articles to be sold was translated into hours in order to calculate a projected budget of both materials needed and labour necessary to make the required furniture items. LS explained: 'it was not long before all management right down to the foremen on the shop floor, were put completely in the picture and, in fact, assisted in compiling their own budgets. Thus, top management possessed a master plan and could watch the efficiency of all departments week by week. This enabled standard unit costs to be introduced and for the first time, in the year 1934, the "real" cost of the firm's products was known.' Later, the information produced by this system enabled a complete set of accounts to be issued every twenty days.

Provincial showrooms

In Manchester, a salesroom was established at 33–37 Great Ancoats Street (10,800 square feet) in 1926, followed later by Birmingham at 114–116 Great Hampton Street (10,318 square feet). In Glasgow, a salesroom opened at 5 Saltmarket in 1930 (10,250 square feet) and in Liverpool at 75–77 Bold Street (10,389 square feet) in 1937. Showrooms were open Monday to Friday 9.00 a.m. to 6.00 p.m. and on Saturday mornings from 9.00 a.m. to 1.00 p.m. (except Manchester, which closed at 12.30 p.m.) All of these showrooms were closed during World War Two.

The 1939 catalogue reads: 'Retailer's customers may visit (a showroom) accompanied by a retailer or unaccompanied if in possession of an 'Introduction Card' issued by a retailer (available on application).'

Travellers after World War One

'Scunthorpe, whose name was still in small type on the map I left in my office in Tottenham, but which is today a small town with a population approaching 60,000.'

– Mr. Roland F. Phillips, sales representative

Mr. A. Sinning joined the firm during World War One in 1916 and Mr. A. C. Stark shortly afterwards (LS's *History*). Walter 'Bill' Rowland was also one of the first travellers to be hired after the First World War; in the *Lebus Log* in 1956, upon his retirement, he said, 'When I joined in 1920 there were only nine Travellers, many of those are now dead.' He worked for the firm for 'thirty-six glorious years' in total. 'In January 1920, I went to Dublin and Belfast – they'd not seen a Lebus representative since 1914,' he recalled. This was his first customer and they ordered a bedroom suite. 'It took me seven weeks to get round the South West of England, from Oxford to Penzance to Bournemouth and the Isle of Wight. I bought a car, did both regions for a while, and then went to Ireland to live. When the Irish Free State came into being and a duty placed on furniture, I moved to North Wales but continued with Northern Ireland.' He was later asked to cover London's West End.

The number of travellers increased and patches covered by each were reduced in size. Mr. S. Morgan joined in 1921 and the following year Mr. T. Braithwaite and Mr. H. Bagley. Another two sales representatives joined the following year – Mr. R. Riley and Mr. C. Crawley – followed by three more in 1923 – Mr. R. Holloway, Mr. A. High and Mr. Roland F. Phillips. Richard Longley joined as the Ulster representative in 1926; he had trained in Tabernacle Street before taking up the post. He covered the whole of Ireland from 1926 to the advent of World War Two (he served in the forces during both world wars) and from 1949 covered Northern Ireland. Donald Paterson was representative for the Dundee area from 1928. Henry Brown, Aberdeen-based, was the Scottish Highlands representative from 1929. Tom Jones was the East Kent traveller from 1927, except for a stint in the forces during World War Two.

Export resurgence on a small scale during the twenties

In 1926, exports to Australia, New Zealand and South Africa yielded a combined turnover of £5,879. J. Grace Ltd. was the largest single customer in Australia and New Zealand with

£640, and in South Africa the largest single customer was Mackinlay and Company with £807.

Furniture Production Interrupted Again – The Products of World War Two

World War Two – Albermarle bombers, Hotspur and Horsa gliders, and Mosquito multi-purpose combat aircraft

With the advent of World War Two in September 1939 and given the firm's previous success in manufacturing war supplies and planes, it was almost inevitable that the firm would once again be involved in the war effort. Much as was the case in World War One, the early stages saw numerous orders come in for a range of wooden war supplies: various types of ammunition boxes, two-tier bunks for air-raid shelters, stretchers, tent poles, picket posts, other barrack-room equipment, cable drums, canvas camouflage on wire frames to simulate tanks and lorries as decoys.

Herman Lebus led the search for war contracts. Before the end of September, at the invitation of the Air Ministry, he visited the Gloster Aircraft Company (later acquired by Hawker Siddeley) with Mr. A. Brown (senior) and Mr. H. Hill to consider manufacturing the Hurricane fighter. However, he decided against working on this aircraft at the Finsbury Cabinet Works because it was an all-metal construction.

They next visited F. G. Miles to see the Miles Magister wooden trainer aircraft at Hawkhurst, a large house adjacent to Woodley Aerodrome (which would one day become the home of Lebus Upholstery). Nothing came of the visit.

With their third visit, they were lucky: Armstrong Whitworth at Coventry needed help manufacturing their part-wood, part-metal Albermarle. The Albermarle was Britain's answer to Germany's Stuka dive-bomber and, although still only at the drawing-board stage when production began (the prototype had not yet flown), the aircraft had something of a chequered career and did not see real service as a bomber. Some were sent to Russia for

use on the eastern front; most were used as a tug for the Horsa gliders. LS recorded that 'much effort was undertaken at Harris Lebus in modifications', including a requirement for lengthening the wings from the original design.

Other major plane contracts followed, including a contract from General Aircraft of Feltham, Middlesex for the Hotspur glider. Originally intended as an assault glider, it turned out to be too small for this as it was only designed to hold eight men. However, it successfully found a role as a trainer for glider pilots. With a wingspan of 62 feet (18.90 metres), 39 feet (11.98 metres) in length and weighing in at 3,600 pounds (1,600 kilograms), and constructed completely in wood, Harris Lebus made these in their entirety and, according to LS, 'some hundreds' were produced, many of which went to a glider training school in Canada.

A contract with Airspeed Limited of Portsmouth for the wooden fuselages of the Horsa glider came next. Hessell-Tiltman, the designer, said the Horsa glider went from drawing board to air in the space of ten months. An initial 695 gliders were manufactured at Airspeed's own factory before being subcontracted out to various firms – from the Austin Motor Company (who made around 300 Horsa gliders) to various furniture manufacturers, including Harris Lebus. The Horsas were huge machines, designed to hold 25 troops (fully equipped), a crew of two or three, and other war equipment such as jeeps, motorcycles and field guns. The Horsa AS51 Mark I had a wingspan of 88 feet (27 metres), a length of 67 feet (20 metres), a height of 6 metres and weighed 3,797 kilograms empty and 6,920 kilograms (15,250 pounds) when fully loaded. No record of the actual number of Horsa gliders made by Harris Lebus survives, except to say, 'it ran into several hundred'. A further planned development to produce the planes in India was eventually shelved, after George Thomas Nicholson and a colleague from Harris Lebus were sent to India to support TATA Ltd. Some work began, but the Airspeed chief designer's flight was lost en route and the project abandoned.

During the years 1942 and 1943 the de Havilland-designed Mosquito became the most important product that Harris Lebus produced during the War. LS wrote:

> Five marks of Mosquito were made by Harris Lebus; originally the high altitude reconnaissance plane, then the Mark II which was a conversion to a fighter, the Mark VI fighter bomber, and the Mark XIII equipped for radar and the Mark XVI an extra heavy bomber carrying 4,000 pound bombs. There is no record of the numbers produced by Harris Lebus, but it was some hundreds.

A further contract for the feasibility of a small, unmanned aircraft to be jet-propelled, however, did not mature.

Decoy Sherman tanks

Towards the end of the war, Lord Beaverbrook telephoned Herman Lebus in the middle of the night asking to meet urgently for a top-secret assignment – a contract to build dummy wooden Sherman-tank replicas to be used as decoys ahead of D-Day. A number of workers were carefully selected for the job and sworn to secrecy, working in a bricked-off part of the factory.

Cockles (collapsible wooden canoes)

LS and A. F. Brown (junior) made a trip to Combined Operations under the command of Lord Mountbatten at Hayling Island to discuss a contract for collapsible wooden canoes, known as 'cockles'. A number were subsequently made, although production was haphazard. Cockles, which were stored and assembled in submarines, were launched through portholes with a diameter of only 29 inches. They were used for stealth reconnaissance operations off the coast of France and elsewhere. In the overall scheme of Lebus-made war equipment, this was but a small part, though the liaison with Combined Operations made it 'intriguing', said LS. Modifications were made as the project evolved and the firm produced a three-man version of the cockle which was 'almost

unsinkable'. A book, *The Secret Invaders* by Bill Strutton, published after the war, mentioned Harris Lebus and spawned a film called *The Cockleshell Heroes*.

Landing craft

As D-Day drew closer, the Admiralty needed more landing craft than existing producers – mainly smaller shipbuilding firms without the advantages afforded by modern production methods – could supply. Harris Lebus was approached to come to the rescue and was soon turning out 14 landing craft per month, delivering 200 to contract.

Harris Lebus supplies the troops

One contemporaneous magazine (quoted in LS's *History*) reported:

> On D-day troops in Horsa gilders, the fuselages of which were made by Harris Lebus, were piloted by pilots trained in Hotspur gliders, made entirely by Harris Lebus, towed by Albermarle machines, the wings and tail planes of which were made by Harris Lebus, to make an airborne assault. This was protected by Mosquito fighters, the fuselages and wings were made by Harris Lebus, and the landing places were previously softened up by the Mosquito bombers, also made by Harris Lebus. Preliminary reconnaissance was made by Mosquitos, made by Harris Lebus, the airborne assault was backed up by assault landing craft, made by Harris Lebus, and preliminary reconnaissance of the beaches was carried out from special canoes made almost entirely by Harris Lebus.

A letter from the top

In a letter to Herman Lebus dated 16 June 1943, Louis Mountbatten, then chief of Combined Operations, wrote:

> My Officers concerned have reported to me the wholehearted enthusiasm and willingness to take pain which was shown by your firm in dealing with some recent urgent requirements (for [Combined

Operations Pilotage Parties] in particular). As a result of your efforts, several of the parties in my command who have to use small boats, are able to both train and to carry out their operations with complete confidence in craft which exactly fulfil their requirements. They are highly trained personnel, and it is such a comfort to me to know that they are equipped in such a satisfactory manner for their important duties. I would be grateful if you would pass on to all members of your staff concerned, the appreciation and thanks of all of us who have benefitted by their good work.

After World War Two – A Public Company

Towards a public company

Five years before the inception of the public company, Sarah Lebus had died and there were complex settlements to be made to the partners (as well as family) in respect of the wills of both Harris and Sol.

As the war came to an end, the only furniture items being produced were upholstered; production had been transferred to H/J shop in Tottenham from premises adjacent to Tabernacle Street and leases disposed of in 1943. The most logical choice as war contracts finished was to produce Utility furniture. This was an area Herman knew much about, having been on the Furniture Working Party, which shaped national policy on furniture production and distribution in a time of post-war rationing. There was demand, albeit regulated, for furniture products at the lower end of the market, and in the past this market had served the firm well.

Reflecting on the partnership years

From ledgers meticulously kept by hand and details in LS's *History,* a picture of the commercial success of the partnership can be made with references to gross turnover.

In the pre-World War One era, which was the 'golden age of exports', the total turnover grew to £419,400 in 1913 from £274,700 in 1901. As World War One progressed, contracts became increasingly lucrative: turnover rose to £1,652,400 in 1916 and £1,592,000 in 1917and peaked at £1,187,000 in 1918. Benefit from war contracts continued into 1919 with turnover of £1,255,000 but fell to around half of this in 1920 at £631,400 and £593,300 in the following year.

During 1927 the partnership applied for a bank overdraft (they had previously had a 'no terms attached' loan for £70,000 from Mrs. Sarah Lebus) and had some settlements to make following the death of Sol the previous year. The 31 December 1926 balance sheet showed fixed assets of £489,959: land, buildings, plant, machinery, fixtures and fittings £160,054; less freehold land £22,459; motors and horses £852; canteen £1,550; and stock in trade £342,261. For insurance purposes, the total valuation was £1,119,200.

The firm did not completely escape the effects of the Great Depression and turnover struggled to £850,000 in 1932, but growth swiftly resumed and reached £1,184,700 in 1934 and by 1938 stood at £1,707,300. Post-recession growth was some 10% per annum. Taking the whole of the interwar years, 1918 to 1939, turnover increased nearly fourfold; much of this was the consequence of the post-war boom in new house building. 'Whilst it cannot be claimed that the partners were able to foresee twenty years ahead, it is proof that their policy of going into the mass market was fully justified,' LS concluded. He also pointed to statistics showing the furniture market growing rapidly in most of the years up to 1939, with an average annual increase of between 12% and 13%, significantly better than the overall advance in consumer expenditure. 'The issue of a small catalogue in large quantities was a considerable asset to sales, and it is recorded that the catalogue business increased from £10,000 in 1930 to nearly £200,000 in 1938,' remarked LS.

No turnover figures for the firm are available for World War Two. Indeed, information from this period is conspicuously absent; it is assumed such figures were sensitive and were kept confidential for security reasons.

Flotation of shares – the public company is formed

Fixed assets were valued at £1,974,486 on 31 December 1946 and flotation of Harris Lebus shares on the London Stock Exchange on 21 July 1947 enabled the raising of £1,500,000 funds in settlements – to Herman's brother Louis and his cousin Bob, who both retired at this juncture – and for reinvestment in the business. As the family partnership was being dissolved, the next generation of Lebus brothers – Anthony and Oliver, the sons of Sir Herman – were waiting in the wings. That said, there was never any question when it came to dissolving the partnership to form a public company that Sir Herman would be elected to lead the way. He did so for the first ten years.

Sir Herman – my hero

Knighted the year before the company went public, admiration and respect for Herman was cardinal, and his broad appeal and popularity seemed unquestionable. Peter Baker worked for a short spell for the firm during the 1950s – an experience that formed the foundation of a career in management and consultancy in the furniture industry. 'Every-one should have a "hero" – one of mine is Sir Herman,' wrote Baker in some memoirs to the author, specifically prepared for use in this book. He continued:

> Any family that can land at Hull with little more than their hand tools and create the biggest furniture factory in the world in that time scale, commands admiration for the vision and determination to fulfil their dream. Every now and then one would see Sir Herman's head wandering around 22 Shop with a word here and a little chat there. Sir Herman was only some five feet tall, slight of build but always immaculately dressed. When he arrived at my bench, we would often chat for twenty or thirty minutes about all manner of things, from events within the trade to national developments. On reflection, I

realise that the cost of this was all mine for, when you work on 'piecework', you are only paid for what you produce. At the time I didn't even consider that. I enjoyed the chats and, if questioned, would have assured anyone that the privilege was mine!

A member of the Furniture Working Party paid this tribute at the time of his death:

> I was particularly struck with Lebus' enthusiasm and determination to get something done about raising the general character of the industry. He was particularly keen on the small man and the small firm should have better conditions. One of the things that he advocated was the building of flatted factories[2] for these small workshops.

'He ruled intellectually…'

Jack R. Shanley, another member of the same Furniture Working Party, sharing his memoirs with the authors of *Furnishing the World,* made comments that, whilst being generally complimentary, are also of note:

> He ruled intellectually: he got the answers; he found all the short cuts… I got to know Herman Lebus and became friendly with him… I once went through his research department with him and everyone was giving him the gen of what they were doing and while they were still groping for the answer, he would ponder it and come back with the answer. It was the same on the Furniture Working Party. When we had a good discussion Sir Herman would quietly close his briefcase and say, 'I'm sorry, I've an urgent appointment, I must go now'. He would get the meeting adjourned and come back a day or two later with the answer – a remarkable man, but he killed his family and his staff.

---

2 A complex of industrial buildings, some of more than one storey, usually for multiple occupation with shared facilities.

Difficult period in the furniture industry

It was a difficult period as the firm went public. The Standard Emergency Furniture policy introduced by the government in 1941, which evolved eighteen months later into the Utility Furniture Scheme, was still in force. There were standard specifications for all new furniture production and firms were subject to strict controls that emphasised both good design and the economical use of timber.

In addition, such furniture was rationed and was only available to newlyweds or to households who had been bombed-out and who were re-establishing a home. Prospective buyers had to get an application form from their local fuel office for a permit. Each permit carried sixty units and was valid for three months. The unit value for furniture varied from eight for a wardrobe to one for a kitchen or dining chair. Retailers could only get furniture from a manufacturer against units given over by customers who had made their choice from a catalogue and not from examples held in a shop. (This helps explain why the firm's showrooms were closed during World War Two.)

Price controls remained until 1948, although after the end of the war availability was extended to those outside priority classes. Despite this, supply by the furniture industry as a whole lagged behind demand for several years. Speaking at the firm's First Annual General Meeting on 2 December 1948, Sir Herman stressed 'the formidable problems' of both timber supplies and restrictions on sales: 'If I were to refer to the long-term prospects of your company I could speak with considerable confidence, conviction and satisfaction, but the trading conditions today are still similar to those… in July 1947.'

The first AGM saw the existing officers and directors re-elected: Sir Herman as chairman and managing director, LS as assistant managing director, Cuthbert Grieg as company secretary and Anthony Lebus, Bernard Humphrey, Raymond Lamb, Desmond Stratton, Mr. A. W. Willsmore and Jack Pritchard as directors.

In November 1948 the Board of Trade made a radical change in policy, granting the industry freedom to design its own furniture. Given widespread knowledge of impending change, the announcement had been preceded by falling of orders for Utility furniture. At the company's second AGM on 8 December 1949, Sir Herman affirmed the firm's policy: 'It has always been the aim of Harris Lebus to provide, especially for the low income groups, an ever growing volume of better furniture, of better design and better value, while maintaining a high standard of conditions for its workers.' The firm was manufacturing in the context of meticulous, complicated minimum specifications and price controls. Plywood and veneer allocation was subject to controls, though those on hardwoods had been relaxed from April 1949.

During this period, a disagreement on future direction around design had seen the resignation of Mr. Jack Pritchard as director. Pritchard had been specifically head-hunted to develop future designs for the firm.

Jack Pritchard and design conflicts

Jack Pritchard picks up this story in lecture notes on 'Industrial Design' (Pritchard Archive, University of East Anglia, ref: PP/14/3/1/13) given on 24 April 1985:

> Just after the war I was Director of a very large furniture firm, Lebus… my job was to develop the product. The firm had a reputation for making well-made low-priced cabinet furniture… dark in colour and [of] no particular distinction. It was sold through small and large retailers throughout the country; distribution in those days was very different from today and was achieved through many small retailers. Sir Herman Lebus had been influenced by Gordon Russell (who also sat on the Utility Furniture Committee) and immediately agreed to invite Dick Russell (Gordon's son) to design his new furniture, but first had a survey of public opinion on design preferences.

'Dark, treacly finish and bits of plastic decoration'

Pritchard continues:

> They showed that taste was changing from before the war and strongly influenced by Utility. The survey included calls on young housewives. It was clear that except for a glorious dressing table, they preferred simple straightforward furniture – not with dark, treacly finish and bits of plastic decoration. As Utility came to an end and furniture manufacturers could design as they chose there was a world outbreak of wonderful extravaganza – shop windows were full of it! A typical comment on the survey was 'Why can't we get simple straightforward furniture as before?' They were referring to Utility, designed under the influence of Gordon Russell, the only furniture that was available during the war. In those days it was becoming popular.
>
> Herman was ill for a month or so and came back a changed man. I had an exhibition in the factory of Dick's designs for him to see but he had now lost his support for a new design. I showed Herman the market research; but he consulted his salesmen who had never seen such fine furniture for mass sales and could not believe it would be acceptable to their customer, the retailer. Such furniture might be alright for the few but not for the many. Herman Lebus took their view not mine.
>
> So, I resigned.

Mid-fifties dining suite in a traditional design

Mid-fifties dining suites in more modern design

Mid-fifties dining suite for either kitchen or dining room with modern materials, including surfaces of plastic and enamel-painted metal

'Sideboards with "waterfall fronts" and novelty handles'

Gordon Russell was director of the Council for Industrial Design between 1947 and 1959 and wrote Sir Herman's obituary for *Design Magazine*. Of this, Jack Pritchard wrote in his 2001 book *Utility Reassessed: The Role of Ethics in the Practice of Design*: 'It is significant that in the obituary that Gordon Russell wrote for *Design Magazine* on the death of Sir Herman Lebus in 1957 he felt [it] necessary to point out [that] he did not agree with Lebus' approach to furniture making.' Pritchard then re-quotes a segment of Russell's writing thus: 'His firm had

SPECIFICATION:	THE "VENTNOR" DINING ROOM SUITE	£51 18 0

the means to manufacture the type of mass-produced democratic product the reformers were aiming at, but by the rest of the industry Lebus was merely regarded as the lower C end of the market. And no sooner was freedom of design conceded, even though one of the most radical of the modern reformers – Jack Pritchard – had been recruited as director of design and development, than Lebus returned to a retailer-led design that demanded sideboards with "waterfall fronts" and "novelty handles".' Pritchard then accused Russell of: 'picking out the most uncharacteristic of Lebus' production, the Link range newly launched in 1956 and expressly designed for the more expensive middle-market sector, as the only range worthy of mention because it set a higher standard of design'.

Design as a marketable commodity

The authors of *Furnishing the World* state that, because 'consumers have little knowledge of how furniture is made, and the materials employed in its construction, it follows that purchasing decisions will be based on look – or style. Because furniture, like clothing, is an expression of status and personality, the public demands variety. Individuality was a selling point.' Sir Herman emphasised the functional purpose of furniture in an induction booklet for new workers available during the late 1940s: 'Furniture is an important part of the home; it includes the table we eat off, the chair we sit on, the bed we sleep on, where we keep our camera or our lipstick, our football jersey or our dance frock.'

Following the inception of the Furniture Development Council in 1950, Danish-born Cyril Rostgaard succeeded Kinsley in the post of chief designer in 1951. In a column of the *Lebus Log*, No. 16, in April 1960 (three years after Sir Herman's death), Rostgaard presented a more rounded view of furniture design:

> Nothing being ideal in designing furniture, one cannot limit the specification to only function and beauty, but must consider several factors which fall with dull thuds all around the designer as he dreams

ecstatically – first, often a strangling competitive price required, next a method of making with little versatility, limited or poor materials, and last but by no means whatever least, commercial appeal. Commercial appeal is a term that makes many designers break out in a cold sweat, for it conjures up anything from rather sweet, fashionable cocktails, to a broth laced up with a score of well-tried gimmicks. To clarify the situation, let me explain that all designs sold are not good – some successful designs are bad – some good designs are successful – some bad designs are unsuccessful. This is quite clear but if you have got lost somewhere, read it again because it is quite in order and is the beginning of your understanding of commercial design. An article to be designed, whatever it may be, is determined by several factors – the function of the article, the materials to be used, the method of manufacture, the fashion influences of the time, and one more exceptional factor – the desire to make it visually appealing, beautiful. The last one (visual appeal) is the factor that most people seek when they are out to buy, as in it they can satisfy personal tastes. Most things designed have had the designer's conscious and intentional applications of this last factor, and it is his extra special factor too, because the other factors are instilled by training and are applied by reasoning, whereas the ability to create some form of beauty is latent and must be already there, awaiting only development.

Rostgaard ends his account with the following emphasis:

> Taste is a thing that everyone has – but the difference is startling from one person to another. 'I know what I like' being the axiom, but the real difference is between informed taste and uninformed taste. Taste… is a developed sense and is influenced by experience, fashion and environment.

Approving designs

In the *Lebus Log*, No. 29, Ronnie Boss, cabinet sales manager, stated: 'we are the first to appreciate that many of our requests for products to the designers and to the factory are hard, and perhaps may seem unreasonable… they are dictated to us by the fierce competition in this industry and by varied trading conditions. We in the sales force are constantly in touch with the retail trade.'

Designers sketching a new design worked to a broad specification laid down by the Sales division; a new design was produced practically every day. Sketches were then shown at the weekly meetings of the Design Approval Committee with representatives from Design and Design Development departments, Production Control department and Quality Control department and the Sales division.

The marketing strategy of the early 1950s 'was to fill a small retailer with Lebus furniture,' commented Peter Baker, 'and in ascending price order – Oak; Mahogany; Walnut.' Baker added, 'As a piece was sold the retailer paid for it and was restocked. The goods remained the property of Lebus until the debt was discharged. Simple, because all that stock was held up and down the country while appearing on the Balance Sheet as "Stock and Work in Progress".'

An anonymous article in *Lebus Log*, No. 1, entitled 'Our products' focussed on the plan for 1954, to 'further strengthen our position so far as the conventional products, concentrating round the interchangeable bedroom range' and 'to widen the scope of our range'.

A copy of an undated Lebus promotional leaflet found in the Geffrye Museum Archives stamped 'Appleton's (Kingston) Limited, Empire House, Richmond Road, Kingston-on-Thames' (in a salubrious suburb) and entitled 'Interchangeable bedroom furniture by Lebus – over 50 matching pieces', gives an indication of the style and prices of the firm's products during the 1950s. The style of furniture appears reminiscent of that of the interwar period.

The 'interchangeable oak bedroom range' leaflet explained to prospective customers: 'You can choose a bedroom suite to suit your needs from over fifty well-designed and beautifully finished articles of furniture. Apart from the wide selection of suites, you are also able to purchase any separately and if you so desire, add to it at a later date… All… articles exterior veneer Oak polished Light Russet, or Medium colour, bright finish. Cupboard and drawer interiors stained Mahogany colour… If you require, all… wardrobes can be fitted with a twenty-four inch by twelve-inch mirror at 22s 6d extra.'

The Middlesbrough suite could be purchased for a total of £57 6s 6d. This included:

- A four-foot-and-half-an-inch wardrobe (Catalogue No. Z7717)
- A three-foot-nine-inch Cheval (dressing) table (Catalogue No. Z7755)
- A two-foot-six-inch short fitted wardrobe (catalogue No. Z7750).

A bedside cabinet one-foot-two-and-a-quarter-inches wide, fitted with a shelf, (Catalogue No. Z7753) could be added for an additional £5 1s. There were also bedsteads to match from £5 11s to £7 6s 9d.

Also on offer were 'new' Divan (single as opposed to each-end bedsteads) headboards in three lengths – three, four and four feet six inches, £2 13s 3d, £3 4s 9d and £3 12s 3d respectively.

Upholstery

The article 'Our products' also discussed developments in upholstery that had 'been making big strides forward'. In the autumn of 1953, a lower-priced range had been introduced and was 'very well received', alongside the medium-priced range 'to which has recently been added designs in leather cloth and also a small contemporary range'.

On 26 June 1950, upholstery production moved from H/J shop at Tottenham to Woodley, near Reading, cementing a permanent separation of production with cabinet-making. This included separating the designers: Harry Whittaker was the upholstery designer. When the assembly shop first opened in 1950 it employed 30 people and produced five suites a week. In 1954 operations moved next door into an old aircraft hangar, used by Miles Aircraft and the Royal Air Force during the two world wars, and production increased. Looking back on this period, Ken Bennett, who was managing director in the latter years of Lebus Upholstery, recalled: 'We produced four or five basic designs of three-piece suites which we called our 'Z' range. These were cheaper than most other manufacturers and very good value for money. These ranges immediately became very popular and we were suddenly inundated with orders for three-piece suites, our open arm easy chairs and bed settees.'

The Z ranges of both upholstery and cabinet furniture were the cheaper end. A three-piece suite, fully sprung with hair, woven fibre with felt stuffing and padding covered in cotton tapestry, cost £51 13s 8d in 1950. Ian Fraser, who was marketing director in the latter years, commented of this period: 'Once, the lounge was considered as a "best room" and everyone was very careful with the furnishings' ('Lebus Silver Anniversary – Celebrating 25 Years of Upholstery Production at Woodley' in *Reading Evening* Post, 23 July 1975). Time revealed there were problems with springs breaking and/or padding sagging or shifting.

Maddox Street – a premier West End showroom

To raise the profile of Lebus furniture as part of the marketing strategy, the decision was made to open a showroom in London's West End. This was in keeping with the industry trend at this time of moving showrooms away from the old East End furniture-making area to the West End. In March 1954 the opportunity came up to move into a new building at 17–19 Maddox Street (just off Regent Street) on a previously bombed site.

Sir Herman must have found this an emotionally difficult but nonetheless commercially sensible decision to make. For more than 70 years, the Tabernacle Street

premises of 117,000 square feet had been known in the trade as the Lebus showrooms; it had been a meeting place as well as a place of business, and many meetings of the Furniture Trade Benevolent Association had been held there.

High-profile visitors of the time included Sam Waring, Sir Ernest Benn of Benn Brothers Ltd., Charles Allom of White Allom, and Mr. Botwright, editor of the *Furniture Record*. Until 1939, the showroom manager presided at the dinner table and carved the joint, and customers were welcome to stay for a meal.

The decision to move the showroom was made easier as Jock Boryer and Frank Felce, who had run the Tabernacle Street showroom, had retired after 45 years' service in 1946, just as the public company was formed. Jock's sons Charles and Walter also worked for the

Maddox Street showroom in London's premier West End opened in 1954

The sales team pictured in March 1961

firm. 'To the trade at large, Jock was a jovial figure with a profound knowledge of the business, and with a host of friends among his customers. To his staff he was the "guv'nor", meticulous in detail, severe (though just) to the malefactor, and an overall general Father Confessor to us all,' commented *Lebus Log*, No. 17.

A long lease for Maddox Street was negotiated and the premises were landlord-adapted to suit the firm's needs. The outside was natural travertine marble with the ground floor in green and the window surrounds and lettering in matt stainless steel.

There was a small reception hall on the ground floor and seven floors with 12,000 square feet of display area. Individual floors were divided into bays by the use of curtains and showrooms decorated in different wallpaper and paints to display furniture.

Tim Healy was Maddox Street manager for the first ten years, succeeded by Sam Perrett, who joined in November 1958. Perrett had been an apprentice with the Evans and Owen department store, Bath, from 1926, and had spent several years with a firm called Woodhouse (where he first met Ronnie Boss, cabinet sales manager, in 1936). After military service in World War Two, he had spent the

last ten years as Oxford branch manager of John Perrings.

After Sir Herman – Oliver elected chairman

When Sir Herman died in December 1957, he was still chairman and managing director of Harris Lebus and had been for its first ten years as a public company. From boy to man, he had been with the firm for 59 years; he celebrated 50 years in the firm with a party in 1949 and celebrated his 70th birthday in 1954. Just as the spotlight had been on Herman and Louis half a century ago, when their own father Harris died, the spotlight would again inevitably have been on the next generation of Lebus brothers – Anthony and Oliver.

On the death of Sir Herman, a split was made between the roles of chairman and managing director. Sir Laurence Watkinson (who had been vice chairman for two years and deputy secretary to the Ministry of Fuel and Power before joining the company) became chairman; Oliver was appointed as joint deputy chairman alongside LS, who was also joint managing director alongside Desmond Stratton. Alf Brown, a special director, was made an ordinary director, and Sir William Palmer joined the board. A little over three years later, at the end of January 1961, Oliver was 'unanimously' elected by the board of directors to the role of chairman when Sir Laurence

Watkinson retired. The following year Anthony became deputy chairman when LS stood down in planned semi-retirement (he remained a director on the board until his full retirement in December 1964). John, LS's eldest son, and his younger brother, Peter, joined in September 1956 and November 1958, respectively; both had a degree in economics from Cambridge, along with experience in the furniture industry in the States.

Erratic profit figures

Compiled from press coverage of the chairman's presentation to shareholders at autumn

Annual General Meetings using *The Times* online, profits in the first ten years as a public company were fairly erratic. In 1947, profits came in at around £455,350 and in 1948 they were £421,148. They dropped to £320,022 in 1949 and peaked in 1951 at £701,107. In 1957, the year of Sir Herman's death, profits dropped to £395,091.

Despite this, the company steered ahead with an air of confidence and optimism. 'By 1966 there was a Sales Force of sixty-seven men… seven permanent showrooms… Lebus had a huge list of 12,000 stockists… this brought in significant turnover,' wrote Rex Winsbury in 'How Lebus Turned Round' in the July 1968 *Management Today*. 'Our issue of catalogues to the trade runs into six figures annually, leaflets highlighting our various ranges run into millions,' recorded the *Lebus Log*, No. 19, June 1965.

'For those who make by those who sell'

In June 1965, the *Lebus Log*, No. 29, produced a special supplement 'for those who make by those who sell'. This was based on a conference on cabinet sales policy held at the Regal Ballroom, Edmonton. The article outlined the structure of the Sales department and investments made since 1957.

Mr. A. H. 'Mac' Maclean was general sales manager with two specialists reporting

to him: Mr. R. F. Burton, upholstery sales (Woodley) and Mr. Ronnie Boss, cabinet sales (Tottenham). In addition, Mr. Jack Thomas had responsibility for mail orders, plus the clearing of obsolete designs.

There were now five area sales managers: Mr. Glen in Scotland, Mr. Wightman in the north of England, Mr. Harold Chadwick in the midlands, Mr. Reg Holloway in the London area and Mr. Ernest Lashbrook in the south.

The travellers, or sales representatives, in the field rose to 66 (or 67, according to *Management Today*). Trainees from Maddox Street were often promoted to travelling sales representatives, such as Mr. K. Spencer, who had gone to west Kent, and Mr. R. G. Harrowven, who had gone to Norfolk. Some of the last batch of new sales representatives welcomed were Mr. E. Burton in Lancashire, Mr. F. Crossley in Leeds and Mr. W. C. Wright in Hampshire.

'A Traveller for this company very quickly becomes "Mr. Lebus" in his own parish if he is doing the job effectively and calling on his customers as frequently as we demand.'

– *Lebus Log*, No. 29, June 1965

The article explains how each sales representative sent in a daily 'call sheet', so the Sales department knew 'exactly where he has been, who he has seen and how much business he does day by day'. Each member of the Harris Lebus sales force had to work to a sales budget, just the same as the factory worked to a production budget:

> [T]hey are expected to work as necessary to get the maximum amount of orders every day… In addition to selling the furniture we make, he [the sales representative] must accept complaints on all aspects of quality and service, listen to customers' particular problems, probably give them advice on many and varied things affecting business, in other words generally represent Harris Lebus, maintain and improve the company image.

Evolving list of permanent provincial showrooms

Plans to roll out a network of permanent provincial showrooms started under Sir Herman continued with Oliver and Anthony – by the early 1960s there were seven in all. When the programme began at the beginning of the 1950s, Glasgow was the third-largest city in Britain; a new salesroom was opened in Watson Street in 1952, where it did well, but proved too small. In 1957, Tom Sneddon founded another at 84 Bell Street. It was in the middle of the main shopping area, twice the size, with a ground floor and basement, its own goods lift and loading bay. It was officially opened on 21 September 1958. Along with Tom Sneddon, the staff team were David Shaw as manager, William McCartney, Ian Nairn and William Redpath. Similarly, Liverpool was targeted for a showroom, which opened on 27 September 1954 at 40 Hope Street. It had six floors and 25,000 square feet of sales space. Mr. W. T. Hiscock was the manager – he had also managed the pre-war salesroom in Bold Street, after a period as the West End of London's sales representative, and worked in Tottenham's Sales department (then known as A department) during the war.

A Plymouth salesroom had opened in October 1955 and was announced by Mr. J. H. Dashwood, Cornwall sales representative, in the *Lebus Log*, No. 6: '[I]t is enhanced in the attractive decorations which repeat, in modified form, our well known Lebus colour scheme of red, blue and grey.' However, this salesroom does not appear in the listing in 1965 and presumably had been closed by then. Showrooms were also established in Leicester at 5 Wellington Street and in Hull at Brook Chambers, 91 Ferensway. However, after a short spell both were subsequently closed as they were deemed too small with no capacity to develop. Larger cities were targeted instead.

According to the *Lebus Log*, No. 29, by the mid-1960s there were permanent showrooms in London's Maddox Street, Glasgow's Bell Street, Liverpool's Hope Street, Manchester at 76 Deansgate, plus Bristol and Edinburgh. There were plans in the pipeline for a Birmingham showroom, but these did not materialise.

Marketing designs – New Elizabethan, Contemporary, Modern or any other name…

Catalogues were produced three times a year and benefitted from much improved illustrations using a Rotaprint machine. However, these still relied on in-house photographs. Photographer Bob Hewett's job (in part) was to photograph them: 'whilst ensuring that he does justice to the designers, he must avoid excessive flattery otherwise the retailer might complain he was misled by the photograph!' ('Spotlight on: Bob Hewett' in the *Lebus Log*, No. 15, December 1959) The Design Programme meant some 250 negatives and 25,000 prints, 12 inches by 10 inches. With a limited number of props, 'Huge boards of wood would be lashed together and whitewashed as a backdrop for the furniture to be photographed – it was all quite primitive and makeshift!' recalled Henry Jacobs, photographer apprentice, in an interview with the author in 2008.

In the 1950s, furniture manufacturers across the country organised themselves into a trade body – the British Furniture Manufacturers' Federated Association. The inaugural show was in 1950 and was attended by H. R. H. Princess Elizabeth (before becoming Queen a few years later); it was the first exhibition of any significance since the end of World War Two. The first show was only open to the trade but in the following years the public were welcomed to annual shows held at Earls Court, London.

The company also held its main exhibition of the year at the Maddox Street Showroom in January–February to coincide with the Earls Court Exhibition. According to the *Lebus Log*, No. 29, June 1965: 'It is at these main exhibitions that we launch our new designs to the trade. We also show them to some of our selected accounts before they go on the market at two previews at the Regal Ballroom, Edmonton in June and November annually.' According to J. L. Oliver in *The Development and Structure of the Furniture Industry* there were additional annual national shows in Glasgow in April and Manchester in August.

Harris Lebus held an exhibition at the Manchester showroom at the same time as the Northern Trade Exhibition at Manchester's Belle Vue. 'In Manchester in August 1963, new bedroom suites and dining sets were introduced, and business done there was nearly double that of the previous year', said Ronnie Boss, cabinet sales manager. And some designs were more commercially successful than others; for example, the Henley – in stripy mahogany (also sold as the 'American' suite with a high chest of drawers) – 'has sold over 200% above expectations since it was introduced in May 1958'. Boss felt this success was attributed to 'good, clean, up-to-date design and finish, on a well-made article sold at the right price' (*Lebus Log*, No. 13, December 1958). He went on to say that a sister suite, the Paladao, would be introduced in January 1959, in a 'stripy veneer from the Philippines (and a relation to the mango tree)'.

Alongside the interchangeable bedroom range and upholstery, the article 'Our products' (*Lebus Log*, No. 1, 1954) gave some hints as to future plans, though interestingly it is written in the past tense and in parts comes across as a 'wish list' unfulfilled:

> We planned to increase the range of kitchen furniture which had made such a promising start last year with the original kitchen cabinet… [W]e planned to… introduce a range of contemporary furniture. We felt whereas there existed a potential market for contemporary furniture, hitherto it had had two main limitations. First of all, it was too expensive, and secondly the designs had been too extreme for the majority of people. I will not enter into arguments here as to whether the furniture should be called New Elizabethan, Contemporary, Modern, or any other name.

The development in the firm's marketing approach was especially evident with the launch of the more edgy Link furniture

advertising, which was produced from the mid-1950s. This emphasised 'Link' as the brand name rather than 'Harris Lebus furniture' or 'Lebus furniture', and the retailer was more likely to make the connection with the branding and the firm than the end customer. (This was also the case for the later Capitol and Europa ranges.)

Advertising continued with the theme of 'interchange-ability' – characteristic of the firm's furniture promotions for its oak ranges, whilst emphasising the contemporary feel of the Link range and introducing the notion of 'mix and match' in furnishing in the contemporary home.

A promotional leaflet at the time stated: '"Link" Furniture – is graceful, modern and so easy to live with, [which] serves to demonstrate "Link" is entirely original modern furniture for modern homes, but with all the grace and charm of a bygone age.'

The leaflet continued:

> Just look at 'Link' – at the pleasing curves, at the strong but slender legs. Classic in its simplicity, contemporary in its compactness and adaptability, 'Link' furniture represents a new approach to modern design.
>
> From the range of 'Link' pieces in these pages, you will find plenty to choose for every room for every home. Each piece can be bought separately, and you can devise innumerably lovely room arrangements – all with astonishing variety-in-harmony. Furnish a complete house with 'Link' or start with a few essential pieces and build up gradually – either way you'll be delighted with the elegance and versatility of this new furnishing idea.
>
> A special point about 'Link' is the way it will blend with other furniture you already have. Few people can afford to set up a home that is completely new throughout, and the modern fashion is, of course, for blending good traditional

with good modern furniture. That's one of the charms of 'Link' – it looks so well with older furniture… To achieve the variety-in-harmony which is characteristic of 'Link', all the pieces are completely interchangeable. There are four variations of the sideboard, six different dressing tables. And the chests [of drawers], in many designs, are adaptable for living rooms, halls, bedrooms or bed-sitters.

Marketing was clearly developing, becoming more innovative and sophisticated. This built on the experience of Oliver Lebus as sales director. Mr. Jacob Zinkin, who had joined the firm as marketing manager in 1961, was elevated to the board as marketing director on 19 January 1962. At the same time, Mr. E. L. Richards joined the board as a non-executive director, replacing Sir William Palmer. Tony (as he was known) Richards was the husband of Barbara Richards, Oliver and Anthony's sister.

'The larger manufacturing businesses of today can command the services of specialist advertising consultants and of the agents of mass publicity', pointed out J. L. Oliver in his book *Development and Structure of the Furniture Industry*.

Advertising manager Peter Barnett initiated cinema advertising for the Link range. 'Thinking of Linking' was the common theme of five one-minute Link films made at Elstree Studios. Magnificent sets were built for each film – streets, shops, houses and gardens. Pearl and Dean, who were famous for cinema advertising, were the producers. In the spring of 1958, the films appeared in 450 cinemas up and down the country.

Advertisements for the new Link range used many catchy marketing straplines such as 'contemporary smartness with ageless glamour' and Link 'enlarges every home – it hasn't given us a spare room, it has given us room to spare'. And '"Link" has enlarged our purse! We've actually spent less than we had allowed, on more than we intended'.

Link in more detail

Lounge and dining room furniture was available in either 'Hazel Oak' or the slightly more expensive 'Sherry Walnut' finishes. Prices for this range were:

- A three-foot-nine-inch sideboard cost £24 5s 9d or £26 5s 6d
- A dining table £12 2s 6d or £12 15s 6d
- Dining chairs £4 10s 6d
- Carving chair £6 5s 6d
- A two-foot-six-inch bureau £19 3s 3d and £20 2s 3d
- Settee from £18 13s 9d
- And easy chair from £12.

Bedroom furniture was available in a wood colour described as 'Tola', which was priced:

- A four-foot wardrobe cost £35 5s 6d
- A three-foot-six-inch kneehole dressing table £25 11s
- A two-foot-six-inch four-drawer chest £19 18s 6d
- A four-foot-six-inch bed £13
- A dressing stool £5 11s
- A low-back armchair from £15 18s 9d
- A high-back armchair from £16 13s 9d
- And a three-foot-nine-inch occasional table was £10 19s.

Link furniture featured in an exhibition in 1960 to showcase British furniture, held at the Coliseum, beside New York's Central Park and opened by the Duke of Edinburgh. This generated orders in New York as well as in Vancouver and Winnipeg, Canada. 'A great many compliments were given on the quality and workmanship of the furniture, but generally speaking (and we were conscious of this before we went) the designs were not thought likely to find great favour with the American public. They prefer larger, more decorated pieces, as opposed to the simple modern line of the "Link" range,' Oliver Lebus commented in *Lebus Log*, No. 18, December 1960.

Top left: Link furniture catalogue

Top right and below left: Advertisements for Link furniture placed in magazines such as *Woman*, *Woman's Realm* and *Woman's Own*

Link dressing table recently for sale on an online auction site

(photo courtesy of fish4 Junk http://www.fish4junk.co.uk)

Link trademark plate in blue plastic inside a drawer

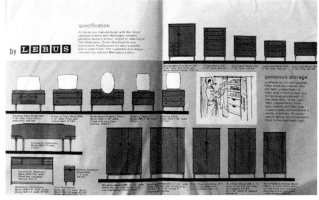

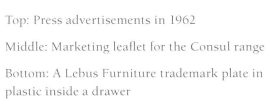

Top: Press advertisements in 1962

Middle: Marketing leaflet for the Consul range

Bottom: A Lebus Furniture trademark plate in
plastic inside a drawer

through something of a purchasing boom, which proved to be short-lived, and from 1960–1963 our Tottenham-made cabinet sales dropped rapidly and alarmingly. We were forced into short time working, and although business in the trade was generally difficult from 1960 onwards, our volume was even more severely hit. Competition was extremely fierce.

Hire-purchase regulations and changes in part explain the higher-than-usual turnover figures for 1960 and 1964, with profit at £513,978 and £424,219 respectively. Profit was at its lowest in 1962 at £136,489, despite extensive national advertising. Boss continued: 'In 1964 the Tottenham factory avoided short time in several years… some parts of it were almost on continuous overtime almost throughout the year. We finished 1964 well ahead of our sales budget and somewhat higher than our 1959 level. At the same time the year 1964 was also a boom year with conditions much the same as they had been in 1959.'

In the *Lebus Log*, No. 29, June 1965 (which would be the last edition of the in-house magazine in this format until a re-launched smaller version in February 1968), Boss cited three key reasons for the decline in cabinet sales: 'Methods used by the Sales Force in their presentation of the company's products were no longer as effective as they had been; many other manufacturers' products had become more competitive and more appealing in design; we were giving poor service, resulting in poor company image. Or, of course, it could be a combination of all three reasons.'

It is noteworthy that Mr. Boss stated: 'From 1959 to 1963 the sales of our medium oak interchangeable ranges alone, which we had been making and selling so successfully for so many years, declined by about the total amount of the Tottenham turnover decline… public taste was changing rapidly, and the popularity of medium oak was declining as quickly as the popularity of the black motor car.' Ironically, it was Cyril Rostgaard, chief designer, who had identified these changing tastes in an article in

the *Lebus Log*, No. 16, back in April 1960 – five years previously.

Interestingly, Boss added: 'During this period, this same Sales Force, which is engaged in selling our Cabinet furniture and Upholstery, had sold considerably more Upholstery and Factored cabinet furniture than they had lost on Tottenham-made designs, so that the company turnover overall was continuing to go up, and the loss was wholly on the Tottenham factory section.'

'Beaten by modern design and modern materials'

In the 1965 article, Ronnie Boss said:

> Cyril Rostgaard, Mr. Buchanan, at that time in charge of Sales Research and now our Product Manager, and myself were out and about all over the country and seeing for ourselves increasing evidence of new materials, such as chipboard and melamine, being used by many other manufacturers who were moving very fast towards modern, well-made and well-finished contemporary furniture, away from traditional designs and that we were not keeping up with this trend. It was significant that the designs of a number of our main competitors in the cabinet field could be seen in almost any shop we visited anywhere in the country. These were reported to us as being the fast sellers which were taking our business.

In a national survey of eleven furniture manufacturers, including Lebus, that covered company image, design, quality of representatives and attention to complaints, Ronnie Boss wrote that 'our own sales force rated number one'. The company was also rated number one in respect to complaints and ranked number three overall out of the eleven firms. 'I have no hesitation in saying that our number one overall requirement can be summed up in one word "communications"; internal, within the Sales Force, with retail friends and with the public', wrote Boss. The conclusion was that the firm should focus on dealing with faults better, ensuring quality finishes and improving quality control generally, better handling of returned faulty goods by retailers and not displaying any faulty products in showrooms or retail outlets. It was not until 1958 that the company elevated Customer Services after renaming the Correspondence department; Barry H. Freeman joined as office manager, Customer Services on 1 March 1962.

Desmond Stratton established a Tottenham Long Term Plan, covering the next three years, which aimed to restore turnover to higher than 1959. In the Long-Term Cabinet Design Programme, the three desired outcomes according to Mr. Boss were:

> To simplify and streamline our standards so that, for example, we make wardrobes to only two depths – which we are now doing; to work on two constructions, framed-up for the lower end and chipboard for the better end; to keep all our designs in a price bracket where we could get quantity sales and long-term runs, essential to the success of a big production unit. It must be remembered also in these days of fierce competition, there are a number of sizable manufacturers who specialise in, say, one bracket of our own design spread, firms who concentrate on bedroom ranges, others on individual suites, others on individual dining sets, and because we are so much larger than anyone else, we have to make in all of these brackets in order to get our turnover, so in each of them we must be as good as any other individual manufacturer.

A marketing committee considered the option to have sales representatives with large geographical patches and handling a significant amount of work in all areas – Upholstery, Factored, Cabinet furniture, experimenting in specialising in either one of Cabinet or Upholstery; this required having two representatives within the same area. Pilot schemes were tested in three locations: south Wales, Essex and Liverpool. These proved unsuccessful. Another option explored was 'ground concentration', which worked on the

basis that more representatives would cover a particular geographical area, each covering smaller patches. This meant that they could spend more time with every customer or outlet. Pilot schemes proved more successful, so the travelling sales force increased and territories were reconfigured.

Rumours and hearsay

Shop Steward Sissy Lewis recalled:

> We were asked to pull our socks up or we'd go under… I knew that something was wrong as soon as Sir Herman Lebus died, and the two young boys took over in the 1960s. This fella came in, I've forgotten his name, but he was given a beautiful house and a snooker table in a beautiful snooker room. They said he had come to try and put the firm back on its feet. We realised that something was wrong.

It is easy to see things through the eyes of the workers and those unfamiliar with the vagaries of the furniture industry in general, and how, on the death of Sir Herman and the subsequent departure of Sir Laurence Watkinson three years later, there appeared to be a correlation between declining sales and the appointment of Oliver as managing director, and then chairman and managing director.

Former employee Peter Baker recalled:

> In 1979 I was putting bonus schemes into the whole factory at Bluestone Furniture Ltd., in Walthamstow and discovered that the Accounts clerk there was also a 'Lebus Boy' and had been working at the Factory when Sir Herman died… He told me that the business had been divided between the two sons, Anthony and Oliver. Oliver having taken the Upholstery factory to Reading in 1950, retained this as his domain while Anthony took control of the Cabinet works as his. For some reason Anthony had hired a retired Civil Servant as Managing Director. The paperwork had multiplied within a very short time and, apparently, orders began to decline at the same time. The Managing Director did

not know what to do in a very commercial enterprise and took his eye off the ball. This is, of course, third party information and may be biased. But I am a 'Lebus Boy'. And that ship was run very efficiently when I was there.

Parts of what Peter said may contain elements of truth, but this had become blurred and the facts misconstrued; now is an opportunity to state the facts and set the record straight.

Restructuring, Reinvestment and Scaling Back

'In 1966, Harris Lebus, the largest UK furniture-maker, was an inch from disaster. Drastic pruning of people, products, premises and operations under new management just saved the day.'

– Rex Winsbury, 'How Lebus Turned Round' in *Management Today*, July 1968

According to Rex Winsbury, Leonard Grosbard was the man to 'put the firm back on its feet' – he was appointed chief executive in May 1966 with previous experience with John Wallace and British Aluminium. In the article, Grosbard stated: 'Two years ago we were up against our borrowing limits; we were bound to make a loss that year; we couldn't put our prices up, because we were 25% overpriced on value anyway, against our competitors; we had to work at 98% of capacity just to break even, and relied on overtime to make any profit; the July 1966 squeeze was only three months off; and we had a dividend to pay.' To quote Winsbury, Lebus had 'chased volume at the expense of profits'.

One possibility was to simply sell out at Tottenham Hale, quit cabinet-making and turn Lebus into a hire purchase and transport company. But land with buildings on it was hard to sell so consideration was given to turn the Tottenham site into an industrial estate through a £1 million injection of investment to make the factory buildings suitable, with a long-term view to sell on at £4 million. However, aside from the fact that £1 million would be difficult to raise, the idea of losing cabinet-making was just unthinkable. And some contemporaneous furniture firms – such as Gomme (after a bad spell) and Parker Knoll – were still profitable. The master plan was to continue cabinet furniture-making, converting a labour-intensive operation based on individual craftsmen to a capital-intensive operation based on machines. Leonard Grosbard, in turn, appointed Robert Mahlich in July 1966 – then a consultant with Harold Whitehead and Partners – as director of production; both were engineers by training.

The value of land on the books stood at £1.2 million but was considered to be significantly undervalued, and on revaluation of all fixed assets in 1967 the figure was raised from £2.8 million to £4.6 million. Then the Greater London Council – keen to acquire industrial land for social housing and incentivise relocation of industry and people to expanding towns beyond Greater London – offered the firm a 'going concern' rate of £3.6 million. Island A was sold for £800,000 on 8 December 1967. Island B was sold £1.5 million on 1 April 1968. Island C was under contract to be sold for £1.3 million. With cash in hand, Grosbard tackled internal problems – management, products, production and marketing. As part of a planned major disposal of assets, loss-making or non-essential activities were either sold or liquidated. This included the chain of garages in White Hart Lane originally bought to service the transport fleet in-house; Eventide Bedding (Grosbard said this venture was 'just nonsense – the lease on its Brentford premises was falling in') was sold to Charles Fox, more as a name than a going concern; Bentwood Chair Supply was liquidated; C. F. C. Lagos – the Nigerian furniture manufacturer that the firm had a major investment in – was also sold. The exercise of forming a leaner, slimmer outfit, along with the disposal of old plant and stocks, cost the company £500,000.

A holding company and two subsidiaries

As part of the reorganisation, Harris Lebus was converted into a holding company, effective from 16 July 1966, with two operating subsidiaries: one for cabinet-making and the other for upholstery. The total cost of this exercise was £1.8 million. The board of the holding company was reorganised, comprising Oliver Lebus (chairman), Anthony Lebus (deputy chairman), Leonard Grosbard, Desmond Stratton, Arthur Tunley and Tony Richards. At the same time, G. P. Fox retired on health grounds, Alf Brown relinquished his directorship and LS's two sons, Peter and John, left during this process after ten years with the firm.

The board of Lebus (Cabinet) Furniture comprised: Desmond Stratton, who became chairman and managing director, Alf Brown, deputy chairman and deputy managing director (in day-to-day control), and Ken Bennett as financial director.

The board of Lebus Upholstery comprised: Anthony Lebus, who became chairman and managing director, Ken Nash, director and general manager, Frank Wooliams and Harry Whittaker.

Lebus of London Ltd. and Merchandise Funds were also retained.

Mass redundancies

With expenses mounting, the real cost of redundancies would have been £450,000. The firm had to find only £120,000 plus some extra payments; the rest came from the national fund in accordance with the Redundancy Payments Act. Because of the industry's lengthy and cumbersome arbitration procedure, disagreements meant some workers had nothing to do during the process. This was, in part, responsible for the firm's interim results for 1966–1967 being worse than expected. A pre-tax loss of £372,000 was more than forecast, and losses continued up to the middle of April, by which time they totalled £550,000. The actual cost of reorganisation in the financial year 1967–1968 was £125,000, plus £400,000 in 1968–1969.

Production and reinvestment in machinery

In search of market intelligence, and shortly after his appointment, Leonard Grosbard visited Germany where per-capita expenditure on new furniture was then three times that of the UK, over £8 a year compared to £3 at manufacturers' prices. There was a higher rate of new house building in post-war Germany, fuelling demand for furnishings.

Traditionally, furniture was a small-scale industry in the UK, with craftsmen, often in small or one-man home-based businesses, specialising in particular bits of the manufacturing process – panel-making, handles, legs, etc. In the 1960s the industry was still fragmented, with 1,500 firms – even this large figure was half the number there had been twenty years before when Harris Lebus had gone public. 'It also explains why, with a mere 8% of the market in its heyday under Sir Herman Lebus… Lebus was the biggest firm in the business' wrote Rex Winsbury. In the article, Leonard Grosbard commented, 'we were twenty years behind the times when I came – now we are a few years in front of the best'.

Marketing and targets

Kenneth Dean (of Pearl and Dean), who had helped market Gomme's G-Plan brand from losses to profitability, was recruited. Winsbury added:

> It is unrealistic to think of one brand e.g. Europa with a dominating share of the market, it is more feasible to think of several brands, each with perhaps 5%. A 10% share of the £150 million furniture market is much bigger than any other firm at present possesses or has ever possessed. But the firm will need to reach or hold something like Lebus's old maximum market penetration to get its 15% return on capital, and that is the measure of the challenge still facing the company.

Under the management of John Thornton, it was Merchandise Funds' target to double its business capacity over the next three to five years. At that time, outstanding hire-purchase balances amounted to £5 million a year – the target was to go through the £10 million mark by the early 1970s.

As well as assisting Lebus and other furniture retailers – making up 60% of the business – Merchandise Funds also dealt in the hire purchase of electrical goods and cars. In addition, various small sailing craft were handled, as well as financing a twin-engine Cessna aircraft. John Thornton commented: 'Although the large finance houses deal in the same way as ourselves, we compete effectively because, I believe our service is more personal and often faster.' ('How Lebus Turned Round' *Management Today*, July 1968)

New products – available only through selected outlets

As a maker of affordable furniture, the question being asked by management was – was this the right place in the market to be? At first, the intention was to stick to the lower end of the market, where the Lebus name was at least well known to the trade (though hardly known to the public – in furniture, few manufacturers' brand names are, apart perhaps from Gomme's G-Plan, which had about 3% of sales). As discussions progressed, the product range was upgraded. Having developed and invested in provincial salesrooms, the decision was then taken to close them all, except for London's Maddox Street. The sales force was cut to 26 and some 1,350 stockists were selected, on the basis of size, position, service, display standards and credit worthiness.

'Europa: grace without fuss, simplicity with staying power'

The Europa range was launched in autumn 1967. It was the first salvo in the firm's new product policy and was pitched squarely in the middle of the market, the 18–35 middle-income housewives who were only 10% of the population but bought 30% of furniture. The marketing strapline was: 'The Europa challenge: show us any other furniture that looks as beautiful, that's made with the same degree of care that you can buy at anything like the price. It can't be done!'

'The big gamble', wrote Rex Winsbury, 'was whether retailers, which had to stock the new line before it could be sold to the public, would accept the idea that Lebus could make good furniture. In the end, it did… The actual design of the new Europa range is rather conservative and has been criticised as such. But this was more or less forced on Lebus. It could not in the circumstances take any affordable risks on the acceptability of the new range.'

The press reaction to Europa was reported in the first edition of the re-launched *News from Lebus*, No. 1, in February 1968: 'Marketing is a heart-breaking trade,' said the *Observer* newspaper. 'Launch a product, feed it, nurse it, push it, stay up all night with it, even cry tears over it and the odds are it will still flop. Of every 100 new products launched every year it is reckoned that only two smell the heady scent of success. Harris Lebus gets into the finals on the strength of its new Europa range launched at the start of the autumn.' The *Tottenham and Edmonton Weekly Herald*, 17 February 1967, said, 'Lebus introduce new ideas into battle for sales… The styling of the pieces owes a lot to the recent Scandinavian influence which has recently caught hold in England, though it resists the temptation to be "way out" since it is meant for a mass market. Europa has severely simple lines with a lack of obtrusive decoration.'

Not a single splinter of wood

The tub chair was the first of the Europa range, produced by Lebus Upholstery in the spring of 1967. The tub chairs were upholstered in polyether foam, covered in a knitted stretch fabric with reversible cushion and zip cover, and had a swivel pedestal base of mild steel finished with satin chrome.

The *Tottenham and Edmonton Weekly Herald* commented: 'People who want a quick and cheap change might be tempted to swap their old armchairs for futuristic "tub" chairs… produced in a range of gay colours, they cost 16 guineas each although you can see similar designs in West End shops at £25 or more. There is not a single splinter of wood in the chair – an odd departure for a furniture firm which has been dealing in wood for seventy years.'

Top: Advertisement, Europa bedroom suite

Top right: Europa dressing table recently for sale on an online auction site

(photo courtesy of http://www.etsy.com/uk/shop/ DurstonDelights)

Above: Europa Furniture trademark sticker in plastic inside a drawer

Europa tub chair

Photographed in famous European locations

'A creative team crossed the channel to photograph the furniture against a backdrop of some of Europe's most exotic locations – St. Mark's Square in Venice, Padua in Italy, Taormina in Sicily, a bull ring in Spain. The results were seen in highly effective selling in Women's magazines and the mass-circulation national Press.' (*News from Lebus*, No. 1, February 1968)

The San Remo sofa units of modular designed upholstery and matching chair in yellow ochre were photographed on Capitoline Hill, Rome: 'They're how to get as much or as little sofa as you want and shaped just the way you want; as traditional two-armed sofas, or filling a whole wall if you put two units side by side, or curved – in two different ways, because you've 1-seater or 2-seater or 3-seater units to link with it.' (Wording from an original whole

The San Remo sofa
units of modular
designed upholstery
and matching chair
in yellow ochre,
photographed on
the Capitoline Hill,
Rome

(Paul Collier private
collection)

page magazine advertisement from the author's
private collection.)

Interchangeable San Remo sofa units were
priced as individual pieces:

- A one-seat unit – with either a left or right
  armrest – from £27

- A two-seat unit from £36

- A three-seat unit from £51, with each
  additional arm from £6

- A corner unit from £46

- And an armchair from £31.

The San Remo corner group, consisting of two
two-seat sofas linked by a corner unit could be
purchased from £130. Other pieces could be
added, such as teak-veneered modular shelving:
base units from £20, other units from £7, with
a round coffee table at £12 and Terranova
recliner chair from £55.

Sales and meeting consumer demand

Europa furniture was available in shops by
September 1967. Initial demand was good,
so much so that the sales targets were raised
by 60% and a double shift was introduced

Europa success reported in a new look in-house
magazine, *News from Lebus*, February 1968

FEBRUARY 1968   No. 1   HARRIS LEBUS LTD., TOTTENHAM & WOODLEY

Princess Margaret to visit Lebus

PRINCESS MARGARET is to pay a
visit to the Tottenham works of
Harris Lebus Limited on Wednesday,
April 10.

Details of the programme for the visit,
which will take place during the morning,
are still being worked out but it is known
that Her Royal Highness will be seeing
the new plant in operation before having
lunch with the Company directors. Princess
Margaret will be the first official visitor to
be shown Europe's latest and most modern
furniture-producing operation.

This will be the second post-war Royal
visit to the Tottenham site. The Lebus sports
ground and pavilion were opened by the
Duke of Edinburgh in 1956.

Introducing . . .

This is the first issue of *News from
Lebus*, a quarterly review of events
and comment for the interest of employees. Extra issues will be produced on special occasions. Contributions or letters will be gladly considered and should be addressed to
the Group Personnel Manager.

Sales of Europa are beating all the forecasts

THE biggest success in the recent history of cabinet furniture: that is the story of
EUROPA which in seven months has achieved a position of clear domination over
its section of the market. To quote from " The Europa Challenge "—

*The Europa range is beautiful, as you'll see in the shop. But look
close. Look hard. Not just at the front but at the back. In the drawers,
at the hinges, underneath. Then look at other furniture. Show us anything
that matches Europa at anything like the price. It can't be done.*

If the language has a hint of self-congratu-
lation about it there are more than enough
hard facts to bear out all the claims. The
trade, who are not to be won by smooth talk
but can recognise a good thing when they
see it, gave their instant approval to Europa.

It was calculated that Europa would
require 1,000 outlets within the first year of
operation. The figure was exceeded in six
months. After retailers had seen Europa for
the first time in the Maddox Street showrooms the initial orders were so large that
provisional sales targets had to be raised by
57 per cent.

The average stock (or re-ordering) rate

for cabinet furniture is between five and six
times per year. The figure for Europa is
19 times per year. For the upholstered
ranges the figure is 15 times. Instead of a
retailer selling stock every two months, he
is selling Europa every two to three weeks:
overwhelming evidence that the big response
by the trade to the introduction of the new
range has been fully backed by subsequent
orders from the buying public.

Like the successful introduction of almost
any product, the Europa achievement arose
from an integrated team effort in which prob-
(Continued on page 2)

*Looking over the Europa fleet : Mr. Oliver Lebus (chairman) and Mr. Leonard Grosbard
(chief executive); followed by Mr. Robert Mahlich (production director) and Mr. Kenneth
Dean (marketing director)*

at Tottenham to keep up. Kenneth Dean, Lebus's group marketing director, said: 'It has been a tough first year for the furniture but Europa – which had to get volume to justify the expensive new plant that makes it – is now running 50% ahead of its sales forecasts… and things are still going well. The prospect is that by next summer, Europa will be the biggest brand in the business.' (Rex Winsbury, *Management Today*, July 1968)

The Soviet Embassy in London bought £4,000 worth of Europa furniture – both cabinet and upholstered for dining rooms and bedrooms to furnish embassy staff houses and flats in London. An order for £35,000 worth of upholstered furniture was placed by a Swiss firm through 'Lebus of London Ltd.', the firm's export division. Peter Sheldon, general manager of Lebus of London, commented: 'It is very encouraging – we have recently been making fresh efforts in the Swiss market.' (*News from Lebus*, No. 2, May 1968)

Named after European (and Scandinavian) towns and cities

The *Daily Mail* Ideal Home Exhibition held at Olympia in the spring of 1968 showed Europa furniture on the Waring and Gillow stand. Mr. Ben Pomerance, joint managing director of Waring and Gillow, said: 'We chose Europa this year because of the exciting sense of challenge of this new and reasonably priced range. Our policy has always been to feature the latest and the best.' More than forty lines of Europa bedroom, dining, occasional and upholstered furniture were on show, including the newest upholstered groups, Malaga, Verona and Andorra, and new chairs Bergen and Madrid. There was a swivel chair called Malmo, covered in dark brown Acrilan jersey.

Changing winds of taste, choppy seas of hire purchase

The confidence shown by Rex Winsbury, when he started his *Management Today* article saying they had 'just saved the day' rather than with the caveat '*may* have just saved the day' is of note. Published three months after Princess Margaret's visit, the new-look Lebus was well

into its stride and the future looked bright. '[G] rappling with this future will be far easier now that Lebus has shrugged off its weighty history,' said Winsbury later in the same article.

Lebus's financial reporting year was June to July. Total turnover for the year ending July 1967 fell from £17.6 million the year before to £11.2 million (the businesses sold off or closed were a factor). Europa sales reached 3% of the total furniture market and, with the boom in consumer expenditure between devaluation and the last budget at a crucial juncture, this ensured the success of Lebus's new sales season. The company conceded that the extra sales generated beyond its original projections were 'almost an embarrassment' as demand outstripped production capacity.

There had been three much publicised resignations along the way: Ken Nash had resigned in January 1967 and Harry Whittaker at the end of June 1967. On 3 August of that year, Leo Martin resigned as director of Lebus of London, the export subsidiary; he had taken exports from £60,000 in 1962 to £565,000 in less than five years. In a statement, he said he did not agree with the firm's policies.

A combination of luck and capitalising on opportunities offered by public policies and turning them to Lebus's advantage had kept the ship on a steady course. With the Industrial Reorganisation Corporation looking into the still-archaic structure of the furniture industry, and the Prices and Incomes Board looking into retail margins on consumer goods, the list of public policies that might yet come to affect Lebus had not yet evolved. The firm only emerged from its loss-making period in 1968, but still had to meet Leonard Grosbard's long-term target of 15% return on capital.

Much like the *Titanic*, the modernised Harris Lebus steadfastly steamed full ahead to its 1973 destination – a new-town factory. But icebergs lay ahead in the form of changes in consumer tastes and purchasing power, hire-purchase regulations and competition. And Harris Lebus was on a collision course with one issue in particular.

Hitting the iceberg of financial liability

Just as the warning from the look-out in the *Titanic* came too late, so too did that for Harris Lebus. The company had tried to make the ship lighter; it was reported (according to *The Times* online archives) on 24 February 1969 that Hampton and Sons had sold the long leasehold interests in 17–19 Maddox Street – about £200,000 was being asked. Merchandise Funds was sold to Triumph Investments for £1.3 million; negotiations had been ongoing since July 1969.

The *Tottenham and Edmonton Weekly Herald* of 29 January 1970 reported that early in 1969 Lebus doubled its total borrowing powers to an upper limit of £7.7 million (the trading loss for 1967–1968 was £927,000). In its interim statement for the year to July 1969, the firm reported a loss before tax of £484,000 and had passed its preference dividend (preferred stock is a special class of shares, e.g. preference in assets in the case of liquidation; dividends accumulated and not paid within an agreed

period is described as 'passed'). Losses announced for the 52-week period ending 31 October 1969 were £1,010,117. That iceberg was eventually struck at Christmas 1969. By Easter 1970, machines in Tottenham went quiet, dust gathered on the neglected glass roofs, leaves blew across the concrete of the East and West walkways, and swans and wild geese swam on the River Lea and walked on the towpath beyond the periphery walls; their flapped wings in oblivious abandon to seventy years of history that had gone more quietly than it had come.

The mesmerising stillness of an affixed notice on the permanently closed, rusting front gates reading 'Acquired by the Greater London Council for housing' belied the swirl of impact felt far and wide. 'Such a sad ending', commented Peter Baker, a 'Lebus Boy', 1950–1954, to the author. 'Many, many retailers must have regretted the closing of Lebus, for many small retailers were, in truth, only salesmen for the company, even though they controlled and maintained their own premises'.

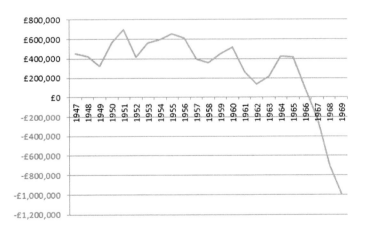

Public company years: profit and loss

CHAPTER FIVE

How We Did It: From Designer's Sketch to Finished Furniture

'It was well made, I will say that. It was all wood and the backs were stained ply, wood shelves. Down there they was ahead of their time.'

– Ron Turton, polisher, 1954–1967 (Coombes Croft project)

Tottenham and Edmonton Weekly Herald, 30 January 1920

By Order of Mr. H. Lebus… WITHOUT RESERVE, FINSBURY CABINET WORKS, TOTTENHAM.

Henry Butcher & Co., F.A.I., have received instructions to SELL by AUCTION at the above premises, on Wednesday February 25th, 1920, commencing at eleven o'clock a.m. the EXTENSIVE SURPLUS AIRCRAFT STORES, MATERIALS, PLANT and MACHINERY, as follows: -

TOOL SECTION – Large quantities of new and nearly new STANLEY PLANES, HAMMERS, TURNSCREWS, STOCK AND DIES, WRENCHES, PLIERS, HAND and BREAST DRILLS, HACK SAW FRAMES, TENON SAWS, FILES, WIRE CUTTERS, RULES, SQUARES, SPRING DIVIDERS, MORSE DRILLS etc.

AIRCRAFT WOODWORK – Enormous quantities of each, WOOD BENCHES, TRESTLES, TEMPLATES, STOOLS, FORMS, COUNTERS, ERECTORS, STANDS, WINGS, CENTRE SECTIONS etc.

35 SINGER SEWING MACHINES… EYELETS and WASHERS, about 50,000… 400 lbs, CAMPBELL'S NO. 40 LINEN THREAD, in 2oz reels…

....

Evolution and Reinvention – Towards Progressive Flow Production

At the end of World War One, the factory was strewn with redundant materials, tools and to some extent machinery, having lent itself to the manufacture of war-related equipment and planes. Not a stick of furniture had been made in four years and the partnership was at a crossroads. Sol and his nephews Herman and Louis embarked on a new strategic plan

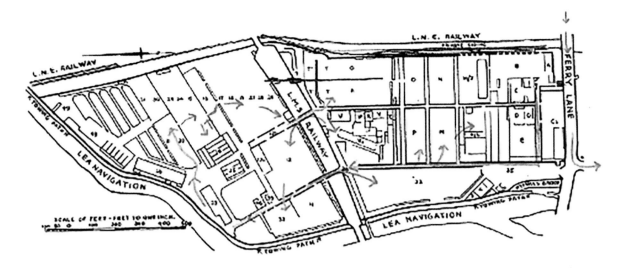

The route of the Duke's tour

for Harris Lebus. In part, this would be an evolution deriving from production methods and skills learned in plane manufacture during the war. In many respects, it was a reinvention. By comparison, emerging from World War Two and recommencing furniture production seemed relatively smooth; it was not long after this that Lebus evolved, with relative ease, into a public company. Arguably the most momentous reinvention was that of 1966, though it would ultimately prove ill-fated.

The contrast in manufacturing methods between this reinvented Lebus manufacturing plant post-1966 and that of Clifford Tee's Finsbury Cabinet Works could not have been greater. 'It looks more like a car factory with its robot machines and conveyor belts turning squares of man-made timber (chipboard) into household articles and finally packing them into boxes' was the description given by the reporter in the *Tottenham and Edmonton Weekly Herald*, 12 April 1968, on the occasion of Princess Margaret's visit. 'The Princess was told that Lebus are ahead of all competitors in technological achievement. She learned how an ancient hand-made craft industry had been turned into an efficient production line.'

A little over a decade earlier, Robert Hawes, reporting in the same local newspaper, was equally as impressed with what he saw on the Duke of Edinburgh's tour on 10 November

1955. The Duke's tour of Harris Lebus in November 1955 was expressly designed to take him sequentially through the flow of production at the factory exactly as it then was. Consequently, the tour moved in a zigzag fashion following an itinerary choreographed by Mr. H. Coles (known as Bert) and Ernest Frederick Powell of the Time and Motion Study Engineers. (Powell had joined the firm in 1931 and developed 'piecework'.) The tour began in the timber field at the end of the East Main Corridor where the Duke watched a barge of timber unloading. It then progressed to the Layout in 31 shed. Next was the Dry store where fork-lift trucks were loading and unloading the Kilns, on to the Planer with its lumber lift and stick conveyor and then the Parts Store in 29. Next came the Mill 28 (connected by conveyor under the railway) and to the Machine shop. With a stop at the Powerhouse and Engineers' department, the Duke then followed the West Main Corridor southwards, back under the railway to see the Sub-assemblies shop 12. The tour emerged to cross the East Main Corridor for the Veneer shop 32 and then back under the railway northwards for the Assembly shop 22 and the laboratory. The conveyors of the Polishing shops on the ground floor of K/L building were next, then the Research department in C2 before concluding the tour in the Warehouse section.

Production through Clifford Tee's original, compact factory masterplan from Z to A compares favourably to the 1955 plan, despite its reliance on labour-intensive batch movements, since he had designed purposely to facilitate the making of furniture in logical progression through the sequential location of buildings and workshops. From the Mill and Machine shop Q/R (any intricate carvings were expertly done in T), makers collected parts in small batches from the Parts Store – hence giving rise to the term 'batch production' and used glue cramps to add pressure and hold joints in O and assembled complete furniture items in M and N. The makers then took their made furniture pieces to the French polishers in K/L. When the polishers had finished, they took items to the fitters who collected knobs, handles, mirrors, glass and so forth from the general stores in G. Then onwards for a final touching up of any blemishes in H/J prior to warehousing and distribution. Movement was aided by the use of 'skates' – basically, small platforms with four castors attached – a pair of 'skates' being used for each article to be transferred.

A mixture of batch and flow mass production prevailed

Undoubtedly, the introduction of mains-powered conveyor belts from the 1930s onwards significantly assisted mass production and the movement of heavy goods generally. There was, however, the imposition of both a railway and a road running through the factory's expansive site. Progressive production became increasingly awkwardly staggered through an expanded and much-altered factory complex – with much necessary loading and off-loading done by hand. Production can only be regarded to have moved to a mixture of both batch and flow methods. Thus, despite all the scientific and technological advances made by the firm, plus the availability of electricity and conveyor belts, the need to move furniture items around manually throughout the factory remained. 'You had porters shifting the furniture with "skates" – "window cleaners", that's what they called it, just up, down, across, it was so easy it was like cleaning windows!' recalled Ron Turton, polisher, as part of the Coombes Croft project. 'Every time you move a product you add something to its cost but nothing to its value,' said Peter Baker of the

Progression of mass batch and flow production in the adapted factory post-World War Two

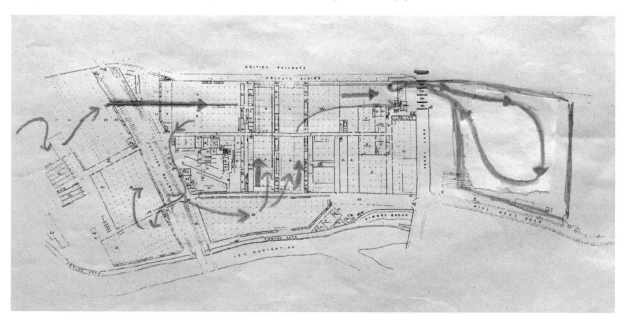

Collecting parts from the Parts store using a 'skate', pre-World War One

'Skates' are evident in the Maker's workshop pre-World War One

company's 'time and motion study' ethos, adding that 'when something is moved it is placed in danger; Oh, the things that I learned at Harris Lebus!'

Towards progressive flow production

On the development and introduction of progressive flow production for firms in the furniture industry, Jack R. Shanley, union leader, commenting some years after the events (for the book *Furnishing the World*), made some interesting observations around the impact of mains electricity – both on the order of production in a factory unit and specifically around the influence Lebus's methods had on other furniture manufacturers: 'But he [Herman Lebus] was trapped like the others with the belt and shaft,' said Shanley, adding:

> So, he had a magnificent machine shop, but each machine had to be placed according to the source of power. And so,

the machine shop could not production-wise be in the right order. So, there was lots of toing and froing. But it was a complete machine shop. But what was clear to me, again by talking to the people concerned, is that when the electric motor was attached to the individual machine something fundamental had changed. Now I estimate that it took from ten to fifteen years for the wholesale furniture trade to realise the significance of that change. Gradually the machines were put in line according to the requirements not of power but of production. But he was committed thoroughly to his system; his whole structure was built on it. The individual powerful electric motor enabled other firms to do the same thing on a smaller scale.

Shanley's point that electricity liberated the order of production flow from constriction by attachment to fixed steam engines, belts and shafts, thus giving rise to freedom of machine location, is only a part of the equation. Harris Lebus was, as we know, constrained by the position and size limitations of its pre-existing workshops.

In the 'new-look', reinvented Lebus post-1966, a compact layout of new machinery, section by section and with automated assembly led to efficient progressive flow. Including the section of island retained and used for storing solid components, the whole operation had been reduced to 450,000 square feet of covered space as against 1.3 million square feet, plus a timber yard, before.

In his article for *Management Today*, July 1968, that set out observations of the company as it was in 1966, Rex Winsbury wrote:

> [T]he actual method of manufacture at Lebus… was simply that of a large number of separate craftsmen linked under one roof. 'We were using essentially the same methods as our smaller rivals,' said Mr. Leonard Grosbard. 'So, there was great extravagance, not only in the use of space, but in the use of labour; and with it, a low degree of automation.

Thus, at the time of the Duke's visit, the manufacture of the furniture had evolved such that modern precision techniques had been developed to enhance traditional hand-crafting skills.

'How we do it…'

In 1960, a series of 14 articles in the *Lebus Log*, 'How we do it…', aimed to explain the manufacturing process and how departments of the company worked together before, during and after the production of cabinet furniture. The *Lebus Log* also regularly kept employees at Tottenham Hale and at its dedicated showrooms and other satellite hubs updated on how their upholstery colleagues 'were doing it' under the heading 'Woodley Whispers'. Dovetailed with these was another series, 'Spotlight on…', which shone a light on key employees and their area of expertise. Some

of those featured were: Frank Stuckey, chief inspector/quality control; Sid Bracken, foreman Makers shop 22; and Wally Baker, foreman stainer. Combined, by implication these articles informed employees how factory production was organised in three distinct zones: Zone One – mill, machining and veneering; Zone Two – sub-assemblies and assemblies; and Zone Three – polishes and finishes. Activities in the timber field preceded Zone One; warehousing and distribution succeeded Zone Three. Attention was drawn to a raft of less-visible aspects of furniture manufacture, such as the purchasing, storage and treatment of raw materials, design development and drawing, research and product development, quality control, and production planning – production control and pre-production planning.

Pre-production Planning – Production Control, Research, Purchasing, Drawing

Pre-production planning had evolved into a slick operation by the 1960s as compared with the factory's early years. A significant amount of planning was undertaken before an article of furniture was put into production. Thinking, pondering, comparing, researching, discussing, sharing; long gone were the days of 'secret culture', when information sharing only went as far as the partners who opened all correspondence in the mornings and issued instructions accordingly. Pre-production planning had evolved in such a way that decision making was ultimately achieved through a number of individuals and departmental heads working in collaboration.

Reg Griffin, pre-production manager, wrote (*Lebus Log*, No. 28, December 1964):

> By the very nature of the work, we (Pre-production department) are one of the earliest departments to know the new designs, materials, techniques and construction and one of our responsibilities is to discuss and acquaint everyone concerned with this information so that a satisfactory conclusion is arrived at for its implementation. How we achieve

this in the development of new furniture design from the designer's sketch to when it is ready for production is the main theme.

In the early years of the Finsbury Cabinet Works, discussions around design, drawing and purchasing of raw materials with the partners generally took place in the general office, building A. Basil Archer thought through designs in conjunction with the partners, then Dickie Porch produced more detailed drawings. In an early extension, T1, sample pieces were produced as and when required, all traditionally hand-made from any new designs sent down by Archer and Porch.

Sample-makers – Alf Brown (senior), Fred Trew and Mr. Holman – also made the highest grade, expensive pieces when ordered by customers, such as the six feet and seven feet mahogany, Sheraton, satinwood and walnut bedroom

suites. Jimmy Garratt, described by LS as 'endearing', was in charge of the workshop T1.

If carvings were required, these would be done in T under the direction of Foreman Alfred William Perrin. Hand-carving was already becoming machine-assisted at this time and machines that had served well at Tabernacle Street were initially moved over to the factory, along with additional new machinery imported from America. These enabled the carving of the same design twice, in a simultaneous process. One such belt-driven machine consisted of a floating vertical column with three fixed horizontal arms – the higher centre one followed contours of a metal casting (an original design, hand-carved) while the other two carved the design in two separate pieces of wood as the operator guided the motion through the use of a handle on the top; roughly cut replicas were then smoothed out by hand. Albert Church, the early-morning gas-lamp

The hand-carving workshop pre-World War One with Foreman Alfred William Perrin on the right of the image

The machine-assisted carving workshop pre-World War One

lighter at Tabernacle Street, was a carver; next to cabinet-makers, carvers were regarded as the most skilled employees. However, the elaborate hand-carved and machine-assisted features characteristic of pre-World War One furniture never resurfaced afterwards.

Before the development of part sheets, cutting lists for the parts required to make a furniture item (such as a chest of drawers) were made in U from the drawing board in S and instructions given directly to the mill and machine shop Q and R. Mr. Flatau was in charge of timber purchasing, working alongside Sol. In 1904, John Rollings, then a 16-year-old, joined as timber buyer; he retired in 1954 – just one year before the Duke's visit to Tottenham.

Production Control

E. O. Payne was in charge of Production Control at the time of the Duke's visit and when he retired at the end of 1956, John Lenton succeeded to the post. With reference to the 'How we do it…' series, the role of the

Production Control department was to decide what quantity of furniture would be made and in what timeframe. The daily 'Quota' or 'Factory Load' was a documented sequence of production as furniture progressed through the various operations before being sent to the warehouse to await despatch. As a result, it was possible to track the progress of a furniture batch or any individual customer order. Production control was arguably at its most effective in the reinvented Lebus post-1966 when Robert Mahlich was director of production; changes and fluctuations in demand could be met quickly because large stocks of furniture were warehoused in part-form (flat-packed) with just one week's supply in complete form.

In the early years at the Finsbury Cabinet Works, eight 'runners', men who were employed to chase the progress of customer orders as they passed through successive stages of manufacture, were a precursor to what became Production Control. If a telephone enquiry came in, since there were no facilities for broadcasting and hardly any internal telephone extensions, an office boy had to go and find the particular runner who had responsibility for chasing that particular order. Some customers were prioritised over others: Maple and Company had what they wanted without delay, even if that meant it created problems in meeting other customers' orders on time. This order came right from the top at Tabernacle Street, down through the chain of command to the workshops at the Finsbury Cabinet Works. A call would be made to the factory and Charlie Oliver, the Maples runner, had instructions to 'steal' goods to make up the order for Maple and Company from wherever he could find them. A runner would frequently get his batch up together as far as the loading floor only for Charlie Oliver to steal it for Maple and Company, and the poor runner would have to start all over again. Perhaps this, more than anything else, exemplifies the difficulties of operating a 'sales strategy' and a 'manufacture and distribution facility' from split sites.

Production Control had begun to evolve during and after World War One. Mr. G. Gosling, who had originally trained as a pharmacist and joined after the war, was given this glowing accolade by LS: '[T]he first scientist, or any individual with a trained mind to enter the firm he became head of an evolving Production Control department, bringing an analysis daily of all orders received the previous day to the dining room each lunch time, and… enjoyed the confidence of the Partners'.

The laboratory of the interwar period

Research department and laboratory

Gosling suggested a 23-year-old former pupil, Archibald Ernest Lain (known as Archie), as the man to establish a Harris Lebus laboratory. He was appointed chief chemist in 1921 (a position he held until his death in 1959) to help develop synthetic glues and understand the chemical complexities intrinsic in cellulose manufacture such that effective, adequate supplies could be produced in-house. 'He travelled throughout Europe and the United States and contributed greatly to Harris Lebus finishing processes,' acknowledged LS. Lain pioneered the use of synthetic glues and was well known as a writer and lecturer on these subjects. He served on the Furniture Development Council, Paint Research Association, Oil and Colour Chemists Association and the Plastics Institute. During World War Two, Lain played an active part in the production of aircraft, especially the Mosquito.

Dr. W. D. Douglas retired in April 1955, after nine years in charge of research. At the time of the Duke's visit, Vic Gellay had succeeded to the post. The Kite Mark Scheme, a national quality symbol, was attached to all furniture pieces from 1953. In 1955, Robert Hawes described the Research department: '[W]here new lacquers are formulated and produced in bulk and glues measured for strength and endurance, the Duke watched as scientists were making deliberate efforts to wreck, spoil and generally ruin samples of good furniture: this was all part of the application of British Standards Tests to the company's products' (*Tottenham and Edmonton Weekly Herald*, 11 November 1955).

Furniture inspection and quality control

In the early days at the Finsbury Cabinet Works there was no structured system for quality control. LS wrote that 'oak was more prone to splitting, especially at glue joints and the tops of chests of drawers and sides of wardrobes', and such defects were discovered, it seems, by chance rather than process.

Arthur Franklin, product development manager, and Reg Griffin, design development manager, jointly writing in an article in *News from Lebus*, No. 2, May 1968, exalting the benefits of the raw material chipboard over solid wood, had this to say about the firm's earliest furniture pieces:

> Looking back, we see furniture made of thick pieces of solid wood, and today, even on casual examination we find that these parts are split and warped, joints have come apart, doors and drawers are badly fitting. Moreover, many priceless antiques have literally fallen apart when introduced into the centrally heated homes of today. This is because all wood will swell when it gets wet and shrink when it gets dry. Plywood was invented to overcome these problems.

During World War One, given the volumes produced by Harris Lebus, government inspectors were permanently based at the works to inspect, pass and stamp each item. Herbert Barnes was appointed as head of Inspection/Quality Control in the years following World War One and, as the firm moved away from batch production to a combination of mass batch and progressive flow production, inspection took place at all stages in the process.

As part of the Coombes Croft project, Hilda Hewitt spoke about her husband, Bill, cabinet-maker and inspector:

> My husband, Bill Hewitt, came out of the forces in 1946, he was a carpenter and started out on building sites, but it was such a cold winter in 1947 that he couldn't stick it and so he started at Lebus as a cabinet maker in 1948, at the age of 36. People needed furniture then, so the trade was picking up. He was at Lebus nineteen years before he was made redundant in 1967 – he was made an Inspector eventually. He had been a cabinet maker in the East End from when he left school; he could make tables, he made a cocktail cabinet that opened up, but we couldn't

take that with us when we moved. As an Inspector, furniture that wasn't right should've been sent back but he used to fix it, little jobs, rather than send it back.

Peter Baker had various experiences with Inspection/Quality Control throughout the firm. He said he worked for a while as a 'Goods Inward Inspector', which entailed the inspection of all (factored) goods entering the factory for what was stated on the invoice in volume and for the adherence of the item to the specification issued. Fred Cullen was for a number of years known as 'Goods Inward Chief'. According to an article in the *Lebus Log*, No. 11, 'He received everything… be it a tin tack or a steam engine' until he retired in 1950, after 47 years with the firm.

Purchasing raw materials

> 'If the buyer brings off the most brilliant piece of business, nobody can possibly know but himself, but let him make the slightest mistake and he is playing to a packed grandstand!'
>
> – Roy Dand, timber purchaser (*Lebus Log*, No. 17, July 1960)

Purchasing was a slick, sophisticated, well-managed, inter-departmental process in the 1950s and 1960s – a far cry from the early years of the Finsbury Cabinet Works. The role of the Central Purchasing department was to procure goods needed for furniture production, including raw materials, in the right quantities at the right price. Stan Bruce was in charge of purchasing. As well as timber, by the 1950s Harris Lebus was also using hardboards, particleboards and laminated plastics in furniture manufacture.

The Timber department advised Zone One – mill, machine shop and veneer shop – on timbers, veneers and plywood compatible with mass production. The department also worked in cooperation with the Design Development and Quality Control departments on the selection of raw materials and with Production Control for quantities of these to be available at specific times.

Before World War One, wood was the main component for all the furniture made by Harris Lebus. According to LS, cargoes of wood were delivered to the London Docks and would have been examined by Sol Lebus at either Messrs. Esdaile or Bow Sawmills. As an example of pricing, he cites Cuban mahogany, which could be purchased at 1s 6d per cubic foot CIF (cost, insurance and freight). In a regular order with Churchill and Sim, Harris Lebus bought significant quantities of American satin walnut and oak for 2s per cubic foot. In the same order, small quantities of black walnut were almost twice that price at 3s 9d. Other material used included brass and glass. There was both a brass room and a glass store at the Finsbury Cabinet Works; brass would have been for handles and glass for use in display cabinets, bookcases and mirrors for bedroom furniture.

'Around it all revolves the romantic world of shipping'

With reference to the 'How we do it…' series in the *Lebus Log* of the 1960s, contracts were drawn up with care and with goods effectively insured; payment was made in various foreign currencies. The December 1960 (No. 19) *Log* stated: '[And] around it all revolves the romantic world of shipping – liners, tramp steamers and tiny coasters from the ancient trading ports of Bruges, and Rotterdam, from the frozen Baltic and the steaming Niger delta, to the din and clatter of the great port of London.' Supplies were bought in bulk, contact usually being direct with the shipper: '[We] can swallow up the entire production of some of the larger shippers, especially so with African logs.' Crucially, the articles in the *Lebus Log* explained that the crux was to achieve 'delivery of supplies at the right time without tying up capital in unnecessary stocks' and that buying three-to-six months in advance was 'not easy!' It continued: 'Seasons have their say – ice precludes shipment of birch from Russia between December and April, floods in Nigeria produce an abundance of abura during the winter and spring, whilst the same floods create a shortage of obechi.' In some cases, supplies were bought from an importer who had an outlet to sell those grades, thicknesses and sizes not required by the firm; chiefly the

case with birch plywood. At the beginning of 1965, according to J. L. Oliver, the import duty rate on timber hardwoods was 8%, plywood was 10%, and chipboards and other board around 20%.

Hardwood

Hardwood was mainly used in the early years with softwood only for some drawer runners and some interior work. Over time, softwood was incorporated more – LS explained that supplies came chiefly from Russia when the waterways of Archangel opened up and a year's supply could be delivered during a three-month window. The hardwoods favoured over time and used during the 1950s were abura and obeche shipped from Nigeria, mahogany from Ghana, ramin from Sarawak, beech from Romania and a little oak from the USA. For some of the Link furniture range from the mid-1950s onwards, African aformosia was used.

In his book, J. L. Oliver stated:

> In 1958 the London prices of furniture-making hardwoods per cubic foot for quantities of about 1,000 foot were, in general: Sarawak ramin 16s 6d, Continental beech 19s 6d, African abura 21s, agba, guarea, sapele, utile 23s 6d, African mahogany 26s 6d, African walnut 27s 6d, aformosia 30s. American oak 36s, Japanese oak 42s, Honduras mahogany 55s, Australian walnut 84 s – 96s, teak 86s and Indian laurel wood 114s.

During World War One, with a blockade on wood imports, sales representatives were switched to sourcing timber supplies domestically, which required a degree of ingenuity. They clearly did well; LS describes the timber field as being 'jammed with timber, often milled to rough cut sizes for the particular contract in hand and kept in "stick" until adequately seasoned for its purpose'. Silver spruce (normally associated with Christmas trees) had to be sourced, as the Handley Page aircraft being assembled at Tottenham were constructed almost entirely of this strong, relatively light, straight-grain pine (which was then covered with finest quality Irish linen). A small amount of English ash was also used. Wings were constructed with wooden spars and ribs, with stringers threaded through them to add rigidity. Irish linen of the first quality was sourced to cover the whole of the wings. It was much the same for the manufacture of wooden World War Two planes and equipment; for example, the wings of the Mosquito were laminated spruce covered in plywood.

When World War Two ended in Europe in May 1945, 'the firm got well into its stride manufacturing utility furniture', said LS. Despite the strict controls on the allocation of raw materials, 'the volume of furniture permitted to be made was conditioned by available resources of raw material'. Supplies came under the direction of the government's Timber Control Department and licences for timber, plywood and veneers were based on a ratio of pre-war consumption. This control continued into the 1950s, though in diminishing degrees. Manufacturers were allowed, however, to augment their resources by recycling timber from surplus war material, such as ammunition boxes, tent poles and so forth.

Plywood

LS, writing on the early years of the Finsbury Cabinet Works, said: '[I]t was several years later that the firm bought their first three ply from [Millwall-based] Venesta, who imported it from St. Petersburg (Leningrad). [The plywood] was made of rotary cut ash or alder, glued together with albuminous glue'. Over time the firm started to import in a big way through a British agent called Skidelsky, who, LS said, 'became a great friend of the Lebus family'. He continued: 'The Russians were apparently the inventors of plywood, which started its life for use in the chests made for Messrs Brooke Bond.' As time progressed, Finland began to manufacture plywood and, towards the end of the 1920s, birch became more popular with Harris Lebus. Supplies continued to be generated by Russia and Finland, and with a fair amount of lauan shipped from Japan cut from logs grown in the Philippines and Borneo. Plywood tended to

be used for the panels of framed-up wardrobe backs, toilets (a generic term given to items of bedroom furniture to compliment suites, such as smaller chests of drawers), square chests of drawers and blind backs of mirrors. It was incorporated for external use in the panel pedestals of desks and filing cabinets.

Veneers: 'From the knife in Vienna or the backroom of a humblest London merchant'

Over time the firm came to use between 20 and 30 different types of veneers. These came from all over the world, though were cut chiefly in Europe – mainly in France and Yugoslavia. Paris was at one time the centre and the firm traded with many producers all over France, as well as Italy, Germany, Austria and Switzerland. Certain veneers (sycamore, maple and ash) were only cut in the winter. The *Lebus Log* stated: 'When abura logs can double in price within the space of six months and lauan prices can be halved in less than a year, and profits (and losses) of between 5% and 50% can be made on veneer logs, the buyer cannot afford not to know every single supplier and his price.'

Chipboard

By the end of the 1960s in the 'new-look' Lebus, chipboard was the main component in furniture manufacture. 'Chipboard: it's not a glamorous commodity, but it has changed the face of the furniture industry and is a major reason for the success of the "Europa" range of cabinet furniture and the basis of the Harris Lebus business,' wrote Arthur Franklin, product development manager, and Reg Griffin, design development manager, jointly in an article on the 'new-look' firm (*News from Lebus*, No. 2, May 1968). 'Millions of square feet of chipboard are delivered to the Tottenham factory every year; then starts the transformation which turns the board, with the addition of veneers and other materials into Britain's best-known furniture,' they added.

Just before World War Two, Germany had started to develop large-sized boards called block-board, lamin-board and batten-board, based on the principle of plywood and having veneers glued at right angles to a core made up of strips of softwood.

To produce the best chipboard, it was necessary to use freshly cut softwood trees – with the removal of bark, chips were dried to almost half their original weight. Chips and glue, weighed in the right proportions, were combined as chips were tumbled or agitated and resin sprayed. Wax in the resin enabled the boards to be resistant to moisture and woodworm. Consolidation was achieved through cold and hot pressing.

The firm used British suppliers as well as imports from other European countries, especially Finland. 'Particle-boards are now being manufactured in almost every country using suitable local material, from flax shives and sugar cane to peanut shells' wrote Franklin and Griffin in *News from Lebus*, No. 2. They added this prediction: 'Due to the abundant supply of raw material, there is no apparent alternative which could seriously be considered as a competitor. Chipboard will probably remain the basic material for modern furniture makers for some years to come.'

'Sticking-up' – life in the timber field

> 'Back of Beyond – land of mystery – remembered and visited only when the sun shines, that's the timber field.'
>
> – Harry Rainbird, timber field manager, *Lebus Log*, No. 20, September 1961

The timber field the Duke of Edinburgh saw in 1955 was in stark contrast to that of the early days of the Finsbury Cabinet Works – not least because back in those days it looked like a field with clusters of piled-high wood, at a time when literally every aspect of wood handling was done by hand, save for a little help from a horse or two.

Drama: Sometime early in the 1900s, Sol is in the timber field…

Sol is awaiting his cargo of purchases, which is due to arrive anytime soon. He stands on the edge of the River Lea Navigation in the south-west corner of Finsbury Cabinet Works, looking downstream. A pair of swans stand in a disorderly fashion on the wet, marshy bank, gazing in the same direction as Sol, as if in solidarity with him. Cold mists begin to swirl off the water's surface and the late afternoon sky is beginning to darken in the cold mid-winter. Sol's mind is drifting back to that summer's day when he first surveyed this site; but with the reservoirs stretching along the eastern side of the river, it can be bleak in this field in winter. This was all part of a simple division between the Partners: Sol managing operations at the new Finsbury Cabinet Works in Tottenham Hale, while Harris continued to manage the 'business' end – finances and sales – from his beloved Tabernacle Street.

Some factory lads, maybe thirty of them, are waiting too; some standing, some sitting on the trucks – which are no more than pallets on wheels. These factory workers, as individual as they are, appear similar. Each wears dark trousers, a light shirt and a tweed-style over-jacket; it is not a staff uniform, it is just what is expected. They are doing what lads do, allowing themselves some mischief in measured control. One flicks a wool cap off the head of a guy sitting in front; the others look around, anywhere around, in mock pretence that they know nothing. The distraction brings Sol back to the here and now.

But it is not long before he drifts into a daydream once more; in his mind, Sol is back where he was this morning – in the sawmills… Sol takes his role seriously: to carefully source and purchase raw materials to be cut into logs at Esdaile and Company's city sawmills. He is standing in the middle of the mills, in one of the few open spaces, in a dark, damp, cold maze with walls temporarily, haphazardly constructed much higher than any man could see over. The inescapable, heady smell of freshly cut timber shipped to the London Docks from far-flung exotic places pervades the air as if it were a god's pot-pourri; it is not like being in a forest – it is far too claustrophobic for that. That said, the animal-like grunts of the men at work, heaving tree trunks in teams, is not dissimilar to the sounds of a forest deep in the Amazon. Over and above this background noise contrasts the altogether calm, collected but nonetheless gruff voice of the mill manager: 'There's no Cuban mahogany today.' It is unmistakably that of a man who is used to barking instructions as often as needed. His weathered face, as battered and crinkled as log bark, appears from around the corner as if transpired from tree-trunk walls.

Concealing his disappointment at this news – mahogany from Cuba could be purchased at 1s 6d per cubic foot (the equivalent of six or seven pence today) – Sol resigns himself to choose an alternative. He has notched up that there is still a rich, plentiful stock of raw materials from which to choose: basswood (lime tree), sequoia (Californian or coast redwood), oak, ash, mahogany and walnut were staple supplies. Walking round a corner, he smiles as he spots a particular favourite, satin walnut (technically a species of gum tree). This was reputedly given its name by his brother, Harris: having discovered it on one of his American trips,

the name was adopted by the whole trade. Sol decides he will take some; it is relatively inexpensive and would polish to a light golden colour. He also chooses some sapele hardwood to make veneer for quality items… if he selects the best logs. Sol proceeds to make his choices with utmost diligence: some mahogany imported from British Honduras and West Africa – Lagos and Bassam. He knows the best logs and he knows wood well; he has had the best tutor in his brother, Harris.

As Sol emerges from his dreamy state and distant gaze, a rumbling noise gets louder and louder… a steam whistle blowing shatters the relative calm, some swans take flight in fright and a train rattles across the bridge over the river on its way to town. It may even be carrying finished Lebus furniture. 'It should not take them too much longer,' he says, and even before he has finished his sentence, the gaslights of the first lighter barge transporting a forest-load of precious wood can be seen around the bend, guided through the dim light

Barges by Ferry Lane in 1958

The Butters three-ton jib crane at work

A bargee in front of the timber wharf in the 1950s

by the white swans beside. One of the workers makes a whistling sound using his fingers – it is their signal of work to be done before nightfall.

In minutes, the timber field is a hive of activity. It is hard work, with heavy lifting. The lads know all this has to be stacked neatly in piles by hand before they can go home – a process they call 'sticking up'. The iron-flanged wheels of the first piled-high wagon of logs begins to move along iron runners, flanked by three of the workers each side; the horses (there are only a handful of them) are not back from their daily delivery rounds and there is no alternative means of power. Several more wagon loads soon follow behind and everything looks to be on track. But then several shouts are heard, along with a piercing screech that only iron-on-iron can make: a stretch of iron track has buckled – just a little – and sunk into the squishy, muddy marshland, and it is enough to derail the wagon. The lads are just glad none of them were hurt – they know the signs to look out for and then they dodge. The buckled track is only on one of the shorter side-tracks and not the main track – the bulk of the

delivery can still be hand-piled tonight. This is another headache for Sol but one that he knows will have to wait until tomorrow. And as for the lads – they are just glad it is not raining today.

'Sticking up' – natural wood-drying process

To avoid deterioration (especially if storage for long periods was necessary) and to allow the flow of air between each timber board, spacer 'sticks' were placed between them as they were stacked – a process known as 'sticking up'. Wood with a high water content was structurally weak as well as heavier. Square-edged lumber arrived in what was called a 'shipping dry' condition, but with a 30–40% moisture content it needed to be 'normalised' through being left out to dry naturally for a short while, explained LS. The 'sticking gangs', a small army of men, were kept busy sticking up, making sets (6 feet to 16 feet in length) at certain times of the year. There was a tendency to overstock in the early days, according to LS, meaning a significant amount of working capital was tied up in those raw materials. Storing wood in this way was a feature that endured in the timber field throughout its existence, and sticking up went on through almost all of the years of the Tottenham factory, whether timber was delivered by barge or by lorries in the later years – the process just became more sophisticated and mechanised.

Mr. J. Fry was foreman on the timber field for 32 years and witnessed the evolution of mechanisation; he died in April 1955, just months before the Duke's visit. 'We saw cranes unloading trees which had been sliced into boards, from huge barges moored alongside the factory wharf,' reported Robert Hawes on the

visit by the Duke of Edinburgh (*Tottenham and Edmonton Weekly Herald*, 11 November 1955). There was no crane for unloading the timber that arrived on barges from the London docks until 1918 – just before the end of the First World War – when an automatic unloading conveyor (commissioned from Ransome, Drew and Clydesdale) was erected in the south-west corner of the timber field (near to what is now the end of Yarmouth Crescent). Iron channels were set in concrete running parallel with the Lea Navigation to guide the wheels

Moving timber with a tractor on a network of rails circa 1926 with Tommy Armstrong

Below left: A fork-lift truck post-World War Two

Below: Sticking wood into piles for outside storage with the use of a 'conveyor' on rails in the interwar period

Above: A worker 'sticking-up' post-World War Two

Top right: The drying shed in the interwar period

Below: Women working alongside men in the
timber field during World War One

Harry Rainbird and the metal detector in shed 30

for the huge apparatus. Special permission was granted to site the crane on the towpath and allow the cradle to overhang and swing over the towpath to the barges, where it could be stacked with timber boards; the machine was especially suited to square-edged lumber. Through a chain of cogs, the loaded crane was moved to where the cradle could be unloaded into trucks. Over time it was reconditioned and improved, and remained in continual use until 1934, when additional woodsheds were subsequently added.

At the time of the Duke's visit, the Butters crane, which had been in operation since 1929, was described as 'a three-ton jib'. Around the same time as it was installed, horses were superseded by electric locomotive tractors made by the Ransome Company. These ran on a network of rails and eventually the mud timber field was covered with concrete and asphalt. From the outset, to assist with the movement of wood, unloaded by hand from barges moored in the south-west corner of the field, horses (or cobs, to be precise) pulled wagons that ran on a network of iron rails from the unloading corner at the river's edge, through the timber field under the Tottenham and Forest Gate Railway via a tall, brick-built arch to connect with the drying kilns. A tram line also ran along the east of what was then the extent of the site, parallel with Pymmes Brook. According to an article, 'Fifty Years Ago – Thinking Back…' in the *Lebus Log*, No. 6, October 1955, there were six cob horses accommodated in stables (building U).

Fork-lift trucks were first introduced during World War Two, after it had been seen how useful these were to the forces. Initially, a single fork-lift truck with a lifting capacity of one ton was purchased, but by the time of the Duke's visit in 1955 six fork-lift trucks were in use – each with a lifting capacity of three tons. Moving 'parcels' of timber unaltered through various operations – including loading into kilns and supplying the mill – was greatly facilitated by the use of fork-lift trucks.

'[T]he latest mechanical handling devices were being used for sorting and storing lumber,

plywood and veneer' reported Robert Hawes, whilst the *Evening News*, on 10 November 1955, wrote that Harry Rainbird, timber manager, aged 44 and with the company from the age of 15, had met the Duke. 'He was particularly interested in a robot used for detecting nails, screws and scraps of metal in the raw material… the Duke was amused when I told him that we sometimes find bullets embedded in the wood. How they get there is a mystery.' In the 'Layout' shed 31, a conveyor of mechanised rollers accommodated all pre-kilning operations, automatically checking dimensions against supplier's measurements, detecting metal, cross-cutting and ripping to desired lengths and widths as well as sticking into parcels. Each parcel was in total approximately three feet three inches wide and three feet high. They consisted of 18 layers of timber lengths (each of one-inch thickness) stacked, using sticks of one-inch by one-inch timber between them to create air space. Parcels transferred to the kilns were picked up, six at a time, by fork-lift truck and loaded onto a 'bogie' for kilning. 'The known measurement of each parcel was accepted, and no further measuring or manual handling was, therefore, needed'. They could then be sent on to the planers or the dry stores.

Progressive kilns – artificial wood-drying process

The use of kilns reduced the water content of timber (a process known as seasoning or drying) before it could be used for furniture making. In the early years, steam was used as part of the process in the Erith progressive kilns, of which there were three in the building complex labelled V. Green timber stacked in batches on wagons entered at one end and – through controlled, progressive stages of continuous drying, starting cool and humid, ending warm and dry – came out in a drier state. The artificial drying process could take three to five days. Adjacent to the building housing the kilns was a cooling timber shed – V2. In those earlier days, the timber seasoning process was a bit hit-and-miss, and splits would occur. In very dry weather, every so often timber would crack – a sound LS likened to a rifle shot! New drying kilns erected in 1933,

No. 14 and No. 25 on the factory plan (and No. 48 later), were a combination of kilns, progressive and chamber, in which timber could be dried to a moisture content of 9–14%.

Augmentation of a Drawing department

Despite the fact that furniture production ceased after the start of World War One, the firm's designer and draughtsman, Basil Archer and Dickie Porch, remained with Harris Lebus, contributing throughout the war. The manufacture of Army supplies was heavily regulated to Woolwich Arsenal specifications and Herman Lebus's initiative to have these specifications simplified was successful. LS wrote, 'Herman made many hundreds of journeys to Woolwich Arsenal, frequently

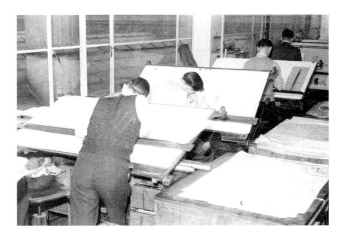

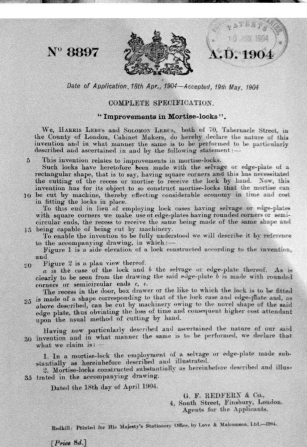

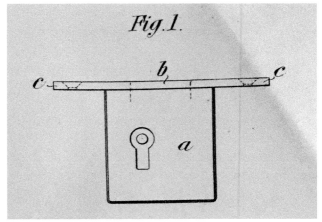

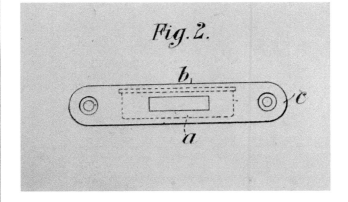

Top left: Pre-production offices in the interwar period

Top right: The pre-production drawing office of the 1950s

Above left and right: A round-edged mortice lock patent No. 8897 dated 1904

(Paul Collier private collection)

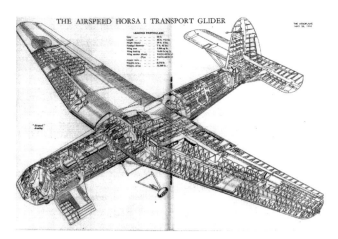

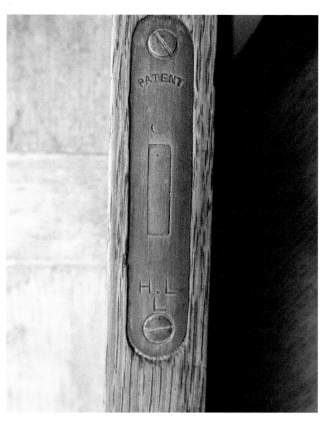

Top: A plan for a Horsa glider
(Mark Bailey's personal collection)

Above: Lock-plate patent No. 8896

Round-edged lock plate

taking Porch… with him'. Porch, in LS's words, was 'a notable character with only one eye with which, it was said he saw more than most people with two'. In 1917 '[t]he parent firm Handley Page sent some hundreds of drawings requiring most careful study,' stated LS. Aircraft blueprints, design drawings, detailed assemblies and sub-assemblies represented a 'new language' to interpret, and it was Herman who spent many hours late into the night to study, digest, understand and articulate their meaning to those charged with transforming plans into planes. The augmentation of a large drawing office staff was a necessary stage in the flight towards the interpretation of these drawings into integral parts and facilitating the necessary machining to fine levels of accuracy. Mr. H. Hill was appointed as its head.

The value of product drawings and blueprints

Mrs. Daphne Bradley (interviewed as part of the Coombes Croft project) recalled her time in

the Drawing department looking after aircraft blueprints in World War Two:

> Everyone had to do what was called 'essential work' if they were not in the forces or were sick or too old or had young children to care for. My job was to keep track of the plans and drawings which the draughtsmen and woodworkers had to use for their work at Harris Lebus. These drawings could have been useful to the enemy if allowed to fall into their hands, so every drawing had to be accounted for after it had been used.

From design layout to jigs and machine set-up

Using early machinery, 'each man set up his own machine,' remarked LS in his *History*; in other words, in the absence of standard part sheets, each machinist sets their own block to make the required parts according to the dimensions supplied. The appropriate wooden parts (size, shape, customer's wood choice etc.) to complete the order were thus machined, ready to be made-up. The evolution in the way part sheets were produced from design drawings, as in the Bart Sheet System, combined with technological advances in woodworking machinery and the way it was powered fundamentally changed the way furniture parts could be cut. Instead of each worker having to set up their own block at their machine individually, reusable standard jigs could be made-up for machinists to use. 'So, what became important,' said union leader Jack Shanley (quoted in *Furnishing the World*), 'was the setting of the machines. The machine set-up became more important than the machine operative because the craftsmen then went to the back of the machine and took off and tested each part against a measuring jig for accuracy. If it went beyond a certain tolerance of accuracy, he would stop the machine.' Only minor adjustments to each machine would be necessary, saving time and improving efficiency.

After World War Two, enhanced drawings produced by the Design Development department went to the Furniture Drawing Office. A full-size design layout (composite drawing) with standard parts identified and a design specification containing fully written details indicating material (especially if new), overall sizes, colour interior details, veneer details, progression and fitting resulted. The Design Approval Committee met weekly with colleagues from Inspection, Production

Jigs for Mosquito aircraft

Methods, Zone Two's Sub-assembly and Assembly, Production Control and the Sales division.

From the design layout, a team of draughtsmen in Parts Section (under the guidance of the section leader) would dissect the article, drawing each individual part down to the last glue block on separate drawings known as part sheets. Each part was then given a numbered code, the first three numbers representing the category, e.g. category 121 – drawer sides, or 120 – drawer runners. All the dimensions were quoted in decimals for greater accuracy. The section leader created a part and metal list, which itemised every single part, wood or metal, which went to make up one article. These part sheets were then distributed to various departments – Time Study for the creation of labour costs, Production Control for ordering, Factory Accounts for material costs, Inspection for maintaining quality and so forth.

There were two jig sections – Zone One, covering the mill, machine and veneer shops and Zone Two, covering 12 shop sub-assemblies and 22 shop assemblies. These sections, on completion of the parts sheets, produced jig drawings, which detailed the various jigs, gauges, fixtures and equipment required for machining, assembly and polishing. These ranged from the simple spindle fixture for a slight curve, to the radio-frequency sub-assembly loading trays for ends or radio-frequency carcase assembly jigs in 12 and H/J shops.

Prototype sample furniture pieces made by hand

Enhanced drawings were passed to the prototype makers in T1 to make-up furniture samples (usually the wardrobe and dressing table of a new bedroom suite) at which point Zone One's mill, machining and veneering and Zone Three's polishers were consulted. A prototype sample of the furniture item produced in T1 from the design layout drawing and design specification would usually be hand-made. The prototype sample was used for proving the construction and was subject to further scrutiny by the Design

Approval Committee. The sample piece was also used for photographing or as an exhibit at furniture exhibitions. Design layouts and design specifications were then issued to other departments, such as Advertising.

In T1, jig drawings were translated into the actual jigs (custom-made tools used to control the location and/or motion of another tool). There were three important factors: safety for the operator, accuracy, and sound construction to last the life of the design. Jigs required a considerable amount of handwork on the part of the jig-maker. Each jig machine was inspected before going into use. The radio-frequency jigs were checked by a dedicated electrician in T1 shop. The sub-assembly and assembly jigs were proven before release for batch production by a first-off sample-maker before going into production, using parts taken at random from the bulk workings in the parts store.

At the time of the Duke's visit in 1955, George Thomas Nicholson was in charge of the Jig and Sample shop. He had joined the firm in June 1924 as a bright 16-year-old, learned on the bench, went to Shoreditch Technical College, and worked under Sid Sawyer, who at that time was the firm's sole jig-maker. He became a first-class craftsman and the pupil succeeded his master to become a jig-maker. In 1937, he was promoted to the staff as foreman jig-maker.

The Albermarle – pre-production in practice

A significant amount of the work involved in the manufacture of the Albermarle aircraft was in pre-production. The firm's expertise in jig design and having the experience and know-how of employees who had been involved in aircraft manufacture in World War One gave it an advantage in winning new aircraft-manufacturing contracts for World War Two. The firm was in a good position with existing departments in drawing, engineering, purchase and production control. Indeed, it was necessary to engage all operations of the factory and there was constant liaison with suppliers (hundreds of metal components had to be bought in) to ensure greater accuracy with the principal manufacturer – Armstrong

Whitworth in this case. Mrs. Constance Walker (known as Connie), who joined the firm in the early years of World War Two in the Purchase department, 'operated a Kardex record of aircraft metal components with quite uncanny skill', (*Lebus Log*, No. 15, December 1959). She chased up parts so that a steady flow of production could be maintained.

As trained engineers in metal, Herbert Barnes, head of the Inspection/Quality Control department, and C. E. Leaman, chief maintenance officer, working with H. Hill, head of the Furniture Drawing Office, and George Nicholson, foreman jig-maker, concentrated on the technical side, with overall management provided by Desmond Stratton and Alf Brown (senior) (sample-maker/Zone One foreman). 'The Chief A.I.D. officer in charge of inter-changeability of all aircraft components throughout the country had the highest opinion of the firm's jigging and accuracy', said LS. Sir Herman Lebus, Archie Lain (chief chemist) and Herbert Barnes became serving members on the government's Committee of Technical Development.

Going through the Mill:

Zone One – Mill, Machine and Veneer Shops

'We use the best machinery that we can find, and I think we have some machines that are better than anything I have seen on this side [America],' claimed Louis whilst visiting Michigan in February 1907 (*Michigan Artisan*, 25 February 1907).

Over time, machinery had to be sourced from American and Germany

Ironically, 13 years later, following the end of the war, it was to America that the partnership turned to purchase machines to re-equip the factory. LS cites a meeting on 23 July 1920 as key to Sol and his nephews' decision to boldly reinvent Harris Lebus. A. C. Harris, who had been the Finsbury Cabinet Works production manager since its inception, was at the meeting and played a part in forward planning. The risks in making products for a different market, changing the type of furniture and method of manufacture were noted and the minutes recorded that 'the new… furniture must be made on American methods'. Further, the minutes note that whilst 'no such factory' had attempted this in the UK, 'in America, large factories are making this class of furniture with great profit'.

Rex Winsbury (*Management Today*, July 1968) wrote that for the 'new look' Lebus post-1966, inspiration came from Germany and their advanced machinery; German furniture manufacturers were turning out 300,000 new pieces of furniture every week – much higher than for any UK producer. No British firms were making such advanced machines and new machinery had to be imported – most of it German. 'It was the usual story of not being able to get the right machinery at the time we needed it from a British firm,' Leonard Grosbard reportedly said.

In the original Sawmill and Machine shop (either Q or R) a number of machines were supplied by Thomas Robinson and Son of Rochdale, who manufactured machines for flour mills as well as for wood working.

The sawmill

Prior to World War One Thomas Robinson and Son of Rochdale supplied the sawmill with large circular carbon steel saw machines used for ripping (cutting in the same direction as the wood grain). Lengths of wood were, by and large, fed manually by the machinist. There were also cross-cut saws (for cutting right angles to the direction of the wood grain); these were of the conventional pendulum type and, with counterbalancing weights, proved hard to operate. In his *History*, LS explained: 'Some very wide boards required a great deal of effort on the part of the operator to cross cut satisfactorily, as he had to draw the saw in a wide arc right across the board, which seemed to be a perilous operation.' He does mention one redeeming feature: 'There was, however, a chain attached to the back of the swing cross-cut, as a safety precaution.' Over time, high-speed steel as well as tungsten-carbide-tipped cutters were introduced; not only were they more efficient but they lasted longer.

LS described the machine-assisted manufacture for tent pins during World War One: '[N]ominally about one inch thick, of hardwood, unplaned, and having been squared to length [they] were put through a four cutter (saw) crosswise and finished in one operation.' They

The mill during World War One

The mill in the 1950s with the Wadkin saws

were packed closely together and virtually formed a continuous block of wood. After World War One, four-cutters (machines that cut edges of a piece of timber – both lengthwise edges and width edges simultaneously) were purchased from the United States; with removable circular, as well as square, blocks they could be set up apart from the machine. Half a century on, when the Duke of Edinburgh went into the new mill 28, Harry Norris was in charge. The deafening noise of crosscut and ripsaws prohibited conversation. 'The fact that Wadkin (a British firm) supplied them with 40 cross-cutting saws, points to a considerable output. These factory machines were for one purpose only,' wrote John Wilson in a letter in January 2007 to Geffrye Museum archivists, enclosing a 1954 copy of a leaflet

Women making tent poles in the machine shop during World War One

for a C. J. Hydraulic Crosscut Saw made by Wadkin Ltd, Leicester – with a photograph of the factory mill.

The machine shop

In the machine shop before World War One, a range of early machines included moulders, spindles, jigger mortices, single tenons, boring and lock machines. Machines ran with an individual V belt connected to the main drive. All turning of furniture legs and columns was still done by hand, and wood was smoothed by manual planer machines – with a recess table top, the edges of up to two boards could be done simultaneously.

A jointing machine smoothed the edges of boards (that were to be subsequently glue-jointed) – a stack of boards would be stood edgewise on the machine table, held together by a form of pallet and hand-screwed together to form a pack. With the machine set in motion as the pack travelled horizontally across the table surface, a cutter in a recess below could cut away any excess, the smallest amount being an eighth of an inch.

Machines purchased after World War One could be driven by compressed air at speeds of 15,000 revolutions per minute (rpm) – more than three times faster than the conventional 4,500 rpm. Some spindles, operated through the use of compressed air, were purchased and, by changing square to circular cutter blocks using smaller peripheries, double spindling could now be done in one operation. Some of the hand-operated jigs and fixtures were replaced to run on compressed air. Cramps, belt-sanders, nailing and screwing machines were also adaptable to work with compressed air. Some other machines were adapted – the American Dodds dovetailing machine was redesigned as fully automatic, enabling it to process a high volume of standard parts. Alexander Dodds set up in 1882 in Grand Rapids, Michigan.

At some point, walls were demolished to create a larger space and workshops S and U were combined in the open-plan area. When the new mill was operational, the machine shop expanded still further. LS described how, finally, 'certain conventional machines were linked together to do two or three operations and thus avoid handling between one machine to another'.

In the machine shop in 1955, the Duke went past the sanding section and the panel sizers, the Mattison lathes (the American, Christian Mattison, had a well-established woodworking machine business in Wisconsin dating from the turn of the twentieth century) and a specialist machine that made cabriole-style legs used often for coffee tables and glass cabinets. The Duke showed particular interest in the machine that produced a turned dining table leg from a square block of timber in one go. Then past the line of four-cutters and the automatic single, double and horizontal spindle-shapers – which moulded half a dozen different shapes at the same time – and a number of items of factory-developed equipment not to be seen elsewhere. The Duke asked about the intricacies of the chain square and jigger mortice and drawer front press and finally watched the double dovetail machine produce its output in a steady stream. The busiest machines were the moulders with four, five or six cutters capable of working at 100 feet a minute; in one operation, the lengths and widths of four sides of a piece of wood could be cut. By 1960, machines were running on electricity at 3,000 to 24,000 rpm using Texrope V belts.

Veneer shop

Originally, affixing mahogany saw-cut decorative veneers to ridged base panels was achieved through pressure of a cramp. However, little veneering was done in the early days and then only on the better-quality suites. As methods progressed, the cramp apparatus for affixing veneer in batches was achieved by a cramp in the form of a rectangular metal frame with a number of hand-screwed clamps suspended on an iron girder above. A three-inch block of hardwood was placed on the bottom with successive layers of glue-veneered panels – about six or eight placed in the cramp, with a layer of hot metal between them. With another three-inch-thick hardwood block on top, the clamps were screwed down and the pressure helped stick the veneer panels.

Across the East Main Corridor, the Duke watched the big single-daylight hot press working to full capacity in the Veneer shop 32 and the line of tapeless jointers splicing leaves of veneer with speed and accuracy. Veneer grading was carried out with a lighting system giving consistent light unaffected by the vagaries of natural light.

Gordon Shepherd remembered working with veneers and the inspection of his work:

> You had to buy your own tools, from Heward and Dean in West Green Road. Lebus trained you, they showed you how you did it, you had to go and get your

Veneer preparation shop – the edges of thin veneer being cut by guillotine during the 1950s (Reproduced from the *Sphere* magazine)

The Duke of Edinburgh being shown the bending press

(Reproduced with special permission from Waltham Forest Local History Archives, Vestry House Museum)

own tools. Small tools like veneer knives, straight edge knives, didn't have to buy much. You could do veneer by hand – marquetry, with a special veneer knife you could cut out a knot in the wood and replace it with the one you'd just cut out. Veneers come off a roll, got to be sliced when soaking wet, off a roll called a 'log'. You had benches either side of the rollers. You worked at bench for veneer cutting and repairing. I worked standing up, can't do it sitting down. You'd stand at your bench and you've got racks in front of you of ready-prepared veneers, cut to size. Veneer is very fine wood, walnut, mahogany, 'birds-eye' walnut. Very thin and you use tape to joint it. You pull down your backing veneer then you lay on the next layer, the face veneer. You'd get a pile of veneers, glue with Scotch glue on the edges, push it down tight so you didn't get any glue on the face of it, then peel them off, put them together edge to edge. That's put on the big metal plates of the veneer jointing machine. Big presses,

used to be ten feet by six feet hot plates, they were aluminium plates, same size as the press, loaded up with pre-glued work, usually eight layers of those, and all the work would be put through the machine. Then they're put on the press and pressed down. That was electric power, but I think the plates were steam heated. They were pressed, hot plate would melt the glue and it fastened them together. Small work would be pretty quick. Plates were pushed out, too hot to handle, you had to wear big thick gloves – they supplied those – you just pushed them through onto a barrow and we took the plywood off, and then the plates were taken round to the other side.

Then another gang takes them out and puts them through a light box for any faults, then chalk them up. They supplied… plenty of chalk! Any faults, cut them out and replace them, by hand. When you're passing them through the light box to look for faults, you had to work really quickly because the next lot was coming through!

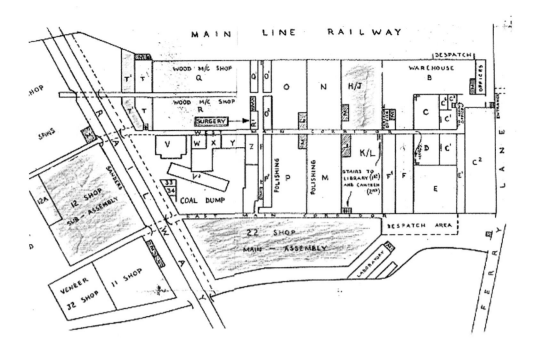

Piecing it all Together:

Zone Two – Sub-assembly and Assembly

At the time of the Duke's visit, makers undertook the assembly of the furniture parts prepared and machined in Zone One in two phases – sub-assembly operations in 12 shop and main assembly operations in 22, as well as some specialised production in several smaller shops. Colin Brown was in charge of the makers in the early 1960s. The machined parts were issued from the parts store, metal components, including screws and locks as well as piecework ticket wallets, stubs for the identity of articles and so forth from the main stores.

Similarly, in the early years at the Finsbury Cabinet Works, pre-cut wooden furniture parts were stored in the parts store P and allocated by the parts storekeeper in batches of five at a time – hence giving rise to the term 'batch assembly'; LS suggested that Joseph Clohosy, the parts storekeeper, 'kept most of the records in his head'.

There were no power presses in the glue cramps shop (O shop in Clifford Tee's original works design). Glue for affixing wood was made from heating up animal derivatives in the early days; the edges of boards to be affixed were glued and left in cabinet-makers' cramps for 24 hours to completely dry. Many Arts and Crafts pieces, particularly cabinets, had a logic of assembly that employed the simple strategy of assembling all components in one direction, with all cramp pressure being applied in one direction too.

The concept of sub-assembly preceding final assembly developed out of the firm's experience of plane manufacture during both World Wars.

The jointing workshop pictured pre-World War One

Women making the wing of a Handley Page 0/400 through sub-assembly and assembly of Handley Page aircraft pictured in C2 shop

Women making wooden parts for shells during World War One: the machines in the makers' workshop are driven by belt and shaft

During World War One, Harris Lebus made the entire Handley Page 0/400 aircraft, including fuselages; crucially however, the final assemblies were sent to other factories to be mounted and have the engines installed. LS explained how the sewing workshop, complete with 36 Singer sewing machines, had been established at the works to 'join the material and tailor it to the required shapes and, in the case of the wings, the bag was pulled over the frame as tightly as possible'. The two wings were kept apart by struts attached to the spars of the wings and the whole made rigid by an assortment of wires and cables. The fuselages

Proudly standing in front of a completed Handley Page 0/400 wing are the production team: Fred Trew, sample maker, is seated on the front row, first left; Frank Geary, works manager, is seated third from the left; Edmund Zala, inspector/quality controller, is seated third from the right; James (Jimmie) Douse peers over his colleagues from the back row, third from right; Sherb Warman is on the far right; from Tabernacle Street sales are Charles (Jock) Boryer seated first on the right and Frank Felce is seated fourth from right; Alf Brown (senior), sample maker, is on the back row eight from the left and Alf Brown (junior) is seated front row between Trew and Geary

Makers assembling Handley Page aircraft in C2

Stretching canvas over a Vickers Vimy night bomber frame

were constructed in a similar fashion to the wings, and the linen 'bags' stretched over them.

Pioneering sub-assembly – the Airspeed Horsa glider

LS described the Horsa glider as being 'designed on the monocoque principle, with wood members and stressed plywood skins, transverse frames and bulkheads and longitudinal stringers'. In essence, this means the plywood skin must be strong enough to keep the fuselage rigid and support the load. It was originally assembled on one jig as a complete unit. At 67 feet long and with a 7-feet-and-6-inch diameter, the fuselage was a large beast to manoeuvre.

Herman believed assembly could be done more efficiently and suggested to Herbert Barnes that the firm switch to constructing six individual barrels instead – a further sub-assembly – and abutting and bolting these together in a final assembly. With this change agreed, adequate manufacturing space was needed. Prior to World War Two, the sub-assemblies shop 12 did not exist so three open-ended field sheds immediately south of the Tottenham and Forest Gate Railway were commandeered. These were enclosed to form one huge workshop to perform the intricacies required for Horsa aircraft manufacture, with Alf Brown (senior) in charge. The fuselages, completely circular, were covered in Madapolam, a soft, absorbent cotton fabric weaved in such a way to give

equal tensile strength and shrinkage in any two directions.

The interiors were also fitted out by the firm – seats for personnel and fixtures for equipment. This included a flap door incorporated in the front section for use as an exit ramp and a sliding exit door in the rear section for parachutists.

Sherman Tanks – replicas in wood… of course

A brick wall was built around a section of 'K/L' ground floor and with C. E. Leaman, chief maintenance officer, in charge, an exact wooden replica of a Sherman tank copied in every detail was constructed. 'At a distance of 100 yards it was impossible to tell the difference between this and the real thing,' commented LS. Two or three were made and after the war were paraded through the Tottenham streets to promote the National Savings scheme.

Landing craft

LS, Alf Brown (senior) and C. E. Leaman visited a shipbuilding firm in Portsmouth that was producing landing craft to gain knowledge of production, first-hand.

At its production peak, the manufacture of landing craft employed 90 men and women. At 38 feet long with keels made from fine-quality English oak, they were made in two halves – each of 20 feet 14 inches wide and 31 inches thick – spliced together. The first 50 were made with 5-inches-by-one-quarter-inch mahogany planking criss-crossed at an angle of 45 degrees with a sheet of oiled linen between and a quarter inch armour plate bolted through. With the next batch, the planking was replaced with half-inch-thick plywood – painted, camouflaged and numbered to speed up the process. Power was from two Ford supercharged V8 engines capable of propelling the craft to speeds of 11 knots when carrying 40 soldiers and equipment. The landing craft were launched on the Lea Navigation fitted up ready for action, except for the guns, and taken downriver to the Thames at Wapping led by a Thames pilot, 'one of whom went by the excellent seafaring name of Heyhoe', says LS.

The launching of the first landing craft on the river at Tottenham Hale was to be a special occasion, though it turned into an embarrassing, albeit humorous, one. It is an incident best told in the words of LS: 'Various Brass Hats came from the Admiralty and everything was carefully prepared. By some mischance the mooring rope broke and the craft launched itself suddenly into the river and embedded itself firmly in the opposite bank!'

De Havilland Mosquito

The Mosquito was the fastest aeroplane in the Royal Air Force. According to LS, during 1942 and 1943, around 90% of the workforce was engaged in aspects of manufacture of Mosquitos. The firm were now adept at manufacturing military aircraft and there were similarities between the Airspeed Horsa gliders and the Mosquitos; both had fuselages constructed entirely of wood on the monocoque principle, covered with Madapolam and doped. Aside from special fastenings and minor features, the Mosquito was made entirely of wood and the firm made everything but the tail-plane. The fuselage was a plywood and balsa wood sandwich. To enable it to carry required equipment and electrical wiring, the structure was stiffened with reinforced hardwood and bracing ribs.

Similarly to the Horsa, the Mosquito was made in two halves on huge jigs; these were subsequently glued together using a gap-filling synthetic glue made from beetles, with reinforced plywood over the joints. 'The firm also fitted up and connected the highly complicated network of electrical and other mechanisms', said LS. This included the instruments in the cockpit (which included

Working on the hull of a landing craft

A landing craft on the River Lea

Sub-assembly of a Mosquito
frame

Makers installing internal
fittings to a Mosquito fuselage

Final fitting of the Mosquito

radar screens in later variants), armour plate protection and the Perspex hood and nose. The wings formed one continuous component containing spars 54-feet long constructed entirely of laminated spruce with plywood skins, which were affixed to the spars and ribs using wooden screws. The plywood petrol drop tanks, which could be jettisoned after fuel was used up, were also made by the firm, as were sub-assembled fuselage parts to be distributed and assembled by other companies.

'My father, Harry Tallman, made Mosquitos'

As part of the Coombes Croft project, Marlene McAndrew recalled when, as a young girl, her father was employed at Harris Lebus during World War Two:

> When war was declared my father, Harry Tallman, who was a cabinet-maker, was not called up into the armed forces because he was in a reserved occupation. What this meant to us was that he was out of work for a long time, waiting for the government to send for him; during this period, he did any temporary casual or labouring jobs he could find, and life was very hard for us. Eventually he found out why he hadn't been called up – cabinet-makers were considered to be the most highly skilled wood workers, used to very fine work, and the government had a special role for them. Dad was sent to Lebus's in Tottenham and found himself working together with the designers on the prototype Mosquito aeroplane.
>
> They were allotted a screened-off section of the plant and had special security passes. He told us how they made very small sections then hung around for hours while each section was put through stringent tests. In particular, skins were applied to the wooden parts with special, very new glues. If the tiniest bubble appeared the whole section was smashed up and they started again. He was proud and excited to be associated with the Mosquito but found the hanging around was tedious, although not so bad in the summer when they strolled along the Lea Navigation waiting

to be called. He told us his amazement when they first saw a couple of men carrying a whole plane through the factory – it was a balsa wood glider!

> He used to bring home small off cuts of balsa and I found it very strange to squeeze this wood into a pulp. He made my sister a balsa-wood rattle, so that she wouldn't hurt herself, but he filled it with nails and screws, so it weighed a ton! My Dad also told us about a good-looking redhead who worked in their section. Sometimes he brought some large, coloured redundant record cards for me to play with. They were called 'job cards' and 'jig cards' and had people's names on them. I now wonder if this wasn't a security risk, but the office staff gave them to him, and I loved them. When the war ended and the men came back, the wartime workers were sacked, and dad was on the dole again until the furniture trade picked up and back he went to small workshops in Bethnal Green.

Beyond World War Two, veneered panels were first sanded in the sub-assembly shop 12, which was established during the war for plane sub-assembly. Gordon Shepherd originally found work at Lebus during the war because of a family connection – his older sister (to his adoptive parents) already worked as a 'forelady' in sub-assembly shop 12. At the age of 18, and with several years' experience 'making ammunition boxes… and petrol tanks for fighters' during a stint at Brasted piano manufacturers (who also switched to making war products), he joined Lebus under the watchful eye of his sister. As part of the Coombes Croft project he recalled:

> I was in 12 shop, they had so many shops there. I was on the back of the machines. I was too young to do machine work there. I cut the ribs and did all sorts of different parts… our clothes prop in the garden, that's a bit of a Hotspur glider! I worked taking stuff off the circular saw. It was interesting – they had sanders, belt-sanders and drum sanders. Belt-sanders ran in a continuous loop that did specialised

sanding. Drum sanders, three rollers and you'd push the sandpaper on diagonally because of the grooves in the roller, then tighten it up so there's no edges. There were three rollers, course, medium and fine. Sanded mostly the plywood when it was cut to size, put them through, check there's no grease on the surface, and after that someone with a special gauge would measure; you'd put your plywood in there and they'd measure the thickness of the plywood.

By the 1950s there were more than 30 sanding machines in the factory, which prepared the surfaces ready for staining and polishing. The butting of hinges to doors and the making of mirror frames was also done in the sub-assembly shop. Thus, parts were brought together to make component sub-assemblies, such as ends, backs, tops and bottoms for all products, including wardrobes, kitchen cabinets, sideboards, chests of drawers and so forth. The Duke was particularly impressed with the Russell screwing machine and bending press. '[H]ere too, the latest ideas in automation were in use,' wrote Robert Hawes (*Tottenham and Edmonton Weekly Herald*, 11 November 1955) adding that this 'demonstrated that the firm was keeping abreast of the space age, for they were almost supersonic in operation'. The Duke said to Joseph White: 'You are the first man I have seen using a hammer. Everyone else seems to be using machines!'

Radio frequency presses and the 'secrets' of H/J shop

Solid constructional parts, including veneered panels, were either issued to the nailing machines or radio-frequency presses – there were around 20 of these throughout the factory.

In his personal reminiscences, prepared specially for this book, former employee Peter Baker said:

> I worked in H/J shop during the 1950s and it was made strictly off-limits to all employees except those with special access rights. On one occasion the entire Arsenal football team was given a tour of the Factory; they were not allowed to linger or ask questions about H/J and what took place there.
>
> When I returned after late-entry cabinet-making training, I worked in H/J Shop and was inducted into the very modern world of radio frequency curing of glue lines. There were peculiar machines and presses all around and trolleys loaded with piece parts and plywood panels. We were being placed in the forefront of furniture-making technology. The whole concept was the product of the firm's Experimental and Development Engineer, Chaim Schreiber, who later set up his own furniture business. Being of an inquisitive nature and always asking questions, I learned a lot about synthetic glues and the productivity potential of radio frequency.
>
> I operated three different radio-frequency presses which were: a press in which I formed end panels with round corners for a dressing table and chest of drawers; a press in which the whole carcass of a sunk-centre dressing table was assembled in 14.75 minutes – the curing time for the glue was ninety seconds; a press in which I assembled a drawer in four minutes – the curing time for the glue was thirty-five seconds. The industry still does not use these marvellous inventions, I am sad to say.
>
> Sir Herman would invite certain people, of whom he would acquaint us during the morning. He would suddenly appear in H/J shop, walk around to each of us and tell us who was coming. Sir Herman always told me to 'give them a good show' – I could unload the press of an assembled carcass and glue and assemble the next whole carcass into the press within five minutes.
>
> With drawer making, there was a standard assembly time of four minutes per drawer. During the curing time of thirty-five seconds I would have the next drawer glued, assembled and ready to be placed

into the press and always knock the stop button with my knee (before the curing cycle was finished) to unload and reload the press. It was just showing off, really – this was my 'piece de resistance'.

H/J shop produced some specialist lines and separately the production of drawers took place in K/L shop. Although by comparison these were small sections, in terms of volume of output, 20,000 or more drawers a week were manufactured by the early 1960s.

It is interesting to compare the manufacture of chests of drawers over different time periods. According to LS, the first big order put through the works was indeed for one thousand chests of drawers in satin walnut wood, three feet six inches wide, with three long and two short drawers, with a wholesale price of 39s 6d. This provided an opportunity to put Clifford Tee's original factory design and facilities to the test. Chests of drawers were a mainstay, a staple manufactured Harris Lebus item. They came in many models, were used for a variety of purposes and made for different rooms of the house. One, known as the 'Scotch' chest of drawers with a very deep top drawer known as a 'bonnet box', was popular in the early years. Harris Lebus had a reputation for producing such pieces and had patented a framed-up drawer side with a 'floating' bottom panel slot dovetailed at each end to allow for flexibility, which helped prevent them expanding and sticking. The making of chest of drawers bucked the usual trend of production in small batches, and larger quantities could be put into production. According to LS, standardisation of furniture pieces scarcely existed at that point.

After World War One, an American automated jointer was purchased from the Linderman Machine Co, a company established by Bert Arthur Linderman in Michigan in 1909. This was designed to cut, glue and slot dovetail joints (drawers were the only manufactured item needing dovetail joints) but was not efficient, according to LS and proved to be an expensive investment: it did not always work to plan and wasted wood in the process.

Writing about furniture pieces with drawers made at the factory before 1966, Rex Winsbury (*Management Today*, July 1968) observed:

> It made 42 different sizes of drawer, and every drawer had to be individually fitted, so that it might not match any other drawer hole. Every item had to be hand-finished. In all there were over 600 separate pieces of furniture being made. According to Mr. Grosbard, 'a big computer firm spent two years trying to sort out the paperwork involved and gave up!'

The main assembly shop, 22, was the largest on the Tottenham Hale site. The assembly of wardrobes, dressing tables and chests of drawers took place in this building. Some furniture pieces – dining room, kitchen and occasional items – were assembled in E and F shops. Sub-assemblies were marshalled together and the loads of component sub-assemblies were delivered from here in 'kit' form. For example, all the parts required to make 50 dressing tables of one design were brought together immediately prior to final assembly.

The actual assembly, or 'cramping', was carried out by one of 35 cramps, each being worked by two men. '[C]apable of curing glue lines in one minute or less, these machines make a valuable contribution to flow production,' commented Robert Hawes. The process required good operational skills and involved the use of pneumatic, as well as electric, hand tools. In the case of a wardrobe, two workers assembled the carcase and another hung the doors at the next operation. In the assembly of dressing tables and chests of drawers, one of the crampers assembled the carcase while another would fit or 'bed' the top and fit the column for the mirror if required. Staining was also done in the assembly shop. The fitting of drawers to give a uniform and flush appearance, removal of rough edges and sandpapering by hand any small blemishes or beads of glue took place there prior to completed furniture items being loaded onto the main output conveyor for polishing in Zone Three.

Ron Turton recalled these tasks being performed as the conveyor rolled:

> Fitters worked all the time, taking jobs off the line, fit them and put them back on. Fitting, you put a clothes rail inside a wardrobe, 'scutching', that's a plate on the keyhole you got to put six handles on a chest of drawers while it was moving.

Peter Baker recounts an early experience in which his handy work was inspected:

> When I was working in 22 Shop, assemblies, on the 'wardrobe' assembly line, on my first day I pushed a finished wardrobe out to the inspector who shortly afterwards pushed it back to me with white chalk marks all over it. I turned to the older maker at the next bench and said, 'What on earth is this all about?' (or words to that effect), to which he responded, 'He's only testing you lad, rub them all out and push it back', which I promptly did! And it was then passed. Another lesson learned.

In the 'new look' Lebus post-1966, the Europa product range was streamlined. Standardisation became the order of the day. The body of a typical chest of nine drawers was constructed from a combination of chipboard covered with a simulated teak veneer which was bought in ready prepared and subsequently glued on site. The 'sleigh' base frames were of solid teak timber as well as the scalloped handles. There were now only 40 separate bits of furniture being made, with three drawer sizes, and all drawers would fit any holes of the same size as a result of the close tolerances achieved by the new methods.

Woodley 'whisperers'

Meanwhile over at Woodley, an update in the *Lebus Log*, No. 13, December 1958 informed readers of recent experiments with pneumatic stapling equipment, arising from visits to German factories by Harry Whittaker, upholstery chief designer, and Graham Nash, works manager. Stapling guns superseded the tack hammer and staples were being fired at an average of three to four per second. However, in a comparison between the respective countries, the article continued: 'the German upholstery being extremely bulky and extremely hard, and by and large, their methods of upholstery were not nearly so advanced as ours and included a large amount of hand-sewing, hand-stuffing etc.' 'The men did all the upholstery, and the girls did all the machining,' said Shirley Hiscock. And 'only the men worked on the wooden frames, as they would be too heavy for the girls to pick up and turn around.'

George Ernest Chaplin, who started in Tabernacle Street in 1929 and moved with the work to Tottenham's H/J shop between 1943 and 1950, was in charge of production as the general foreman. Pieces of furniture were built on the assembly-line principle by groups of six men – wooden frames were mainly of beech and, occasionally, birch or oak. 'Oh yes!

Upholstery workers at Tabernacle Street pre-World War One

The upholstery assembly line at Hawkhurst House, Woodley pictured during the early 1960s

The tub chairs – I remember them well,' said Shirley. Teams were known by the names of the articles they normally constructed. Thus, there was a tub group and a Grecian one (they once built so-called Grecian chairs and the name stuck). The work was done at a fast pace and various combinations of springs (zigzag or coiled), rubber webbing, moulded latex foam, ready-shaped pieces of rubberised fibre, carpet felt and many other materials were attached. It was a complex operation, but quality was maintained.

Former employee Dave Lewis described some of the processes:

> When you entered the main upholstery shop, you had rows of upholstery groups running down the whole workshop – each group consisted of six workers and there must have been about eighteen groups. In front of each group would be all the frames and covers – foam, springs, everything you need to make a sofa or chair. Behind each group was the area where the finished furniture would be put; beyond that was the warehouse where the finished stuff would be loaded and then delivered.

> As I said, each group had six people and each did a separate job in a process: number 1 tacked the foam to the arms; then he passed it to number 2 who tacked the covers to the arms; he then passed it to number 3 who fitted seat springs and seat; then on to number 4 who did the back, next on to number 5 who covered the outside arms and attached the facings; finally number 6 man who fitted the outside back, fixing underneath and then fitting castors and fringes. That would be it, one item of furniture – a sofa or chair!

In another shop, women were machining the covers made from moquette and tapestry fabrics previously cut out on long tables. Each girl worked at a handy table designed in the factory and incorporating her own private cupboard. Above was an indicator light that she switched on to show when she was about to finish the job in hand. At her side, her

name was prominently displayed on a Perspex plate; this was useful, and anyway, it was good 'to have one's name on the door even if one didn't have a private office'. One girl might be operating a machine turning out fabric-covered buttons; others, using simple but effective equipment, made complex ruches, and cushions were filled with sisal pads or latex foam units.

Shirley Hiscock said:

> I think at one time there must have been about forty girls on sewing machines; so you can tell it was noisy – what with the machines and forty girls talking! I remember, when I started there, we had a training school for the machinist, before we could go in the factory on the machines and production. I can remember there was a repair section, where there were two men; if the girls were busy and they needed something done, the men would have a go on the machine if one was spare. The girls were on bonus so didn't want to stop and do repairs. But at one time I did the repairs still on bonus!

Polishing with Pride:

Zone Three – Polishing and Finishing

In the polishing shops, the Duke's party watched a dozen slow-moving conveyors taking the furniture from the spray booths to the final hand-finishing section. Robert Hawes was prompted to observe 'the word accurately describes the impression one gets of output at the end of the production line – out into the polishing shops, where they are sprayed with polish whilst still moving.' (*Tottenham and Edmonton Weekly Herald*, 11 November 1955)

Some polishers, such as William O'Hare, who, after joining the firm aged 15 in 1897, had stayed for 49 years until his retirement in 1946, would have experienced all the changes in polishing, from French to spraying. In the early years at the Finsbury Cabinet Works, polishing was done in K/L workshop; as a skilled,

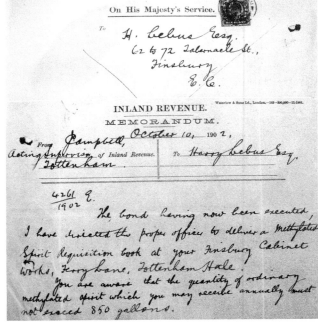

labour-intensive process, French polishing was done only by trained men. A school for indentured apprentices was located on the first and second floors of K/L workshop.

A revealing statement is made by LS: 'All the cheapest products, namely satin walnut and cheap square chests [of drawers] and some desks were polished by women'. Thus, it would appear that the 1,000 chests of drawers, the first order, fit within the category of 'cheaper' product.

Polish store and manufactory, pictured before World War One

Elsie Lambert's reflections on her French-polishing experience

Former employee Elsie recalled:

> The men used to make the furniture and it came down to us to be polished; bedroom suites, dining room suites, sideboards,

Permit to store methylated spirit at the factory, dated October 1902

French polishing bedroom suites before World War One; it is mainly men working on the quality furniture suites

A sizeable workforce of women pose for this photograph in one of the polishing shops

cabinets. If they wanted something very highly polished, we used to have to do it so far and then they would finish it off. Some of the furniture used to be very highly polished years ago... we used to do a lot to it then. We always had to rub it down until it was smooth. Then whatever colour sort of wood it was, if it was ash, we had to rub it all with goose fat and if it was walnut, we had to rub it with brown, and if it was mahogany, we had to rub it with black. And after a time that all had to be sandpapered down again, and then it was varnished then sandpapered down again before we started to polish it. There was all

that preparation. The polish used to stain your fingers. I don't suppose it's done like that now.

French polishing – the high-gloss finish most suited to hardwoods such as mahogany – was produced using shellac (a resin secreted by the female lac bug) diluted with methylated spirit and applied gently using an oil-lubricated cloth. It served to fill wood grain and many thins coats were necessary, each applied a layer at a time. The final coat needed some time to harden completely. Although this method produced a beautiful finish, it was fragile. A permit was granted in October 1902 by the

Inland Revenue agreeing to the storing of methylated spirits – not to exceed 850 gallons annually – at the Finsbury Cabinet Works.

Raymond Shard's trade insider knowledge of French polishing

In a piece sent to Oliver Lebus, French polishing enthusiast Raymond Shard shared his knowledge of French polishing:

Staining and filling:

Their mahogany furniture was first water stained and then coated in a colour plaster, which was rubbed down smooth prior to polishing. The fashionable colour of mahogany at the turn of the century was a rather nasty opaque muddy brown, which virtually obliterated the entire figure in the wood. This revolting practice persisted well into the 1930s and lasted even longer among the piano manufacturing fraternity.

Fadding up was done in two stages:

The furniture was first coated in polish using a special brush known in the trade as a mop. Next it was treated with a fad, which was a rubbing pad consisting of wool cloth or absorbent cotton wadding inside a soft cotton cloth. This prevented the polish dragging as it was worked into the wood. The polisher worked in rhythmic circles from end to end to build up the desired surface. This was known as bodying up. It was hard work, and once the process started it had to be completed without interruption.

Cutting down:

After the furniture was left overnight to harden it was then cut down (rubbed over) the following day with fine 400-gauge flour paper sprinkled with a little linseed oil from time to time, until it was smooth as silk; the residual oil was cleaned off with cotton rags.

Finishing and fitting:

Finishing was done with a rubber, which was made with upholsterer's wadding folded into the shape of a cone, and then covered with good quality sheeting which was lint free; the rubber was used in a similar fashion to a fad working from end to end in a continuous pattern, paying particular attention to the edges. Once again, a little linseed oil was added with discretion otherwise the oil could be buried under the polish. Whilst this might look quite acceptable at the time, within a year fine cracks would appear and disfigure the surface. This was avoided by slowly reducing the oil and adding a little methylated spirit, which cleared the oil

Women in the polishing school on the upper floor pictured before World War One

and thinned the polish at the same time to give a smooth glossy surface. This process was known in the trade as 'spiriting off'.

Other finishes

Not all furniture was French polished: 'No oak or satin walnut was "filled",' said LS. Oak was treated with water-based stains. Some items were fumed – placed in a chamber to be infused with ammonia for 24 hours. Fuming was a relatively new process, still at an experimental stage. The backs of cheaper items would be painted in greenish yellow ochre, as was customary in the trade, while the more expensive ranges were left white.

Doping planes with a paintbrush

During World War One, Handley Page aircraft were finished by being doped. Dope was a plasticised lacquer, which, when mixed with colour pigment and applied, tautened and stiffened Irish linen stretched over wooden wing frames – much like an artist prepares a canvas for painting, except that dope is airtight and weatherproof.

As a highly flammable substance in liquid form, special precautions were necessary and controlled conditions were required in its application. A dedicated workshop for the purpose was erected on the additional land acquired in 1911. This was located north of the Tottenham and Forest Gate Railway between the Lea Navigation on the west and Pymmes Brook on the east, where workshop 22 would later be established. The workshop had to be heated to create the right conditions for application and ventilated to protect the workers from fumes. When placed vertically on trestles, wings and fuselages could then be painted with the dope. During World War Two, camouflaged dope was applied to the Airspeed Horsa glider in a specially erected workshop at the southern end of the site.

Cellulose spraying introduced after World War One

After World War One, thoughts were geared towards the resumption of furniture production for the mass market. The partners made a series of visits to the States. They brought back a host of information about modern methods, new machinery and many samples of new finishes for furniture – one of these being cellulose spraying.

Early spray polishing and conveyor line

Spray polishers in the early 1960s as pictured in the *Sphere* magazine

Compared to labour-intensive French polishing, the potential of cellulose spraying was quickly appreciated. If adopted, the new process had the potential to reduce costs and increase efficiency – both of which fitted with the emerging Harris Lebus strategic business plan.

Proposal put to workers

In December 1920 all polishing workers – both women and men – were assembled and addressed by Louis about the proposed major change. According to LS, his cousin Louis 'explained the nature of the materials to be used and the various processes to be employed, and emphasised the reason for introducing it was the necessity to cheapen the cost of polishing and bring down the price of furniture'. LS did not reveal if the talk also explained the fundamental shift the firm was intending to take in the type of furniture to be manufactured or the change in target market. Clearly there was some apprehension on the part of workers, who, according to LS, did not give their immediate approval. However: '[W]ithin a few days, the employees agreed to co-operate with the new scheme.'

Early experiments in automatic spraying F1 shop

Reciprocating guns, moving horizontally and vertically, suspended above a slowly moving conveyor were introduced with the flow of cellulose spray controlled by an 'electric eye'. This was initially tried on the upturned blind backs of mirrors for chests of drawers, then with whole furniture carcasses. With a spray gun filled with dark Jacobean cellulose colour, 'only the cheapest furniture was treated in this manner' commented LS and it was discontinued after many trials. To be effective, a large volume of the same line of furniture items moving progressively would have been needed, and as it was, this interfered with the production balance. That said, 'it was most ingenious and did, within limits, an excellent job,' conceded LS. In the *Lebus Log*, No. 13, December 1958, Charlie Holland, a crate-maker since 1908, shared his memory of making the first spray-polishing booth, 'a wooden box

about four feet square' in the days when a wardrobe was a month in the hand-finishing section. The introduction of spray polishing started in a small way with hand spray guns and individual booths, with elementary fume extractors and an adjustable height turntable.

Conveyors and spray flow production

By 1930 the firm had developed flow production through 12 lines of conveyors, initially made of cotton belts and later converted to wire mesh. At first, internal spraying of carcases on moving belts was attempted before developing methods to achieve spraying of whole items, inside and out.

An article in *Lebus Log*, No. 6, entitled 'What is "lacquer"?' explained that there were three types of ingredient used: cellulose nitrate, resins and plasticisers. Cellulose nitrate was the basic film-forming ingredient – it looked like cotton wool and was soluble in a number of liquids called solvents; resins – both natural (from a Malayan tree) and artificial (made from glycerine and by-products of the coal industry) were used, one for gloss, one for toughness; and a group of materials known as plasticisers, which moved with wood to prevent cracking. 30% of lacquer consisted of film-forming ingredients and 70% was solvents (manufactured by fermentation) and non-solvents (diluents for the resinous compounds). It was the liquid components that helped the film-forming components to be sprayed. Lacquer dried in 15 minutes, with around 15% evaporating during the spraying process.

Sissy the spray polisher tells how she did it

Sissy Lewis spent 42 years in the Polishing shop, taking her from the interwar years (she joined in 1928) through World War Two and right up to her redundancy in 1970. She had followed in her mother's footsteps. Her husband, Tom, was a maker in shop 22. An account of her experience was published in *Furnishing the World*. She began at the bottom as a cleaner of the spray booths before being offered a job as a spray polisher, which she put down to her mother's influence.

I got a job on the new runway… a moving belt where the furniture comes to you, you spray it, and then it went away from you. I was fifteen when I first started to spray. Somebody showed me how to do it and the very first bed I was put on, LS came and stood behind me. I was scared and couldn't pull the trigger. I didn't get any practice. I went straight onto beds – it didn't matter much about beds, especially the back of them. It was easy to learn, and I got into it very well. I worked alongside girls of my own age and some a little older. The older ones were professionals as they had been spraying in the booths. There were no men sprayers at that time – all women and very friendly.

The furniture would come through from the assembly shop on a wide conveyor:

[F]rom this they were [hand] sorted onto smaller belts that came through our shop. The two spraying rooms were huge with different moving lines for beds, chests, chairs, tables and wardrobes respectively. They were positioned on the belt about two feet apart in such a way you could spray the sides, the front, the top, but not the bottom or the back.

So the first job was to spray the stain to the colour of the pattern. You had no control over the colour as it was all done special [set-up centrally] according to the work you were on. The stain dried quickly and then you'd lacquer it. It could be either a shiny or a matt finish. Some pieces of furniture like wardrobes were big to do, so they got the tall girls to do them. How they got me on there I don't know but the better sprayers were put on wardrobes. I was always a wardrobe sprayer. We used to do a lot of shading. I remember doing a dining room suite for America. All you could see of the colour was just an egg shape in the middle, all the rest was shaded. I had to alter the air in my gun so it spitted out little spots, so it looked like it had woodworm.

The first job I did in the Second World War was white wardrobes and cupboards for hospitals in France. It was white enamel inside and out. I got covered like a snowman. Then we went on to ammunition boxes; they were khaki with white letters on the front. Then on to tent poles and then telegraph poles; the telegraph poles were done with khaki paint, the tent poles red. Even our hair was red and these poles were ever so long. You had to do them on a rack, turn them and spray them. You had to walk along to spray them 'cos they were so long.

Then I went into the dope shop where I spent the rest of the war… on nights…

Moving a Mosquito main frame into the doping shop

Women doping the wing of a Handley Page 0/400

we worked on the Horsa glider, which was very big, like an underground tunnel about 30 feet across. You moved it round as you worked. Put your back under it and shift it round. We worked in a gang of six, first the 'madap' [the linen stretched over the plywood of an aircraft] and then the dope… like a reddish paint… terrible smelling stuff. We used to do four of these fuselages a night, which was marvellous really. We were the best gang. They put me in charge.

We also made this framework of a lorry in wood – just the framework. It was then covered in canvas and I had to spray the windscreen, the radiator, the wheels and the numbers. It was then put on the road so the Germans would bomb that convoy of artificial lorries, so the real lorries got through.

Later I worked on the Albermarle airplane where I put on the red, white and blue. The Mosquito was different: we just did the wings, and that was all wood and every square inch a screw-hole.

Ron Turton's recollections of spray polishing

As part of the Coombes Croft project, Ron Turton, who joined as a 21-year-old in 1954 and stayed until he was made redundant in 1967, recalled:

Mostly women did the spraying. Best shop was the walnut shop. I worked in there a while – you had to be special to work in there. Bedroom suites; thirty minutes for a dressing table – you'd paper all the inside, lay it in the rack and do it, then tilt it over so you could do the two ends. You'd go in there; I like being early, some used to rush in, roll your trousers up and change your shoes. I rolled my trousers up because they could catch on the conveyor belt. I'd change to boots because your shoes could catch. Some would change their trousers, so they'd go home presentable. One bloke used to come in a suit, homburg, briefcase and umbrella – make people think he worked in a bank!

You had an apron, 6d a week, clean one every week. The polish builds up on your apron; you wipe your rubber on your apron. Some people had like a boiler suit. I started on the line; the line goes on and you're polishing. It [furniture] goes on a conveyor – there's a gap between each wardrobe, so the line would go along accordingly, so many inches a minute – with chests of drawers it would be speeded up. There'd be a wallet stapled on the furniture, on a wardrobe it'd be on the top, others it was round the back. You had a ticket for papering, spraying, pulling over and fitting.

My job was 'pulling over', using 'pullover'. We used to have a kit, like a box on a frame, and you had your rag, your wadding, two bottles and sandpaper. We used to use 'pullover' solution and a rag – you had the tap on the wall to fill your bottles with 'pullover' solution, bloke used to get big sheets of rag, cut it up and sell it – good bit of rag you could do the job quick. We got more [pay] for pulling over a wardrobe. They would change you from time to time, according to where there was work. You may be on bedroom suites for days – couldn't do them on a line, they was stacked on the floor, and if the work dries up, you get put onto something else. And the spray booths, they'd come and clean them all and tip the stuff away. There was no stuff left in the ground, it was all taken away, it wasn't dumped.

Turton also remembered Quality Control also in the spray-polish shop:

[S]prayers, they was colour spraying. Bring the colour pattern, put it against the job; if it's no good, take it back, strip right back and do it again. If the charge-hand spots it, it'd be chalked up, no good, and do it again. Put it on the line, if it's 'ok' charge-hand chalks it up. Do the next one. They had a doctor there; a doctor of science or something, and he'd come and sort out any problems with the solution or the lacquer.

Metal fittings store

Glass fittings store in the early part of the twentieth century

Below: Fixing metal fittings to bedroom suites

Below right: The office furniture fitting shop of pre-World War One

He added: 'They had everything there. They brought a three-rubber job, this new lacquer job. It was so advanced with these lacquer jobs.'

Sissy Lewis also recalled how inspection was done and mistakes corrected in the polishing shop:

> [I]f you weren't careful the spray could run if you didn't control your gun. If the air pressure was too high and if you pulled the trigger back too far then you'd get a lot of runs and you'd get told off. This furniture you'd take off the line and it would be taken to a little place where men washed it off with a stripper. It was a very nasty job. It would then be put back on the belt and you'd have to do it again for nothing [in the system of payment by results]. If it was somebody else's fault it would be put back on the repair line and re-sprayed there by one girl.

Preparing and Packing to Send –

Warehousing, Invoicing, Packing and Distribution

At the time of the Duke of Edinburgh's visit in November 1955, the new north warehouse was still in the planning stage; it would not become fully operational until mid-1957, just before Sir Herman died. Furniture warehousing and preparation for distribution were still carried out in D, E and F. The building known as B had loading arches giving direct access to load carriages using a private railway-siding platform. The complex of extended C buildings facing Ferry Lane was for packing – either for the home market or export. As the favoured mode of transport moved from rail to road over time, the extended C building complex incorporated loading bays for an ever-expanding fleet of vans.

When the new warehouse came into operation under the management of Tom Waring, it had the capacity to store up to 35,000 items of completed furniture. Post-1966, with the addition of a mezzanine floor, the building was large enough to accommodate a new production unit and office functions, as well as warehousing when the majority of completed furniture stocks were held in part-form rather than made-up and taking up air space. The entire frontage of the new warehouse was designed to park the fleet of Lebus vans.

Invoicing for products purchased by Lebus customers

Marian Cotton worked as an invoice checker in the late 1950s and gave the following account in her recollections as part of the Coombes Croft project:

Section of warehouse with finished furniture in storage

We didn't have telephones on the desks, but the section head had a telephone. We had pencils, rulers, we didn't use typewriters. There were a few typists there to do the special invoices. It was a huge factory and they also had a big factory elsewhere – one lady used to type out the orders for the upholstery section in Woodley.

And we'd be handed a batch of invoices by the woman in charge, or the head and we'd work through and then get another batch. We'd have a pile of orders come through and they were transferred onto the firm's sets, and we'd check them against the orders for the delivery addresses throughout the country.

In an adjacent room was a section known as the Addressograph department. Here there were racks upon racks of name and address plates which operators pulled out one by one to be ink stamped onto the firm's invoices. There were about ten of these machines all making a great clatter.

The furniture was supplied to hundreds of customers, including chain stores. The delivery address was often different from that of the head office, so although many of the plates were colour coded, it was all too easy for the wrong ones to be pulled out and stamped onto the wrong invoice set. It was the job of the invoice checker to return incorrect sets (after checking the order requirements) to the operator concerned. As you can imagine, this was often met with displeasure! Checking the invoices was a responsible but boring occupation.

Ted Eastland was in charge of the invoice section of the Sales department, having joined the Railway department in 1929, returning to Lebus after service in World War Two.

Packing and Despatch department – the early years

Harry Thornton had fond memories of his time in the Packing and Despatch department before World War One, and in particular the export

Top: Workers prepare 'knocked down' (disassembled) furniture and pack for export in the period leading to World War One

Above: Export packing cases: the destination of Buenos Aires (spelt 'Ayres') is stamped on some crates

market, which he shared in the *Lebus Log*, No. 21, December 1961:

Furniture for export was sent as 'knock-down' (K.D.) – prefabricated with instructions for assembly on arrival at its destination – but came through the factory in exactly the same manner as furniture known by us as 'TIGHT' (fully assembled and glued etc.) for the home market. It was assembled, polished and fitted perfectly, no gluing of course, all glue blocks were screwed into position. Each packer had a man or lad working with him whose job it was to take the furniture to pieces and wrap the polished parts together in waxed paper and brown paper and generally prepare everything for packing, each separate part having to be lettered and numbered.

I can recall some parts of the globe to which Lebus furniture was sent – South America, Australia, New Zealand, Nigeria, Sierra Leone, South Africa and India were among those that remain chiefly in my memory. We also had a continental trade, chiefly with France, Germany and Belgium. Our main export to South America was six feet solid oak bedroom suites. Australia and New Zealand seemed to favour fancy goods, such as writing tables, delicate looking drawing room suites and inlaid mahogany card tables complete with packs of cards, cribbage board and beautiful cut glass wine decanters and glasses. What I remember most for South Africa is three feet satin walnut suites – six suites would be packed in one case.

Packing cases were well-made, strong affairs and before use were lined with tarred, waterproof paper. Packing material varied according to the customer's specifications and consisted of straw, wood-wool, coconut fibre, horsehair and Italian grass – no doubt, except for the straw those materials were used afterwards for upholstery. Coconut fibre came in tightly packed bales and had to be loosened up for use and for the purpose we had a carding machine standing in an old tin shed by the East Gate. Wood-wool was produced on a machine which stood in a corrugated shed in the timber field. It was one man's job to keep us supplied, carting the wood in a huge box on wheels and dumping it into a corner of the workshop. Boys could not resist the temptation of diving headfirst into that soft pile.

Furniture for our continental trade was not K.D. and was packed in crates. As far as I can remember there were about 16 packers

The Shipping department pictured in 1914, just before World War One: Harry Thornton is in the middle row, third in from the right; Fred Cullen is to the left of Harry; on the back row is the father and son team of G. Mason junior (third from the left) and G. Mason senior (to his son's right)

employed and each would pack two, three and sometimes four cases a day. The outbreak of the war in 1914 put the damper on exports and during the war years it gradually petered out.

Mr. Brooks was in charge of the Packing and Despatch department in the early years. On a good day, nine or ten railway carriages would be filled and he was, according to LS, 'interrogated' each morning about how many trucks he could manage to fill that day. But, as LS reveals, 'as he had very little control over what was sent up from the factory, he could not always be sure of achieving the maximum'. This fits with the wider policy of the partners of 'non-disclosure' of information. LS explains: 'As was common in those days, all figures of output and the limited statistics produced were considered confidential and managers down the line had little or no knowledge of what was going on.' However, Brooks developed a sneaky way around this, as LS explains he 'had a feeling that he would save an odd truck or two up his sleeve in order not to go below a certain minimum'.

'Goods were sent at the company's risk, packed in straw and canvas, with some battens, and all packing was charged and returnable,' described LS. However, the 1939 catalogue stated:

> Packing materials are free and not returnable. Delivery is free of charge to customer's address in London. Delivery is undertaken only on the condition there is an adequate road to premises and that delivery can be easily affected by means of ordinary staircases and doorways (in the case of cost of tackle then charged to customer's account).

For delivery abroad, cases, crates and packing materials were charged at cost.

More administration than envisaged

Using the railway entailed a vast paper trail. The general office was unable to deal with this in addition to its other functions, which were fast expanding at the time, for instance with

Goods train being packed on the Lebus private rail sidings just south of Tottenham Hale station

the addition of a telephone switchboard in 1908.

Consequently, administration associated with this had to be fitted into the despatch space B, and E. C. Parford was made manager of rail distribution administration. Disagreements between Parford and railway officials over how much should be charged for the freight led to him fixing his own rates. To protect the firm in case of a challenge being mounted by the railway, Parford kept much additional paperwork This, in turn, led to further pressure on space as goods waiting for despatch could no longer fit in space B. Eventually this led to the expansion into the newly built C2 building.

Parford's caution proved beneficial. LS's *History* describes how, in 1936, the Great Eastern Railway eventually issued a writ of £2,000 for 'deductions not allowed'; it went to court and the firm won its case.

Arthur J. Easter joined Lebus as a 14-year-old in 1906. An article in the *Lebus Log* commented: 'Looking back over the years, many of us can remember Arthur as the

absolute authority on all railway matters – in fact he was the Railway department.'

First road delivery van

The first road van, for London deliveries, was a horse-drawn vehicle with Jo Noblet driving, in 1902. Later there were up to three Foden steam trucks – difficult to steer and prone to accidents.

By 1908 the firm had five Thorneycroft lorries. These had a chassis with detachable open body and solid tyres. While one body was in use, another would be loaded, and when one returned empty the other would be lifted into the chassis for the next journey. Furniture was piled about 12 feet high and held down with canvas and heavy webbing. The drivers had no windscreens to protect them. These were later fitted by the works carpenter, Mr. Dibnah.

Gradual change from rail to road

While the railway continued to be the chief method of distribution, by the early 1920s, lorries were being hired from outside providers. By the end of the 1930s, these amounted to 125 lorries. The East Yard and Gate (to the east of E and south of C2) were developed and extended to accommodate lorries ranging from 800 cubic feet to 1,250 cubic feet.

Lorries and trailers pictured during the interwar years

By the time of the Duke's visit, distribution was entirely by road and almost all within the British Isles. The firm's export market, which had been growing in the period leading up to the outbreak of World War One, was sadly a thing of the past – most of the furniture produced was for the home market.

The Lebus fleet of the 1960s

By the early 1960s, when the new warehouse was functioning to its full capacity, the firm's vehicle fleet had grown to 140. Many of these could be seen lined-up in front of the new warehouse building. These vehicles were a mix of the firm's own and those of its subsidiary, Merchandise Transport.

White Hart Lane Garages, which had joined the Harris Lebus group in March 1961, took over responsibility for the fleet's maintenance and repair. Their premises housed a modern petrol filling station. They provided a full maintenance and repair service for private cars, and they were Vauxhall agents but could also supply any other make of new car. Fred Forrest, transport manager, was ultimately responsible for this, 'the youngest HL interest'. A. W. Jackson was the manager, H. Ryder the assistant manager and Jim Pickavance the technical foreman.

Big, highly polished wooden boxes… by Bob Rust

In a piece written especially for this book and sent to the author, former employee Bob Rust described the Lebus fleet:

> As 'the largest furniture factory in the world', Harris Lebus had the largest fleet of C-licensed goods vehicles. This licence allowed the vehicle owner, usually a manufacturer, to carry goods to anywhere in the British Isles (though they were not permitted to bring anything back, except material for use in the industry).

One of the Lebus lorries of the post-World War Two era

The fleet of 1960s lorries, re-branded 'Europa', pictured in front of the new warehouse north of Ferry Lane on the occasion of Princes Margaret's visit with Oliver, chairman, Leonard Grosbard, chief executive (front), Robert Mahlich production director, and Kenneth Dean, marketing director

Lebus's vans were unusual: the large, flat area on the side – perfect for eye-catching artwork or much-favoured decorative scripts – was never used; just plain grey vans and two words – 'Lebus Furniture'. Anyone passing the factory in Ferry Lane could not miss the row of Luton vans backed onto the loading bank of the huge warehouse.

In the 1950s and 1960s, furniture transported was, in essence, 'big, highly polished wooden boxes'; the volume it occupied led manufacturers to either make or deliver only when it was ordered, say by a retail outlet. This explains the infamous 'six-week wait' for the new dining room set and the row of vans constantly loading. Given its vulnerability to damage in transit, finished furniture items had to be wrapped in special covers, old blankets or hessian wrappers and packed in the van in reverse order to which they would be delivered. Loading was generally done by the driver – as he was responsible for the load – with the help of one or two loaders. This lengthy and skilled process invariably took all day!

I worked with Percy Edwards, Assistant Transport Manager (from Dec 1959). He had the most phenomenal memory for deliveries and geography. As an 'outsider' you were given whatever load was available – a delivery trip could take up to a week. You could put the deliveries in order yourself or, better still say 'Percy, lay this

out for me!' With his help you would be able to go from start to finish and avoid half-day closing – still common then – and in many cases coming up to the delivery so that it was on your nearside or finishing the right street for a back door delivery!

Because of his skill, if management wanted to get hold of a particular driver, Percy was asked. He would check what run they were doing, look at his calendar, think for a moment, then say 'all being well, he will be at…' then name three deliveries.

With the growing cost of transport, and to obviate vans 'full of air', Lebus employed a new carrier with A licences – which allowed picking up return loads. Eventually they took over the fleet, forming the subsidiary Merchandise Transport.

Flat pack finally killed the 'proper' furniture trade.

Rust laments the emergence of flat-pack furniture items of chipboard construction, with hand polishing and finishing consigned to the history books as modern equipment automatically 'finished' furniture pieces. As automation replaced manual workers, union leader Jack Shanley wrote: 'So, can we pause for just a moment to recall an era that is passing before we get on with the job of ensuring we effectively meet the threat of those who would "make robots of us all"' ('Lebus Closes' published in the National Union of Furniture Trade Operatives magazine, *Record*, April 1970).

CHAPTER SIX

Work, Rest and Play: Welfare, Pay and Performance, Break Times and Leisure

'Being in a very large works was a new experience too. After working in small workshops all his life my dad was for the first time very well looked after at Lebus. There was a full medical unit with qualified staff to tend every injury, and a canteen.'

– Marlene McAndrew (recollections as part of the Coombes Croft project)

Drama: Bruce Castle Museum, 24 September 2008: The Lower Levels of Lebus

It is 7.28 p.m. and the room is still filling. The last few people are taking their seats and only a few chairs remain. The talks at Bruce Castle Museum are always well attended and this one is particularly so; unlocking the lower levels of Lebus – the archaeology of the Harris Lebus air-raid shelters – has a wide appeal. The presentation will shortly begin; a buzz of excitement and ripples of anticipation pass through the assembled audience fuelled by the rumours that the Lebus family are here.

LS's sons, Peter and John, are indeed in the audience as guests of honour, along with Oliver Lebus, who wears the crown for tonight. And just as the presentation starts, I gaze at him in awe – just as others may be doing; I have the honour and privilege to sit beside him, and not just because I invited him personally, but because I feel I want to be with him, and right beside him on this occasion. I feel a bond with Oliver.

As Peter, John and Oliver are introduced, the crowd shows its appreciation in the customary way. With planning consultant Jon Lowe introduced and the lights dimmed, I glance again to my right – a twinkle in Oliver's eye is as bright as any star.

Jon Lowe's presentation takes the audience archeologically through the underground chambers of the Second World War bomb shelters; rusted helmets, frayed lighting cables, painted signage and graffiti, wooden bunk beds and toilet seats were all afloat in muddied water – the tunnels that time seemingly forgot.

Except, at least one of the audience had been there… back in time, and Oliver remembers vividly. And when invited to share his recollections, he does so eagerly and with relish: 'Soon after the war started it was decided that the time taken to reach the shelters and return to work was too long both in terms of personal safety and waste of war effort. So instead, we built reinforced concrete shelters, enough for all our employees next to each major workstation. We had electric signs in different colours installed throughout the factory showing employees what to do. As time went on people didn't go to the shelters until the buzzers actually sounded!'

Perceptions of Lebus as an Employer

The firm's attitude to its employees is perhaps most obviously demonstrated through its building of a very fine example of an air-raid shelter. To construct a network of shelters 530-feet long, five-feet wide and seven-feet-and-three-inches high, complete with camouflaged over-ground look-out posts, an underground control room with telephone connection to the factory and to the local gun-sites for early warning, was a monumental commitment by the firm for the welfare and protection of its employees. There was adequate space for each and every worker, accessed through a safe tunnel under one of the arches of Ferry Lane humpback bridge. A considerable amount of work was undertaken in the shelters' construction. A visit by the then home secretary, John Anderson – creator of the 'Anderson shelters' – in the summer of 1939 praised the firm for its achievements.

As the war progressed, this network of underground shelters was, apparently, given over for the use of local residents to protect

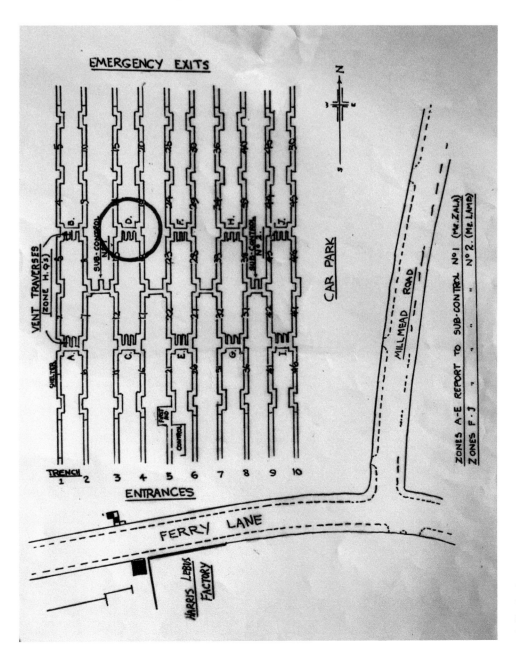

A plan of the company's air-raid shelters north of Ferry Lane

Inside the air-raid shelters

against night air raids (although there is no official record of this). The other set of reinforced concrete war shelters that had subsequently been constructed next to every workshop were used by employees instead. Those shelters constructed for exclusive use by senior officers on night duty sited within C2 shop acquired the nickname 'Millionaires' Row'.

Whilst a cynic might argue that the provision of air-raid shelters on site was merely an investment to save valuable production time from being lost as a consequence of air raids, providing protection to all employees may be viewed as an acknowledgement of the valuable asset they were to the firm.

'We were in great danger'

As part of the Coombes Croft project in 2008, Mrs. Daphne Bradley recounted her experience of the shelters during the war:

> Quite frequently there were air raids and we had notices all over the factory that would light up when the air raid sirens sounded. We had men on the roof who were called 'roof spotters'. When the sign 'ALERT' lit up, it meant that the air raid siren had sounded. We wouldn't have heard it with all the noises in the factory. We carried on working until the sign 'TAKE COVER' was lit up. Every machine had to then be turned off and I had to lock up the drawings and we had to make our way to the brick-built shelters which were all over the factory. We were in great danger because we were a target for the enemy because of all the things which were being made at Harris Lebus. When the danger was over and the all clear siren had sounded, the words 'ALL CLEAR' would

An employee stands between Handley Page fuselages with his foot on what looks suspiciously like ammunition!

light up. We would then return to work. Sometimes we were in the shelters for half an hour, and sometimes for two or three hours, maybe more.

Contrasting perceptions to reconcile

LS wrote: 'Both pay and working conditions were ahead of those existing… in the trade.' He continued by saying that firm achieved this 'long before such things became the commonplace of the welfare state'.

On the other hand, a statement made by the authors in *Furnishing the World* contrasts with those of the firm: 'It may have been the largest furniture factory in the country, but trade unionists reckoned Lebus to be "as bad as the worst in this country" for working conditions'.

The dissentient view needs to be balanced by consideration of actual provisions made by the firm around welfare, conditions, pay and performance, break times and leisure activities, combined with recourse to available reminiscences made, importantly, in the employees' own words. And alongside any influence exerted by the unions, the firm was, in any case, obliged to comply with legislation, such as the Factory Acts.

Welfare at Work

'The following notice is posted in the works: "The firm offers advice and assistance in cases of serious illness, or other serious trouble to ALL employees, their immediate family or dependants. In such cases Mr. A. C. Harris should be approached personally and without delay by those concerned or others on their behalf."'

– 1939 Lebus employee handbook titled 'Something about the works and the workers'

A worker's 'friend'

Between the wars, a worker's 'friend' service was provided by A. C. Harris, who was at that time assistant works manager. LS explains that from the early days of the Finsbury Cabinet Works, 'welfare was looked after in

some measure by the partners through the benevolent individual named Alfred William Perrin'. Perrin, the manager of the Carvers' workshop, was not only renowned for his wood-carving skills but 'his ability to cut fingernails with exacting precision to remove obstinate splinters!' He also provided some emotional support to workers.

'Call the witness – Mr. Alfred William Perrin'

The firm was making compensation payments to an ex-employee (subject to court rulings) who had suffered an injury at work; Alfred Perrin represented the firm in Tottenham Courthouse as the firm disputed a specific 'welfare payment'.

With reference to the *Tottenham and Edmonton Weekly Herald*, it was the week beginning 1 April 1912. The background to the case was that Harold Humphreys fractured his leg at work, which had left him with a left leg a quarter of an inch shorter than the right. A compensation order of seven shillings and sixpence a week had been awarded by the court the preceding September; however, this had subsequently been stopped by the firm as from 8 February 1912 because they felt Humphreys had recovered and 'whatever incapacity that was urged could only be "assumed" incapacity' (*Tottenham and Edmonton Weekly Herald*, 1 April 1912).

A fellow Lebus employee, Perrin, had witnessed Humphreys walking apparently comfortably – both lived very near the factory. Perrin told the court this had been on 21 October last, shortly after the compensation order was made: 'In that respect I was somewhat surprised, that he appeared to be walking comfortably. As I saw him, on his feet, walking, and thinking he was recovering, I made him an offer of some light work, just light duties… indoors, but Harold declined.'

Perrin recalled the accident had taken place at the time of the Coronation of George V, a couple of days after; it was 24 June, a Saturday, during the morning. 'Harold was covering some wood in our timber field… it is kept in piles…

in sticks… as part of the seasoning process…
[A]s he was covering this pile with a tarpaulin
and reaching over one of the logs must have
dislodged and struck him.'

Charles Hooper (the solicitor acting for the
firm) told the court that he and Humphreys
walked together 'for some distance' and at 'at
four miles an hour'.

When asked to give his account, Humphreys
told the court that since the accident he'd never
been able to walk properly without a stick.
When asked by the judge why he had refused
the offer of light duties, he claimed that it was
not safe… not safe to walk on his leg.

The *Tottenham and Edmonton Weekly Herald*,
5 April 1912, gives the verdict: '[T]he
respondent was examined in an ante-room by
the medical assessor, Dr. M. Houghton, who
found that there was nothing the matter with
him – His Honour terminated the award from
February 24.'

Personnel department

'Any problems, you could go to the Personnel
Officer, say borrow some money. They'd lend
it to you and stop it out your wages.'

– Ron Turton, former employee (recollections
as part of the Coombes Croft project)

Following the Factory and Workshop Act
of January 1937 and the need to change
from informal welfare work to a structured
Personnel department, Mr. Alexander Raymond
Lamb (known as Raymond) was given
that brief. Lamb established a fully-fledged
Personnel department, which was located in
the old brass room, and he did a great job.
He 'visited the sick and dealt with scores of
personal problems' (*Lebus Log*, No. 27, August
1964). The country was on the cusp of war,
which would test the firm's welfare provision
– the Personnel department 'was enlarged
and carried a tremendous load' during World
War Two, confirmed the *Lebus Log*. Lamb's
background did not readily suggest him for
the role. He had been with the firm for six
years, having joined with previous experience

as a junior manager with Herrburger Brooks,
piano manufacturers. His first job at Lebus was
foreman polisher, before joining Edmund Zala
as assistant inspector in zones Two and Three
and ultimately taking charge of shop 12. In July
1947, he joined the board of directors when the
company went public, eventually retiring in
1964.

Pulling together – help is at hand in World War Two

The firm would employ 6,000 people, in two
12-hour shifts, during the war. Aside from
the obvious need to conserve materials, avoid
waste and encourage maximum effort of
efficiency in production, the emergence of the
'war spirit' meant there was no shortage of
volunteers who could be called upon, on a rota
basis, for various war-related welfare duties.
'The results were outstanding,' confirmed
LS. 'All this was stimulated by the liveliest
propaganda, much of the poster work being
produced by local talent'.

Home Guard

Bernard Humphrey organised the various
air-raid precautions. From the outset, a fully
equipped volunteer Home Guard Service
was established and training lectures were
organised. The first sergeant of the Harris
Lebus Home Guard was A. C. Stark, one of the
firm's Scottish sales representatives, who had
been a captain in World War One, according
to LS in his *History*. Sid Bracken was also a
Lebus Home Guard sergeant. He joined the
firm in 1928 and was trained by Fred Trew
and Edmund Zala. For a while he had been an
MC at boxing tournaments, including at the
Royal Albert Hall, and he had the commanding
voice that went with the sergeant's role. In later
years, as foreman of the makers in shop 22,
he reminisced about the time they 'had only
short guns and wooden dummies to drill with!'
(*Lebus Log*, No. 17, July 1960)

Fire-fighting service

Sensible precautions already existed to protect
workers and infrastructure in what was a
highly combustible environment. There was
a small-scale voluntary fire service, under

Top left: Harris Lebus Home Guard

Left: Decontamination Squad

Above: Volunteer Fire Brigade

the charge of a former London Fire Brigade officer, which was considerably strengthened at the outbreak of war. The 'pukka' Lebus Fire Brigade, as described by LS, comprised 60 employees, including Desmond Stratton, Alf Brown, L. Courtney and Frank Forrest, and its remit was to cover both the factory and Tabernacle Street.

Olive Mayo – who joined Lebus from school in 1935, helping calculate the value of freshly delivered wood stocks – recalls here one of the many talents required of a firefighter!

> When I joined the Auxiliary Fire Service, I ended up some nights back at Lebus where they had organised entertainment for the night workers to distract from the threat of air raids. To my great surprise and embarrassment, I was marched from fire duty to where this so-called 'entertainment' happened and told I was to do an act, tap dancing and community singing. I was not equipped or of any use for either!

Olive Mayo

Sir Herman Lebus next to the main fire-alarm circuit board, which would show the location of a fire alarm when triggered

(Reproduced with special permission from Waltham Forest Local History Archives, Vestry House Museum)

Decontamination Squad and Heavy-Duty Gang

There was also a Decontamination Squad and a Heavy-Duty Gang, all trained for demolition and rescue work, in case this was needed following air raids. Commendably, the Heavy-Duty Gang's service was available to employees who suffered bombed-out homes. And they were indeed called out – in one incident a worker who was unloading a landing craft into the River Lea saw a bomb fall in the vicinity of his home; he ran there to find his house destroyed and his wife killed.

'In addition,' described LS, 'there were drives in aid of the Red Cross' to complement the firm's permanent medical facilities.

First aid and medical facilities

Just as the firm had precautions around fire hazards, the provision of medical aid located in U building was established early on – a general physician was available at set times and not just for work-related injuries. With the advent of World War One, a modern, fit-for-purpose first aid and general medical facility had been developed, which would serve the firm well in World War Two. The surgery, with therapy rooms, north of R workshop, provided separate sections for women and men, and in later years a dental practitioner. Writing of the 1950s (in recollections produced for this book), Peter Baker recalled that it was 'fully staffed by qualified nurses, and a doctor was on call, whenever the factory was working, usually for at least sixteen hours per day, five-and-a-half days a week'. Marian Cotton (Coombes Croft project) remembered: '[The] Section Heads had a First Aid box. I don't know if they were used or not. Just for cuts and scratches. I think it was there by law.' As part of the project, Hilda Hewitt recalled that her husband Bill 'went to the nurse to get some ointment from there to put on our son's bruises. I don't remember he had any injuries himself.'

A nurse provides treatment in the doctor's surgery

(Reproduced with special permission from Waltham Forest Local History Archives, Vestry House Museum)

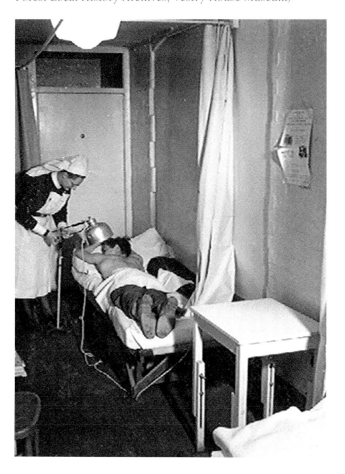

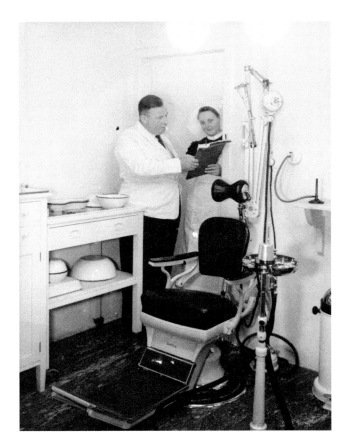

Dentist

(Reproduced with special permission from Waltham Forest Local History Archives, Vestry House Museum)

Minor injuries and risks

Successive Factory Acts made increasing provisions around what would now be termed 'health and safety'. These were consolidated in the 1959 and 1961 acts (the latter being substantially still in force) that imposed more stringent regulations. (Workplace health and safety is now principally governed by the Health and Safety at Work etc. Act 1974.) Despite the potential for injury – Harold Humphreys' fractured leg was one example – recorded incidents are few and far between. This may be due to the fact that no internal records exist and records of the Prince of Wales General Hospital are not available. However, it may also be because the quality of the firm's medical provisions was such that incidents were adequately responded to and very few cases went 'beyond those four walls'.

Ron Turton remembered a minor accident during the 1950s:

> There were twelve polishing lines in there. We had rails, very dangerous. You're holding your job back and doing it, and it comes to the end of the rail and it drops back. One of the women, Annie, had a wardrobe fall on her. Women worked there on the dining line, dining tables – you couldn't expect them to do 'robes, you'd got to lift them on and off, too heavy.

Ivy Eden, a friend of Daphne Bradley (who looked after the drawings in World War Two), worked on a circular saw. Daphne says of her friend: 'One day she did catch her finger under the drill. Probably she was tired, especially if there had been an air raid during the night.'

An open well in the office floor

It was not only in the workshops that risks were evident but also in the office spaces; these were not purpose-built but rather 'squeezed in' – such as those in C building (originally designed for warehousing furniture). LS wrote: '[I]t was somewhat rudimentary; there was an open well in the floors at the time and the offices had the full benefit of ventilation from below!'

Marion Cotton, describing her workspace, said: 'It was pretty cold because it was cement flooring. Our office was in a single-storey building with a glass roof.'

Ron Turton, on the other hand, thought this made it warmer: 'Glass roofs – in the summer they gave you salt tablets. Imagine doing that now!' He added that there were 'great big heaters overhead, big square things; not cold in the winter, used to sweat in the summer.'

Sawdust clouds in the air

Many of the machines were not fitted with basic dust units to collect sawdust and woodchips in sacks; they had pipes that simply blew sawdust clouds into the air and over the floor, from which it was manually swept and carted off in barrows to the furnace for burning.

Spray polishing – walls of continuous running water

The spray-polishing shop seems to have stuck in the minds of those who worked there. Daphne Bradley suggested: '[T]hese people had to drink a pint of milk a day which was supplied to them because of the danger to their lungs.' On the other hand, Sissy Lewis stated: '[P]eople used to say we should have milk on a job like this, but we never did. The spray never made me feel funny. When visitors came round, they used to put handkerchiefs to their noses 'cos of the smell of cellulose. It smelt like nail varnish. We didn't have masks or special clothing either' (*Furnishing the World*).

Gordon Shepherd's recollections (Coombes Croft project) contradict the above: '[W]here they had spraying, masks were supplied. We didn't need them. I had an apron, thick white cotton twill apron and carpenter's apron… they had continuous running water down the walls to take the fumes and the residue away.' Ron Turton recalled: '[T]he fans were terrific, the suction was that good, took all the fumes away.'

'My Tea Trolley Run of Fear' by Phyllis Roberts

Former employee Phyllis Roberts shared her experiences of negotiating through the spraying workshop accompanied by a tea trolley:

> Used to have to take this trolley to different 'shops', you know, like the spray shops and all this. And they had a conveyor belt going across, you know, from one section to another in this corridor and you had to get this… manoeuvre this trolley over, in, between wardrobes that'd be finished there, and they'd be coming up and down to be sprayed, and you'd got to try and get… and that frightened the hell out of me! I thought to myself what am I going to do if I'm on my own? 'Cos I had visions of just going up and getting sprayed and all… along with the wardrobes!

Dodging loaded furniture trucks for a comfort break

Marian Cotton talked of the hazards involved simply in taking a comfort break:

> I remember that the toilets were situated quite some way from our workstation and access to them was through a part of the factory where workmen pulled trucks loaded with wooden furniture parts along metal tracks like railway lines, set into the concrete floors. Huge oval mirrors were set at intervals so that the 'traffic' could be seen and moved with safety.

Open belt shafts – invisible in the flood waters

Probably some of the most dangerous times in the factory were caused by flooding from the River Lea. The belt shafts would fill with flood water and the wooden slatted coverings would float off in all directions, making it impossible to see where they were. Inevitably workers would fall in a shaft, to waist-height. Whilst flood tides were beyond control, it seems surprising that a factory engaged in moulding and fixing wood did not devise a system to secure the shaft coverings with a hinge and lock mechanism.

The inability to see underground shaft pits during flooding, reduced visibility exacerbated by sawdust clouds, poor lighting, early mechanised saws, 'runners' dodging heavy furniture items on 'skates', and vats of ammonia – these would certainly give the risk assessors of today a major headache.

Tottenham and Edmonton Weekly Herald,
30 September 1932

Killed at Lebus' Factory – Ambulance Men Extricate Victim

> This week's budget of mishaps includes a distressing fatality at Messrs Harris Lebus Cabinet Works at Ferry Lane. It occurred at 11.00 p.m. on Monday. William Bolton, aged 20, of 125 Durban Road, Tottenham, was ascending in an electric lift, intending

to take a load of timber from the ground floor to the first-floor workshop. The lift did not stop at the first floor, and the unfortunate employee was caught between the timber and the side of the shafting. He was wedged tightly against the shafting and could not be extricated until members of the Tottenham ambulance service were summoned to the works. The utility van was driven in, and the officers, using grip ladders, secured the pinioned man and applied artificial respiration and oxygen on the way to the hospital. When

Dr. Ross, one of the house surgeons, examined him it was ascertained that Bolton was dead, his neck having been broken by the force of the impact.

Another employee, John Mansell, Kings Parade Buildings, Tottenham, was in the lift with Bolton at the time.

The inquest will be held at Tottenham Court House this [Friday] morning.

The verdict – accidental death – reported in the local paper the following week acknowledged a factory rule 'not to sit on top of the load in the lift' had been contravened by the victim, and that the lever 'must have been out of order'. In his witness account, John Mansell, aged 16, the night charge-hand, said Bolton sat on top of a truck of 330 planks of deal wood that had been wheeled into the lift because 'there was no room on the lift floor'; he confessed that he had told Bolton to do that. Mansell described in harrowing detail how Bolton shouted down 'I'm getting hurt' and how he shouted back, 'Pull down the lever of the switch to stop the lift'. The switch was shoulder-height. Bolton shouted, 'I have, and it won't work. The lift won't stop'. Mansell described how Bolton started screaming for help and then the lift stopped.

The only explanation he could give was that Bolton had dislodged the load while reaching for the switch. During the hearing, the large, brass lift operating lever was actually fully demonstrated – the handle dropped and

stopped the lift when one's hand was removed from it.

Mr. H. Chasteney, H. M. Inspector of Factories, asked Mansell whether he had found the handle 'stuck up' instead of going down the dial when the hand was taken off. Mansell said he 'was too upset to notice whether the lever was turned down or up'. He had never known that to happen – 'the lift would go on climbing if that occurred'.

Bernard Humphrey, the company's chief engineer, told the hearing that all the safety devices were in working order after the accident and that he had 'tested them one by one'; it had been tested by the insurance expert on 23 May and in June. However, he 'found that the spring of the lift lever was broken in two' and said that 'this might have prevented the switch lever from working and caused the lift lever to stick up'.

Under questioning, Humphrey conceded Bolton was 'not experienced enough to realise the dangers involved' but that 'anybody could work that [lever]'. Humphrey stated: 'Had we known in time [he was sitting on the load] we would have taken drastic action immediately.'

Asked by the coroner whether there might not have been a tragedy had the lever operated correctly and caused the lift to stop promptly, Humphrey replied, 'Perhaps so.'

William Bolton had been employed for only five months. Dr. H. Ross, surgeon at the Prince of Wales General Hospital, confirmed that he died almost instantly. Sub-officer Ernest Wakeford of the Tottenham Fire Brigade told the inquest that he had helped to remove the victim 'who was on the floor of the lift in a crouching position with one leg doubled up under him and the other hanging over the side, wedged between the lift and the wall'.

The coroner noted the firm's intention to place 'safety devices wherever possible… so that such a tragedy will not occur again' and added that 'they need not go beyond what they already have in operation'.

Mark Bailey – an ambulance driver's experience

Former fire-fighter Mark Bailey covered an area that included the Finsbury Cabinet Works and wrote the following for the author for use in this book:

During the late '50s, having found my way in and out of several factory jobs, I decided to follow my late father's footsteps and join the Middlesex Ambulance Service. By 1964, I was based at Tottenham Fire Station (next to the Town Hall) working on the Front-Line Emergency vehicle.

It was the practice within the service that the two-man crew took daily turns to drive or attend the patient. And so it happened that the first time we got a call to the Lebus Factory, I (as duty driver) knew exactly where to locate the Surgery.

Six years earlier, although having been aware of the factory for some years, my first, and only, comprehensive visit took place during the early summer of 1953 whilst attending Page Green Secondary Modern School in Broad Lane.

Although having little recollection of the Polishing or Upholstery sections, I clearly remember the long West Main Corridor and adjoining passage to the parallel East Main Corridor.

Continuing southwards, one came to the timber yard with its drying kilns and stacks of timber that were in the constant process of being unloaded from the Thames lighters or barges. These vast steel vessels were a familiar sight along the River Lea (and we were used to constant school warnings never to attempt to board or play on them, as they were very dangerous). The loaded lighters, sitting quite low in the water, had been towed from the London Docks, the timber having originally arrived there on ships from around the world. Once emptied, the lighters sat very high up on the water, and it was not unknown for workmen and

foolish children to fall into the deep cargo hold. Even worse, if one fell into the water, the steep sides and undercut bow and stern made it impossible to climb out. Also… they were often moored two or three deep, [which] meant that a victim could easily be crushed between them.

After the relative quiet of the timber yard, the shock of entering the Mill shop was staggering; the noise, dust and frantic activity. It was at this point that I decided that I never, ever wanted to work in a factory. Certainly, the sub-assembly shop was a little more civilised. But for the life of me I cannot recall seeing any finished furniture during that visit.

I have quite strong memories of the southern end of the works, particularly of the cluttered east–west roadway. I recall that here, as in the main north–south entry road, both lorries and large removal type vans were usually to be seen, along with trailers, factory trolleys and the like, loaded with both raw timber and part-constructed items.

It was via this crowded route that emergency ambulances had to find their way from Ferry Lane to the southern end of the West Main Corridor in order to collect the more seriously injured workers and rush them to the Casualty unit of the nearby Prince of Wales General Hospital in Tynemouth Road.

As you may imagine, given the size and complexity of the factory, the types of potential accidents (not to mention general illness) were unlimited. Fortunately, the Surgery was well equipped for all but the most serious events, and so visiting ambulance crews usually had a fairly easy time. That said, we never did understand why it was located in such an inaccessible position – that long walk along the West Main Corridor could be something of a trial, particularly when dealing with a stretcher case.

Pay and Performance

The Factory Act 1856 had set the working week at a maximum of 60 hours; these had been reduced to 56 for women only in the Act of 1878. LS confirmed the hours at the Finsbury Cabinet Works before World War One were 60 a week, from 7.00 a.m. to 7.00 p.m.; office hours were 9.00 a.m. to 7.00 p.m. on weekdays and 9.00 a.m. to 1.00 p.m. on Saturdays. Days were long and break times were regimented at half an hour for breakfast and lunch – and must have been much welcomed. These evolved as the length of the working day was shortened: lunchtimes were lengthened to an hour, and morning and afternoon breaks of 10 and later 15 minutes introduced.

Timekeeping and discipline were part and parcel of working life; LS mentioned that the firm's clocks were often covered in old sackcloth to prevent 'clock-watching' during working hours. The firm even had a dedicated clock-keeper, Ernest Shepherd (known as 'Shep'). He came to the firm in 1919 to wind all the clocks, numbering some 76 in all. He continued to do so, part-time (he also worked for a clock-repair firm), for 45 years.

'The Foremen were always on the prowl…'

LS described how the foreman in each workshop had offices built up on stilts, giving them a vantage point from which to watch over every worker. Women were employed only as polishers before World War One; Elsie Lambert, a polisher working between 1902 and 1905, said that she 'worked from 8.00 a.m. to 6.00 p.m.', which is ten hours a day and 50 for a week; she does not mention Saturday working. Charge-hands worked to foremen; Elsie remembered: 'The foremen were always on the prowl', although her comment that she 'could talk to neighbouring workers' suggests some relaxation in discipline. A foreman's attire was as formal as his discipline was strict. Frank Stuckey was one such foreman. He joined in 1923 as a general machinist and was soon promoted to foreman of the Machine shop, later rising to the rank of deputy chief inspector, quality controller. The *Lebus Log* described how he wore the traditional garb of the foreman of

the day – a bowler hat and brown suit (*Lebus Log*, No.18, December 1960).

Hourly pay and 'piecework'

LS wrote about pay and the early days at the Finsbury Cabinet Works: 'The majority of workers were paid on a weekly basis in accordance with a signed Indenture; A full rate man took up to £2 12s 6d a week.' However, he does not specify how this figure was calculated.

Makers, however, worked to a piecework formula – a productivity rate based on the number of furniture items processed. In the makers' workshop, Joseph Clohosy was in charge and fixed the piecework prices. According to LS 'There was little or no argument with the men'. If they chose, a maker could employ a boy or two to help and then pay them directly from their own wages.

Charlie Holland the crate-maker

The *Lebus Log*, No. 13, December 1958 sheds light on Charlie Holland's story and his pay within the factory's first decade, which appear to fit an emergent general pattern.

When Holland joined the firm as a 14-year-old in 1903, he recalled earning one penny an hour as a crate-maker, a total of five shillings and sixpence a week. Four shillings went to his mum to pay for his keep and he could have a night out with his girlfriend, taking in a show (it was the age before cinemas), a drink and a fish and chip supper – all for sixpence.

After two months, he left to work at a case-making firm in the East End before returning to the firm again in 1908 to start a 50-year career with Harris Lebus. On his return, he was a 'piece-maker' in charge of nine men making furniture packing crates; after paying them, he made a total, with bonuses, of £2 a week take-home pay (*Lebus Log*, No. 13, December 1958).

Sol's annual bonus scheme

In practice, there was a degree of inequality in the pay structure, especially when annual Christmas bonuses paid at Sol's discretion

– some exceptionally generous – were factored in.

Some surviving pages from Sol's personal notebook quoted in LS's *History* show him effectively working two systems. Perhaps unsurprisingly, Joseph Clohosy was one of the top bonus earners, with a bonus of £10 and a special bonus of £100 on Christmas Day 1902. Basil Archer, chief designer, received £25 plus £40; Alfred Perrin, in charge of the carvers, received £20; Fred Trew, sample-maker, received £12 10s; and Mr. Brooks, in charge of Despatch, £7 10s.

Good boy / bad boy

An apprenticeship as a polisher was a five-year course for young men joining at 15 or 16. According to LS, starting pay was 10s 6d a week, rising by 2 shillings a year. 'If he was a good boy in any particular week, he got extra pocket money of 2 shillings.' LS added that polishers worked to piecework rates: 'After three years as an apprentice a polisher could join the piecework rate scheme whilst still in training but their earnings would be capped at 30 shillings a week, regardless of how many

furniture pieces polished. If he misbehaved, some of them did, he was reduced to his apprenticeship rate.'

Beatrice the polisher

Beatrice Wright started work with the firm shortly before the outbreak of World War One as an apprentice French polisher at the age of 14. For a man, the apprenticeship involved a five-year apprenticeship; for a woman, 'almost as long', and her apprenticeship began at 5 shillings a week, apparently half what a man would earn (*Lebus Log*, No. 14, July 1959).

Early apprenticeship indentures and pay

Some early apprenticeship indentures throw some further light on pay progression. For example, the five-year apprenticeship indenture of Albert Church, who joined the firm on 24 March 1898 (as a new boy, he was the early-morning gas-lamp lighter at Tabernacle Street), stated his weekly pay would rise from 4 shillings to 5, 7, 10 and 14 respectively for each of his first five years. Eight years later, when George Daughters joined the firm on 28 January 1906 (he was the son of Edward

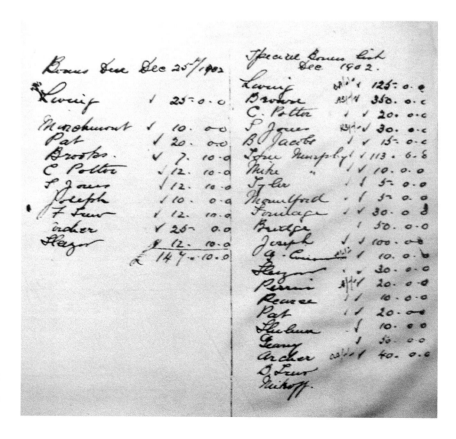

Sol's personal notebook: a list of workers and their bonuses, Christmas 1902

Daughters, the Marshall-engine driver) on a
five-year apprenticeship as a machinist, his
indenture showed his pay starting at 8 shillings
a week, rising by 2 shillings a year for the first
three years, and then to 15 shillings and 18
shillings in years four and five respectively. By
contrast, William Flemming, who also joined
in 1906, starts and remains static at 10 shillings
pay a week.

Indentures compared

From the copies of four early indentures
available, a pattern of pay seems indiscernible.
There are other differences of note: the five-
year indentures of Albert Church and George

Daughters are on a standard template (No. 280)
by Waterlow and Sons Limited, and record
their fathers' consent; those of James Douse
and William Flemming are on a different
template in which the term is specified as three
years and the wages set accordingly.

Harris Lebus personally signed those of
Church, Daughters and Flemming, whereas the
one for Douse is signed by Herman Lebus.

Church's and Daughters' indentures showed
their fathers agreeing to provide 'sufficient
food, clothing, lodging and other necessaries
for the said apprentice'. There are additional

hand-written terms to both indentures such as 'all bank holidays allowed'.

Daughters is required to 'do and perform work during hours regulated by the firm' and his indenture stated that 'no wages will be paid during sickness and if the works should close for any other purpose other than holidays'. For Church (who was working at Tabernacle Street as the early-morning gas-lamp lighter) his hours are specified as '8.00 a.m. until 8.00 p.m. in winter and 6.00 a.m. until 6.00 p.m. in summer; and interestingly, he appeared to be entitled to sick pay – 'doctor's certificate to be sent in cases of sickness'.

Douse's and Flemming's indentures do not specify working hours and have printed, standard terms such as No. 2 – 'No payment to be paid to the Workman whilst absent from work either on account of holidays, ill health, accident or from any cause (similar or otherwise) whatsoever' – and No. 5 – 'The Masters can determine this agreement upon giving to the Workman a week's notice in the event of the Factory where the Workman is employed being either burnt down, injured or destroyed by fire, tempest or boiler or other explosion'.

One commonality between all indentures is the agreement 'not to divulge the Masters' secrets', and in the case of the indenture template used for Douse and Flemming specifically even prohibited divulging 'the terms of this Agreement'. They also agreed not to strike, rule No. 4 of their indenture stating: 'And in consideration of this Agreement the Workman further agrees with the Master to stand by and diligently work for his Masters and not withstanding any trade dispute strike or combination of workmen and the Workman will use his best endeavours as far as he is able to prevent any trade dispute arising or strike taking place at the Master's business.'

Evidence of divulging content to the unions

Three of these indentures came from Lebus family archives. William Flemming's was found in a pile of ephemera at the Geffrye Museum. It had been donated by Jack Moss – a pre-World War One union organiser then living at Myddleton Road, Wood Green, N22 – and may well have influenced the content of the book *Furnishing the World*.

The firm and the unions

The authors of *Furnishing the World* constructed their argument about the reputation of the firm around a specific episode in labour relations. Post-World War One, industrial relations in the furniture industry were particularly turbulent. The specific issues cited at Lebus were union recognition itself and piecework, or, to use the accepted term, 'Payment By Results' (PBR).

The National Amalgamated Furnishing Trades Association (NAFTA) established a branch in Tottenham in 1918 with Harris Lebus in their sights. However, it would not be until 1939 and the advent of World War Two that the firm would eventually become unionised.

Women wanted

Women were employed in large numbers in furniture manufacturing at the beginning of World War One when the immediate impact of large numbers of male workers signing up was felt. This prompted the first push by the unions.

The National Amalgamated Furnishing Trades Association (NAFTA) was formed in 1902 when the Alliance Cabinet Makers Association (1865) amalgamated with the United Operative Cabinet and Chair-makers Society of Scotland. In 1914, NAFTA wrote to the War Office to complain about employment practice at the firm, inferring either women or immigrants were taking jobs from men and being poorly paid.

In a letter dated 22 September 1914 to the director of contracts, War Office, Whitehall, Organising Secretary Mr. F. Bramley wrote:

> We hear also that Messrs Lebus of Tottenham have secured War Office work. It is nothing short of a scandal that East End sweaters should be supplied with orders from your department during which time respectable employers have their factories closed and British workmen walk the streets.

Post-World War One agreements made within the firm

A Tottenham NAFTA branch was organised under the then General Secretary Jack Cohen in 1919 at the same time as the firm was organising meetings with workers to reach agreement on terms and conditions going forward. Some agreements reached in this process would effectively discriminate against the recruitment and employment of women. The agreed rules were made at two conferences held at Tottenham on 13 December 1918 and 1 January 1919 and were then printed and distributed in a pocket-size book, *Lebus's Workers Committee Rules*. Amongst those present at these meetings were Sol and Louis Lebus, Jack Cohen, C. F. Hawkins, J. Dagger, Frank Geary (representing the employers), A. C. Harris (then Finsbury Cabinet Works' assistant manager) and delegates from the various sections of workers employed by the firm – women as well as men.

The rules affecting women were No. 11 – 'that women would be employed only on processes they were engaged on before the war' – and No. 10 – 'the present staff of female polishers to remain, but *no* additional females to be employed, until the male staff equal the present number of females'. The fact that women were empowered in decision making is admirable; they essentially agreed to discrimination – presumably in accepting the inevitability of returning ex-servicemen being given preference for jobs. However, Beatrice Wright – by then Mrs. Briggs and mother of two daughters, Beatrice (junior) and Vera – was re-employed (after redundancy at the beginning of the war) as a spray polisher; she was earning £2 10s. She commented: '[A] loaf was two-and-a-half pence, twenty cigarettes eleven-and-a-half pence, and margarine… we couldn't afford butter… was four-and-a-half pence a pound.' *Furnishing the World* states: 'Women's rates were two-thirds of the male rate'.

A five-day week of 47 hours

Curiously, rule No. 4 of the *Workers Committee Rules* stated: '50 hours to be the working week'. *Furnishing the World* stated: 'In December 1918 a Joint Industrial Council for the Furniture Industry – employers and the main trade unions, was established to regulate and oversee wages, hours, production, grievance, health and safety and education'. NAFTA argued for a 44-hour week, but the employers would only concede 47. That said, LS stated that 'during 1919 the five-day working week was inaugurated' and that 'the full-time hours were reduced to forty-seven'; they had been reduced to 50 by the end of World War One and he adds that when changed, 'the hourly rate was raised so that no one earned less money'.

Pay structure – hourly versus 'piecework' rates

The hourly rate pay structure agreed at the aforementioned winter set of meetings was summarised in rule No. 2:

> A minimum rate of one shilling eight and three-quarters pence per hour, with extra 1d per hour for spindle and four-cutter machinists, to all sections of workers to whom it has been applied by agreement between employers' federation and the trade unions. French polishers to receive the cabinet trade rate agreed to in a similar manner; female polishers to receive 11d per hour (pending a district rate being agreed upon).

LS put it another way: 'Spindle hands and Four-cutter Machinists were paid an hourly rate of one shilling nine and three-quarters pence, while Machinists, Cabinet-makers and Fitters were paid one shilling eight and three-quarters pence, and French Polishers one shilling five-and-a-half pence' (the women's rate was 11 pence).

However, within a few years of agreeing these rates, the firm wished to move away from day rates, which had been in place during and since the war, and revert to piecework (PBR), which had been the norm before the war. The firm put forward a list of rates for 'comment', said LS. In principle, NAFTA opposed PBR.

The firm and unions clash – the strike of 1923

The strike at Harris Lebus in 1923 was part of a country-wide dispute during which local trades unions were galvanised at a national level and clashed with employers over pay and conditions. Of the strike, LS said that 'with the exception of a few old faithfuls the entire works went on strike' in the face of what felt, to some, like an ultimatum. *Furnishing the World* estimated the figure was 600 cabinet-makers out of a total workforce of 3,500. With unemployment rates high, the firm was inundated with applications and LS said 'many of the strikers drifted back'. (It is thought this was in 1923, although a letter by the firm's solicitors refers to it as 1926.) At the end of the dispute, the firm was still non-union with PBR in operation and for NAFTA this felt like a crushing defeat. Meanwhile, at the firm's upholstery production unit in Tabernacle Street, most upholsterers had long worked to a PBR pay structure. The Amalgamated Union of Upholsters (AUU) accepted PBR, thus putting them at odds with NAFTA.

In Tabernacle Street on 3 January 1929, George Ernest Chaplin signed a five-year upholstery apprenticeship – which he had actually begun the previous November. Both the pay and conditions are significant: Chaplin's indenture is on a similar Waterlow and Sons Limited template to that of Albert Church and George Daughters, both signed some twenty years earlier. Version 208*A* of Waterlow and Sons Limited indenture template signed by Bob Lebus has on it, in hand-written script, the following: 'The said apprentice shall do and perform work during the hours as regulated by the firm. All bank holidays allowed. No wages will be paid whilst absent through sickness, nor if the factory or works should be closed for other purposes other than holidays.' Starting pay had not increased much in the intervening period and Daughters' initial salary was still only ten shillings per week, rising every year by a further three shillings for the first eight years and in the ninth year to 34 shillings, and so by 1939 he would be earning 40 shillings per week.

In *Furnishing the World* it was suggested that, by 1930, machinists (making the parts) had become as important as cabinet-makers (assembling the parts), and the full London rate

for a 47-hour week was the same for both at 82s 3d. Looking back at the early indentures, the apprentices were given a variety of titles, for instance George Daughters was described as a machinist and Albert Church as a carver. In the words of union leader Jack Shanley in *Furnishing the World*, machines 'took away the cabinet maker's arms and shoulders. It took away the graft. The machines were far more accurate… [B]earings make the machine… able to run to finer and finer limits. Now each machine was separate, and the craftsmen were in front of their machine feeding it. There'd be a labourer behind taking it all off and putting it on a trolley and conveying it to the next machine where the machinist took it through the next process.'

Rising to general foreman of Upholstery, George Chaplin seemed to have kept relations between management, workers and the unions in check; it seems disagreements never got further than the Production Control office and were always settled quickly. 'As soon as the buzzer went in the morning it was "head down" until dinner,' said Dave Lewis on his experience as a worker during the 1950s (as recorded for the author especially for this book). '[T]hen "head down" until home time. No time to chat – the more the group did, the more we got paid. We would get paid by the amount of tickets we handed in every day; each ticket was sown to the seat cover so when, say number 3 fitted the seat he would tear the part of the ticket he needed and at the end of the day we would hand them in.'

Time and motion study engineers and wages

Ernest Frederick Powell joined the firm in 1931 to assist with rolling out PBR across the business; the makers and polishers were already working to this pay structure, and the firm had the Mill and Machine shop in its sights. 'Piecework prices were expressed at the time as a price for the job but as the Time Study department got into stride, this system was altered and bonus prices were introduced and all work on PBR was expressed in time and not money,' stated LS.

Time and motion study emanated from America and was described as a 'new tool'. LS relates that as far back as 1881 in America, a Mr. F. W. Taylor had been studying separation of operations. Initially, stopwatches were used by the firm's foremen to determine prices/costs of making new products. Ernest developed the firm's Time Study department and became manager. The introduction of PBR in the Mill and Machine shop was deemed beneficial – it also assisted the firm with working to greater accuracy and with inspection and quality control.

The firm and unions reconciled

At the time, Jack Shanley was general secretary of the Amalgamated Union of Upholsterers (AUU) and as World War Two loomed and the Board of Trade was looking for reputable firms to produce Utility furniture, trades union organisers had to approve the firms. In *Furnishing the* World, Jack Shanley said of this process: '[A]s soon as we knew the name of a factory which was to produce furniture under the utility scheme, we sent an official down to meet the management, and told them "we have come to sign up all your work people as you are going on the Utility scheme". The suggestion was that it was a condition of the contract that all workers should be in the union. No one ever questioned it'. There was, in fact, no compulsion about this and approved firms became closed shops. The union accepted the Lebus wage structure (by then based on job times, not prices) and the firm gave the unions full facilities to function within the factory.

In 1947 the AUU merged with NAFTA to form the National Union of Furniture Trade Operatives (NUFTO), with Jack Shanley as assistant general secretary. Shanley had worked with Herman Lebus on the Furniture Industry Post War Reconstruction Committee. He recalled:

> In fact, he [Sir Herman] more or less invited me to apply to Lebus as Labour Relations Manager – he had already asked my General Secretary, Alf Tomkins, who had said no. I laughed. I said, Sir Herman, Sir Herman I wouldn't last six months in your factory. And I wouldn't because he would be going round the factory, and he would see something and he would go up and correct the man.

The experience of Sissy Lewis – the firm's only female shop steward

Sissy Lewis, who was involved in the union, spoke of her experiences in *Furnishing the World*:

> After the war I became the only woman shop steward at Lebus… I spoke at our

Female employees from Lebus protesting to keep the Cost of Living allowance (COL) in 1952

union conference in Eastbourne one year against equal pay for women. At the time it was our union policy because, as I said, by having equal pay for equal work men liked it because it secured their own jobs. Women on the other hand would find it harder to find a job as people would sooner employ men although I insisted that women were better workers. A woman would have her husband and children to look after and could lose time from work, whereas a man was alright.

The 1970s feminist surge was yet to come.

Peter Baker – from union member to shop steward

Peter Baker joined the firm at the beginning of January 1950:

> I was approached by a shop steward with regard to 'joining the Union'. I insisted upon his explaining to me why I should join, which he did quite lucidly and convincingly. The most convincing argument being that, as the firm was a 'closed shop', I could not work there, on the shop floor, unless I joined the Union. So I became a member of NUFTO.

In time, Baker was elected shop steward for H/J shop. He explained how PBR worked in practice:

> [T]he worker accumulates 'time' for all the tasks completed during the week and is paid for that time at the agreed hourly rate, which was the industry standard agreed. Where the employer has not provided continuity of work during the day the employee is paid 'waiting time'. The surplus to the base earnings of the week is referred to as 'a bonus'.

Baker worked on the radio-frequency presses:

> When I tell you that the six of us could produce one hundred bedroom suites a week, consisting of a four feet wardrobe, three feet gents fitted wardrobe, a three-drawer chest and a four feet wide,

sunk-centre dressing table, for which we were being paid a basic lieu bonus of 25%. We were in a new shop, using revolutionary equipment, without any pre-knowledge of how, what or where assembly or sub-assembly times may go. So we were not working at full potential. Perhaps this gives some concept of the potential productivity of this innovative development in making furniture.

Shop steward and time and motion study

Baker spoke of a crucial event in terms of his career with the firm:

> The time allowed for assembling a sunk-centre dressing table was 14.75 minutes. Three of us operated this particular RF press and I had been timed originally, gaining a time of 10 minutes. I was quite happy with this because I could perform the task in less than 5 minutes and earn 100% bonus. The other two chaps could not make a bonus within this time and so the time had to be put 'in dispute'. This required a re-time which necessitated me, as Shop Steward, being in attendance beside the Work/Time Study Engineer. Ron, the chap who was being retimed, was embarrassed and flustered, it was a hot day and he was breaking out in a sweat, also making a ham-fisted job of the whole thing. I was more interested in what the Work Study Engineer was doing and concluded that I could do his job so, after the study was ended, questioned him about his profession. I then discovered that one had to be 25 years of age and a tradesman to be allowed to train as a Time and Motion Study Engineer. I decided to wait. I could afford to wait three years – albeit reluctantly.

> In 1951, I was summoned to a meeting by the Convenor of Shop Stewards (a paid employee of the firm although all he did was Union Work) who informed us that the firm was suffering a downturn in orders and that we were going to commence working a four-day week. As one could not claim benefit for one day

and, to assist in covering the shortfall in income, we would have Friday and Monday off on alternate weekends. In that way we could claim for the Saturday as well and get three days' benefits; even though we did not normally work on Saturday this was regarded as a 'normal working day'.

Convenor of shop stewards

Dennis Gilbert Morris Hurst ('Denny') was convenor of shop stewards. When the Duke of Edinburgh made his visit in 1955, he talked with Hurst, who recounted: 'He was particularly anxious to know if workers have any complaints, and how grievances which might arise in the factory were handled' (*Furniture Record*, 18 November 1955). Frustratingly, no answer was recorded. Hurst was killed in a road accident in October 1958; he was 53 and had been convenor for 17 years. The tribute in *Lebus Log* read:

> Much has already been said about Denny in other places by those who, because of his allegiances, possibly are in the best position to do so. He must have had his faults – who has not? But it will not be for those that he will be remembered. Rather it will be as a man of integrity who, once he had given an undertaking – and he would never do so unless he believed it to be a proper one – adhered to it irrespective of any pressures which might be brought to bear.

> (*Lebus Log*, No. 13, December 1958)

Furniture workers seek wage rise

In December 1955, the *Tottenham and Edmonton Weekly Herald* reported:

> Workers in the furniture industry – thousands of whom are employed in the Tottenham and North London area – have been pressing a wage claim for 4d an hour for those employed under systems of PBR. A claim has been rejected by employers; a Wages Campaign Committee has been organised by the London Furniture Workers and a mass demo in

Trafalgar Square is being staged early in the New Year.

Some of the firm's workers felt strongly enough on the issue to swell the ranks in support of the issue of the day and evidence shows this was not tolerable on the part of management. On file is an open letter to workers from Sir Herman Lebus, dated Thursday 12 January 1956, 'about an incident on Monday 9 January'. An extract from the letter reads:

> Last Monday, in breach of the National Labour Agreement and against the advice of the Union Executive, the great majority of you were absent from work in order to attend a demonstration. It has been represented to me that this expression of disloyalty to the Union and to the Company may have come about because of an impression that the Board and I personally would not disprove of such an act. This is emphatically a mistaken impression… For more than fifty years I have done my best to promote the welfare of all concerned in the Company and in the Industry. To be rewarded in this way is indeed disappointing… in the past we as a Company have done our best to be fair to all concerned.

It seems reasonable to conclude that direct involvement and empowerment of workers to further their cause was not approved of.

Erratic work patterns and redundancies

'We wasn't all redundant at the same time,' Ron Turton said, referring to the mass redundancies of 1967; this statement has a certain resonance, given past history. Redundancies during the two world wars, such as that of a young Beatrice Wright, are easily explicable, as indeed are double shift-work patterns. During World War Two, Daphne Bradley was glad that women did the same sort of work as men (some men with specialist skills were exempt from the forces) because 'the salaries were very high and with bonuses the take-home pay was a vast amount higher than that which was paid to the men and women in the forces – army, navy and air force'.

On the other hand, she admitted the shift-work pattern was hard:

> We had to work from 7 o'clock in the morning until 7 o'clock at night with only one hour for lunch for seven days a week; we then had one-and-a-half days off and would work another seven days and so on – every fourteen weeks we had to do our quota of night work which was for one month when we would work from 7 o'clock in the evening until 7 o'clock in the morning with one hour off to go to the canteen for a meal.

Peter Baker said: 'It was June of 1951 when I was caught in the third redundancy from Lebus.' (Presumably he meant 'third round', although it isn't clear which exact period he was referring to.) Needless to say, it had to do with balancing reduced sales with size of workforce. The fact that Baker was back in employment at Lebus once again a year or so later – and on shift work to boot – suggests that whatever caused the firm to make redundancies at that specific point was short lived, in turn suggesting a re-balancing of workforce to match increasing demand for furniture products. 'Early in 1953 the trade had "picked up" again,' said Baker, 'and I discovered that I would be working a "double day shift" pattern. This meant working 6.00 a.m. until 2.00 p.m. Monday to Friday and 6.00 a.m. until 12.00 p.m. on Saturday for one week; the following week's pattern was 2.00 p.m. until 10.45 p.m. from Monday to Thursday and 2.00 p.m. until 10.00 p.m. on Friday. Although irregular it was practical… and, if it was available, I would also work overtime, with the Union proviso that we had to have a twelve-hour break between shifts.'

Ron Turton was doing shift work when he started in 1954, though he recalls different timings:

> I did 8 to 6 o'clock Monday to Friday, Saturday overtime I did 7 to 11 o'clock, that was alright because I had the rest of the day then. The unions got the hours down (to 40). Friday night finish 5 o'clock.

> Shift-work, you did 6 to 2 o'clock, 2 to 10 o'clock at night. You had to take your turn at it, nobody wanted to do 'earlies', you could change with someone. Most didn't want 'earlies'. And if they was busy or not, they stopped the shifts and you work normal time.

That said, Marion Cotton, who started in the late 1950s, wished for more part-time or flexi-time opportunities for office staff (as recollected during the Coombes Croft project):

> Started at 8.45 till 5.15, I think it was about 37 hours per week. Some did part-time but you had to be very lucky to do that. I was envious of those who could come in at 9.30 a.m. You did the hours they chose for you.

A shift had taken place by the following decade, as recalled by Ada Frost:

> I went back in the 1960s… I think I did part-time at Lebus, the same sort of work in the office. I did the wages and I used the machine. I did different times, only half-days and not every day, odd time really.

Clocking-in cards on the wall beside the clock in the main entrance; Bill Ferris, concierge, is pictured

(Reproduced with special permission from Waltham Forest Local History Archives, Vestry House Museum)

Woodley 'whisperer' – working from home and seasonal work

Meanwhile on the firm's upholstery side, Shirley Hiscock said of the 1950s at Lebus:

> I was away from work bringing up the children, and the firm couldn't get machinists, so they put a call out to ones that had worked before and had small children to do 'out work' – they would bring a machine and work to your house while the children were on school holidays. When the children went back to school, we worked in the factory – it worked for all of us!

Dave Lewis said:

> When a job came up at Lebus Upholstery – I jumped at it! I lived a few hundred yards away and had finished getting my City and Guilds in Modern and Traditional Upholstery and was working for a local rival. I was a master-cutter, but wanted to do upholstery. It was hard work but the people there were fantastic. The two years I had [before they closed down] were seasonal because in the upholstery game you are very busy in the winter, when people are at home looking at their furniture, and quiet in the summer, when people are on holiday. I had two summers where I would be on a three-day week and then laid off, only to be taken back six weeks later. And the winter would be overtime!

Peter Baker was generally happy with his shift work, overtime and bonus pay:

> I was saving money in order to get together a deposit for a house. And working was not a problem. Getting there at 6.00 a.m. was. I always earned enough to make each shift pay around about 100%–120% bonus. Perhaps that is why I was never reprimanded for arriving late in the mornings. Ending the evening shift at 10.45 pm was another matter, however, and I only stopped work at 10.45 p.m., washed up and went home with no rush

whatsoever. What would one do at that hour anyway? Being a night owl and not a morning lark also affects one's pattern of life and thought processes.

Even on a four-day week in early 1951, Baker earned just over £12 after all stoppages:

> I visited friends that I used to work with in a bank when I left school over a Friday lunchtime drink. They did not want me to pay for a round of drinks. I asked Cyril – we shared the same birthday – what salary he was currently earning. It was £6.10.00 a week, gross. I then showed my wage slip from the previous night – it was then understood why I had not returned to the bank after National Service.

Baker left the firm in 1954 when he got married and bought a house in Essex.

Ron Turton described his starting pay with the firm:

> I was only like, you're a 'journeyman' when you're 21, so I wasn't on the full – I was about 20-and-a-half when I went there… You'd get a rise on each birthday 'til you get the 'journeyman's rate' at 21. When you start, so many weeks, you got a percentage, then it dropped and after that you was on your own, earn your own money. Double time, you could get good money, can't remember, but it was more than £10 a week, more than £20. You got hourly rate and the cost of living on top of that. Some of them, they couldn't do it, never earned much.

Gordon Shepherd was not keen: 'They started doing piecework and when they started that I came out – I wouldn't be pushed. Came out about 1949, went to work at Stirling – another furniture place in Phillip Lane.'

And Marion Cotton recalled: 'I was paid about £5 a week', for office work in the 1950s. The furniture industry as a whole was shrinking. The authors of *Furnishing the World* wrote that by '1959 the number of firms working in the East and North East of London had fallen by half and the labour force fallen by over a third compared to pre-war levels'.

J. L. Oliver stated:

> From the beginning of the first full week in April 1963, a new payments schedule in the furniture industry came into effect. The basic hourly rate for a journeyman aged 21 and over was fixed at 3s 9d in London and 3s 7d in the provinces, with the supplementary cost of living allowance at 2s 2d, making the total minimum hourly payments of 5s 11d and 5s 9d for a working week of 42 hours, with reductions in hours and increases in the cost of living allowance to be spread over nearly three years.

The Contracts of Employment Act, 6 July 1964, had given employees the right to a written statement of their terms of employment and setting out minimum periods of notice. 'The Redundancies Payment Act played a crucial part', wrote Rex Winsbury in 1968. 'The real cost of the redundancies was £450,000, a large sum that Lebus could hardly have afforded on its own, but without which the unions (which in the event accepted the redundancies with great realism) could hardly have acquiesced.' ('How Lebus Turned Round', *Management Today*, July 1968)

In 1966–7, between half and two-thirds of the firm's workforce of over 3,000 were made redundant; many of these were second- or third-generation employees. This included both shop workers and office staff. Both Henry Jacobs and Ron Turton were made redundant in 1967. Turton recalled, 'Some they kept back. Lots of men must've found it hard… when they was finishing, redundancy was based on what you earned over the time, you got a week's money. In the 1960s, it was £70, £80 a week they was earning'.

Such low staffing levels had not been a feature of the company since its earliest days. During the Second World War, up to 6,000 workers had been employed, although this was spread over two twelve-hour shifts, and at the time of the Duke of Edinburgh's visit in 1955, the total number of employees at Tottenham was quoted in the national tabloid, the *Star*, on 3 November 1955, as 3,000 men and 700 women.

Rex Winsbury in *Management Today* reports Robert Mahlich, director of production, having said Lebus had a 'nonsense' ratio of 800 staff (managers) out of 3,000 employees, compared to the usual ratio in the industry of eight or even ten to one. The superstructure was trimmed back to one to six.

With only 1,000 or so employees left, the old individual incentive bonus scheme for the separate craftsmen was deemed no longer appropriate to machine manufacture in an automated plant. Consequently, a new pay and productivity deal was worked out with the unions, which substituted group bonuses for individual ones.

Commenting on this, Rex Winsbury wrote:

> Announced in June last year [1967], the agreement was said to be the first of its kind in the industry, giving Lebus a potential three-fold increase in production for the same size of labour force! A double day shift system was introduced to replace the old single shift. A third shift is to be brought in soon.

The agreement increased basic rates to around £25 10s for a 35-hour week for a skilled man on the new shift system (from £24 10s for 40 hours) and gave a degree of inter-changeability between jobs. Holiday arrangements, life assurance, and sickness and accident pay were also improved. The actual pay structure was tidied up at the same time. Interestingly, Yatton (another furniture manufacturer) later made a similar move.

Counting out the wages

'I used to go down the steps on Ferry Lane, bear left, walk through, bear right and keep on and you got to the conveyor belts. You was allowed three minutes over the time, the Mill had five minutes because it was further.'

– Ron Turton, polisher, 1954–1967

Ron Turton recalled his clocking-in card:

> The clock card had the hourly rate, hours you worked, your clock number and any deductions like the savings. Trustees Savings, they'd deduct it from your wages, and it would go in your account… but people would see what you had stopped on your clock card.

On the other hand, Marian Cotton had different recollections:

> I've got a feeling I had to sign in a book. You'd go to your section and sign your section book. They allowed us about five or ten minutes if you had a good reason for being late and you'd be reprimanded. We weren't docked any money if we were late, I don't remember if we were.

'When I think how they must do wages now, it all seems so old-fashioned. I never used them, but they did have adding machines with a paper roll'.

Mrs. Ada Frost

There is a real tinge of sadness and a twist of irony to Ada Frost's story – she was a wages clerk with the firm throughout the 1940s and again through the 1960s after marrying and having a son. She recalled:

> I left because I had angina. We didn't have a phone in those days and my son had to write a letter and take it to work for me. I said, 'I must go to work' but the doctor said, 'you can't'. And he wouldn't give me a certificate. So I had to leave, it was only a few weeks before it all closed anyway.

Frost was born in 1918 and was around 90 years of age when she was interviewed in 2008 as a member of the Coombes Croft group, in preparation for 'The Lebus Exhibition' at Bruce Castle Museum.

Given her advanced years, her memory of some intricate details of her life experiences was quite astonishing:

> I think I went to Porlock in Somerset, with a friend at Lebus; her husband was in the navy… in a farmhouse on top of Porlock Hill, long walk up… with our cases. I think it was full board; I remember having sponge pudding and raspberries.

However, she then casually admitted, 'I don't remember what I was paid, but it seemed reasonable. I think I had some sort of paid holiday as well, but I don't remember how much holiday we had.'

She was able to remember that: 'Each employee had a number, they clocked-in on the big machines on the wall in the entrance. There was a big clock in the cabinet, you put your card in the slot, punch the handle and it registered the time you clocked-in, and again in the evening to clock-off. The time was stamped by the minute.'

Arthur Hickford was in charge of the Wages Office when he retired in 1951 after 49 years with the firm, having joined in 1902 at the age of 15. Over this period 'he experienced the phenomenal changeover from a physical to a mechanical method of producing the weekly payroll' (*Lebus Log*, No. 23, September 1962). In the early years at the Finsbury Cabinet Works, W. H. Wright was the chief cashier, which was one of a number of functions undertaken in the General Office (building A). Wages were paid in cash – gold, silver and copper; a considerable amount of cash was handled to prepare weekly wages. According to LS's *History*, the total annual payroll for the firm had risen to just over £80,000 in 1902 (compared to just over £69,000 in 1901) and by 1913 (just before the war) it peaked at £134,066. Some £2,500 in cash would be counted out on the premises in wages preparation each week with only a paper trail to assist the process.

The Friday afternoon wage-trolley run

Before World War One, a number of mobile cabinets were built for the Friday wage run – in wood, of course. Each cabinet had several trays with 50 holes drilled through at regular intervals. Wages were calculated and the coins and wage slip placed in wooden cups, one for each worker. With a dowel pin turned at the bottom of the wooden cups, they could be slotted into the holes on the tray. This ensured they would stay in place when the trolleys were wheeled to the respective workshops.

E. J. Witchalls (known as Ted) was manager of Staff Wages during the latter years of the firm (he was succeeded by Mrs. Eileen Noble). Witchalls had joined as wages clerk in 1935, working on factory wages preparation in an office in T1 under the direction of Mr. A. Penny, before the section was absorbed into the Cost Office. After a period in the Powers section, Penny became supervisor of the Staff Wages section. In 1951, Witchalls assumed the role.

During the 1940s, Ada Frost was a wages clerk; she recalled:

> It was a big office, in the old building, I was there some years. I would do wages, the clock-cards, with all the hours written on. This was the end of the week job. I suppose people were paid one week in arrears. When I first went there, I used to go in early because they taught us the Comptometer. So I'd get in at 8 o'clock every day, and quite a number of us went in, to learn this machine. One of the experienced ones would teach us, we didn't have a manual, just exercises. My desk was in the same place at 9 o'clock – I would stop and then start my regular job.

> About the Comptometer; there were big and little figures on each key and a little strip on top to show your calculation. On the right-hand side was £s, s and d [pounds, shillings and pence]. It didn't print out anything, there was no record. It was rather like touch-typing, you could add without looking because there were little indentations on the keys, you could feel them. You had to write the answer down on the clock card. If you wanted to multiply something, like 45 x 95, you hold down the '4' and '5' keys and press nine times and move once to the left and press five times and you had the answer. And it

would add and subtract, and you could do division on it.

> The keys were in threes, for hundreds, tens and units. So if you wanted 30 x 20, you'd hold down the '3' key in the tens column, the middle key, and move once to the left and press twice and that was the answer. You had a little handle at each side, only small, that cleared the total from the strip. You could just flick it more or less, not a big thing. And then you could do the next one. And if you use the one colour it was easier. Multiplication was about the easiest to do, division and the others you could be using both hands, and some of the multiplication you have both hands. You still have to think when you're dividing; it doesn't automatically do it for you. I found it hard to learn at the beginning. But you would have a rough idea of what the answer ought to be anyway, it just confirmed the answer.

> Whatever workshop it was, the same people worked on those cards. You added up the hours on the back, marked it against the day, then you transferred the hours to the front of the card, and any overtime as well, and then you had to do the tax and the insurance and everything as well.

> The cards would all be made up, and they went into slots on… well, it was like a board, you could fold the boards. You had to get all the cards in the slots exactly right, one under the other, because you'd got to add them up and reconcile them at the end. You had to keep them straight so all the figures would line up in columns. And then the final figure would be in the bottom right-hand corner after all the deductions were taken off. If one slipped a bit, they would all be out, and it would be wrong in the end and you'd have to go back and find it.

> And that was what I did all through the war. I went back in the sixties.

> The Supervisor had to make the wages up, and we'd go down into the strong room.

I used to help her sometimes with the wages. She'd have to work out how many notes she'd need, and silver and copper. She was good at it. I'd go down in the strong room with her. It had gates. I think she had a key; I suppose so. You could stay in there if there was an air raid and do the money.

The money was out in the wages envelopes in such a way that you could count the money after it was sealed. So many notes and coins, there were little holes put in the envelopes so you could count.

We did the factory wages not staff wages. It was a very big job, a big responsibility. The packets then went into wooden boxes for each 'shop', and the Foreman would come for them and take them to pay out the wages. Sometimes I would have to take them down if they weren't collected, but not often.

We had photocopiers, I think that was after the war, for the clock-cards, I think.

The payroll was on huge sheets of paper and you had to add them up, and I did that more than the clock-cards; how many insurances, things like that, you had to summarise at the end. The pay roll was the photocopy of the clock-cards.

In an interview with the author, Photographer Apprentice Henry Jacobs said:

We produced pages of wage slips – there were 3,000 individual slips. It was two days' work. The prints needed glazing and drying – we used a big machine which produced a lot of heat. Processing was very labour intensive and involved mixing four or five different chemicals by hand, including developing and fixing solutions. Some of these could cause skin rashes if spilt and the fixer gave off fumes! They would be classed as noxious now, but we did have a mask. I did have to go out for air! In the summer it could be 100 degrees in there, and I often worked bare-chested! Sometimes the girls from the office would come up to collect them

– they often waited outside for fifteen minutes or so for the room to cool down as they wouldn't come in with the heat. The wages department would then cut up into individual slips with a guillotine.

'We didn't like the work very much because most of it was uninteresting… the only compensation was the very high wages that we drew at the end of the week.'

– Mrs. Daphne Bradley

Recruitment and Training

The firm looked to encourage school leavers through local arrangements, placing advertisements in the local paper and using the local Labour Exchange (Job Centre). However, more often than not it was the case that someone – a family member or friend – 'put a word in'.

School leavers

Mark Bailey, local historian and former Tottenham ambulance driver in the 1960s, was taken round as a school leaver in the early 1960s. He recalled the following in his memories, written down for this book:

In those days schoolchildren were expected to line up in a file or crocodile two deep, and walk in an orderly and quiet way to one's destination; thus we proceeded to Ferry Lane via Tottenham Hale, over the hump-back bridge, and lined up outside the Main Office building A… It has to be said that the pupils (particularly the boys) were generally considered to be local factory fodder. And no doubt with this in mind, the annual school event visit for school leavers was a conducted tour of the nearby Harris Lebus furniture factory.

The Junior Technical School, which was part of Tottenham Polytechnic (now the College of North East London) on Tottenham High Road, had such an arrangement with the firm. Their in-house magazine, the *Tekton* (Volume 5, Summer Term, 1934) noted that 'on 1 May and

Visits of junior technical school leavers to Harris Lebus from Tottenham Polytechnic, *Tekton* magazine, summer 1934

(Reproduced with special permission from College of North East London)

21 June, Forms 1b and 1d visited Messrs Lebus' Joinery works'.

The Labour Exchange, Scotland Green

Peter Baker went to the firm from the Labour Exchange in Scotland Green, Tottenham, after National Service in January 1950, as did Ron Turton in 1954. Turton said: '[T]hey were advertising for polishers. I had a couple of jobs, and my uncle got me an interview for a French Polishing job with another firm – I didn't get it, not that one. I was out of work for a while 'til Lebus.'

Local newspaper

Just a few months before the major restructuring and mass redundancies of 1966, the firm was advertising in the *Tottenham and Edmonton Weekly Herald*, 1 April 1966, and it is noteworthy that these were mainly for clerical positions in sales and accounting:

> Lebus offer career prospects to boys and girls in the age group 15–17, vacancies in many departments, including Accounts for Calculating Machine Operators, Sales Research and Sales departments for Figure and General clerks. Those with GCE O' levels can advance to responsible posts. Part-time day release facilities are available for further vocational education.

The *Tottenham and Edmonton Weekly Herald*, 9 February 1968, contained an advertisement for the firm, which was again recruiting but this time for machinists:

Lebus, we require wood Machinists and Sanders – to help us meet the huge demand for our highly successful 'Europa' furniture. We offer excellent rates of pay, day work (40 hours) £25 plus, shift-work 35 hours £26 plus (6.00 a.m. – 1.30 p.m. and 1.30 p.m. to 9.00 p.m.) overtime if required, attractive working conditions, three weeks' holiday at advanced pay,

Staff handbook, late 1950s

Train for your Career…

HARRIS LEBUS LTD.
FINSBURY WORKS · TOTTENHAM · N.17.

improved sick pay scheme, pensionable employment, generous free life assurance cover, good canteen facilities.

Training opportunities

'Families brought their sons and daughters in; some did the City and Guilds to learn it all,' said Ron Turton. The creation of training opportunities was important to the firm. J. L. Oliver wrote:

> Trainees are eligible for one day release per week, with pay, to attend classes at Tottenham or Walthamstow, parents being kept informed of progress… recruits are provided with a miniature encyclopaedia of the furniture trade, are encouraged to use the works library containing books on training, technology, factory management and hobbies, in addition to trade periodicals.

City and Guilds in Photography

Photographer Henry Jacobs trained alongside his role at the firm:

> I went to Regent Street Polytechnic for my evening classes, paid for by the firm. I had to leave work early, at 4.30 p.m. to get there – they didn't dock my wages either. I passed my City and Guilds in photography in 1964. Brian Carter (known as Bill) was 'a first-class photographer'; he was 28 years old and in charge of the dark room. Bill really encouraged me; photographic job opportunities were hard to come by. It was a fantastic start, I learned so much from Bill and from the evening classes I was allowed to go on.

Cabinet-making – Late Entry Trainee Scheme

Between leaving Down Lane School and National Service, Peter Baker had worked in a bank in the City: 'I opted to enter the "Late Entry Trainee" Scheme as I wanted to earn real money', said Baker. He discovered the firm operated a scheme for those who had been unable to train as cabinet-makers from leaving school:

[T]here were six of us and we started at 8.00 a.m. on a Monday morning in November 1950 at Worship Street in the City.

Our instructors appeared to be a couple of grizzled old cabinetmakers to us, but then we were all in our early twenties. But they were extremely efficient in their teachings. The first morning we were all provided with a toolbox and a full complement of tools. These we paid for by deduction from our weekly earnings when we returned to the factory. That first day! I had been provided with an oilstone that was, and still is some 60-odd years later, graded 'Fine'.

Our first task was to sharpen our tools; most people seem to believe that a woodworking tool is ready for use as purchased from a hardware shop, and that is not the case. They need sharpening because they have only been 'machine ground'. We were told to take up the plane and were shown how to take it apart and reassemble it, then disassemble again while the finer points of sharpening were demonstrated. Then we had to flatten the back of the plane iron – until this was absolutely flat, we were not allowed to turn over and work on the bevel.

My plane iron had a little hollow, part way into the right-hand edge, which had to be eliminated. It was about 5.30 p.m. before that hollow disappeared. I had broken the monotony by sharpening a couple of chisels during the day.

The value of all that preparation and boring work is that even now, sixty-odd years on, my tools are easy to 'touch up' and hold their sharpness far longer than other people's tools. I cursed those two old cabinetmakers then for being somewhat pedantic, but I now praise them for the same reason. I mention this to demonstrate what a forward-thinking firm it was.

City and Guilds in Cabinetmaking

Peter Baker described studying for a City and Guilds:

> One day, as I was walking along the main corridor, I met Mr. Edmunds Zala, Chief Inspector and my former boss, we stopped for a few friendly words and he advised me to study for the City and Guilds. I followed his advice and enrolled for the course at the Shoreditch Technical College, some six miles away just on the edge of the City. As the course started at 6.30 p.m., I cycled because that was the only feasible manner to get there in time, which meant that I had to leave the factory at 5.30 p.m. – half an hour before normal leaving time.

Interestingly, Baker said, 'there was no "day release"' and that he 'paid his own tuition fees, plus textbooks, drawing paper, note pads, drawing instruments, pens and pencils including final exam!' He continued:

> One evening was purely practical and we had to make a piece of furniture entirely by hand. The other two evenings were theory and drawing. The instructors for these two evenings were all Government Inspectors for the Board of Trade, employed by the college on a part-time basis but having a background in woodworking. Once they had set the task for the evening, they would move around the class ensuring that all were following instructions and on the right track. Every evening they finished this route at my desk and we then spoke about the things which I was doing at Harris Lebus, sometimes for the second hour of the class! They were hungry to learn about Radio Frequency curing of glue lines and associated details, of which I had gained experience with the firm and they had absolutely no knowledge at all. Talk about reversing positions – the pupil, teaching the teachers!

Break Times and Leisure

The year 1939 marked the approximate halfway point of Harris Lebus's period in Tottenham. An employee handbook of the time gives an excellent snapshot of what it was like to work there: the working week had been reduced to five days, the hours had been reduced to 45 (40 for office staff), lunchtime was one hour, breaks were 10 to 15 minutes morning and afternoon, paid holidays had moved from just bank holidays to one week. There were medical facilities offering inoculation against colds and influenza free to employees, access to a convalescent home run by the FTBA at the firm's expense, a canteen and a barber's shop, a team of cleaners worked day and night to maintain high standards of hygiene and repair, and working conditions were generally more relaxed.

Marion Cotton, an invoice-checker in the 1950s, commented that despite the formal set-up:

> We sat one behind the other, we had wooden desks. Our office was just rows of desks, there were about a dozen girls in our invoice checkers office… We could talk, I can't remember if it was only during the break. It was fairly easy-going, but you got on with your work.

Keeping workers 'fed and watered'

Alongside medical provision, another crucial aspect of daily working life was access to meals and refreshments. In the early days at the Finsbury Cabinet Works, to help the day along, 'sometimes cans of beer… were brought in at breakfast time and sold at 2d a pint; "Sherb" Worman remembered doing this many times as a boy,' wrote LS.

Tea, bread, kippers, saveloys

Just before World War One, as the youngest apprentice polisher at age 14, it was Beatrice Wright's job to fetch refreshments from the 'barrow-man' for the other girls. In the *Lebus Log*, No. 14, July 1959, she remembered: 'The tea was not served in cups either, it was collected in one-pint beer cans suspended in a line from a notched wooden pole.' With this balanced precariously in one hand, and a box full of bread and kippers in the other, she would climb the stairs to the women's polishing shops on the second floor of K/L, where the canteen would later be established.

Basic facilities

In the days before the canteen, there were basic facilities for heating up food and tea was made from various hot-water tanks in each shop. Charlie Holland also recalled that during the First World War, a man sold kippers and bloaters in the corridor by the Polishing shop. He would warm them in the boiler meant for steaming beech spars used in the manufacture of war supplies; once he put the fish on the steam valve and caused the boiler to 'blow up' (*Lebus Log*, No. 13, December 1958).

Coca cola machines and cigarette kiosk

In the 1950s, Ron Turton remembered:

> There was old Coca Cola machines in the Mill, 6d I think it was. You could get time sometimes – go outside for a smoke while it [spray polish] dries. Curly, he used to have a little kiosk selling cigarettes, and he'd come in with a little attaché case and sell the cigarettes and sweets; his wife ran the kiosk, he worked for Lebus.

A bus home or a packed lunch

Marian Cotton recalled:

> I believe an hour for lunch. I think we had a certain lunch hour. The office emptied or girls stayed at their desks to eat. You could rely on the buses then, they kept to a timetable, so I came home, only a few minutes by bus, and I knew what time I could get back again. Bus fare would be about 5d home and 5d back. I didn't go home every single day.

> I took lunch with me if I stayed. If there was an urgent job you might stay, if the invoice was urgent. I don't remember where the canteen was, I ate at my desk. I don't remember a communal room near where I worked. A sandwich or soup left over from the day before, main meal in the evening when my husband was home from work. I remember taking a vacuum flask for tea at lunchtime. I read a book or a magazine, some did knitting and we'd chat.

Everyone remembered the 'tea trolley lady'

Marion Cotton remembered:

> We had a tea trolley lady. She probably sold sandwiches and biscuits. We had two breaks, morning and afternoon, about quarter of an hour, I think. The tea trolley would go by and you might miss it. I don't recall them ringing a bell or anything. The trolley came in the office. I can't remember if we paid for the tea at the end of the week, it was only a few pence a cup. They had cups and saucers. I think it was rolls in the morning and cakes and biscuits in the afternoon.

Mrs. Daphne Bradley recollected that during the Second World War:

> [E]very morning and every afternoon the tea trolley would come round and sometimes if we were lucky the tea lady would have thick slices of bread and dripping in the mornings at 1d per slice. That was a real luxury in those days of rationing. In the afternoon we could buy a cake with our cup of tea or maybe a slice of bread pudding. We had ten minutes' break both morning and afternoon.

Ron Turton remembered his break times:

> 10 – 10.15 a.m. tea break; they come round, little money box and write down what you want and then it comes round, roll in the mornings, perhaps cake in the afternoon. You had to pay. Hour lunch time; then afternoon was another break.

For Henry Jacobs, Apprentice Photographer, the tea trolley runs were two of the highlights of his day. During a meeting with the author in 2008 he said:

I loved the coconut cakes with crunchy, white strands on the top. We often played cards at lunchtime. I sometimes used the canteen or ate sandwiches in the darkroom next to all the chemicals. I could heat a can of soup up in the kettle!

Professional catering

Aside from Henry's 'can of soup in a kettle', catering for a hungry workforce of several thousand with hot meals, hot beverages, cakes and pastries became a well-organised affair with the installation of a canteen. The idea for a canteen was originally considered by the partners way back when the Finsbury Cabinet Works began operating; they commissioned a feasibility study on providing hot midday meals.

'Mess Room' proposal

LS's *History* quotes a letter dated 3 March 1902 entitled 'Mess Room' in which Edmund A. Bartlet, who was involved in the feasibility study, wrote: 'The value of the structure would of course gentlemen be a matter for you and your architect, but may I be allowed to say that my experience in this line has taught me that successful catering quality depends on the perfection of the kitchen arrangements, also a good storeroom that purchases may be made as largely as possible… care would always be taken that customers of whatever nationality should have equal courtesy and attention.' Complimenting his consideration of 'equal opportunities', Bartlet's menu sample read:

> [C]ut from joint/meat pie etc., 2d, potatoes and portions of vegetables at a half-penny each, soup during cold weather 1d a bowl, fried fish to be served daily with chips (market permitting) at either half-penny, 1d or 2d, three fried or boiled eggs two-and-a-half pence, baked or boiled plum alternated with rice or tapioca in half-penny portions, half-pint mugs of tea, coffee or cocoa at a half-pence each. Good meals can be provided at tuppence or thruppence a plate.

Bartlet's proposal at that time was rejected, presumably on the grounds that there was nowhere to erect the purpose-built facility that he clearly required.

World War One communal canteen at Hale Wharf

Shortly after the outbreak of the war, Tottenham Urban District Council established a substantial war kitchen in converted buildings on Hale Wharf. Workers from other surrounding factories – Gestetner, Flateau, Eagle – also used the facilities. Whilst a number of workers would be living close to their place of work, the facility offered alternatives to cold snacks and re-heated food or going home to eat. It also prompted the firm to establish its own canteen, exclusively for its workers and staff.

Space freed up for a canteen

With available space no longer required for the indentured school of polishers, which had been discontinued on the outbreak of war, the canteen, with a seating capacity of 1,400, was located on the second floor of K/L building above the 'touching up' workshops. The Advertising department and photographers occupied the other part of this floor.

Subsidised meals

Initially the provision of the meals service was contracted out to an outside caterer and ran along these lines for a year or so. However, as a business venture it proved difficult for the outside caterer to provide substantial meals at a modest price and to generate a profit. Consequently, the firm took the service in-house, with costs being subsidised.

During World War Two, the canteen catered for shift workers, some on nights. Daphne Bradley was one of them: 'It was difficult to eat dinner in the middle of the night, and especially so because next to Harris Lebus there was a slaughterhouse and in the night the smell of horse flesh cooking used to waft through the canteen. It was a sickening smell and I shall never forget it.'

The 1950s makeover

'The Duke of Edinburgh was taken to the Canteen, on the second floor of 'K/L' building. Looking resplendent in contemporary, bright pastel shades following its recent makeover, the canteen can seat 1,400. In the kitchen the midday meals were just coming out of the ovens, along with tiers of pastries and buns for the afternoon tea trolleys.'

– Tottenham and Edmonton Weekly Herald,
11 November 1955

The 1950s 'makeover' was courtesy of Cyril Rostgaard, chief designer. The main colour – 'Moss Rose' (pink) – was 'warming and cheerful' since most of the sunlight came from north-facing windows. The ceiling was painted intense white, including joists and pipes; the dado rails and below were in deep 'Sloane Pink', the skirting and radiators were in dark 'Maroon Red'. Some half-walls, doors, screens and pay desks were painted 'Chelsea Blue' as a relief to the pink walls – 'because however pretty a colour may be, it will become boring and suffocating if it surrounds you without respite. Colour reliefs are like cooling drinks on a hot day – you don't want the weather to turn cold, but you enjoy the cold drink'. The window frames were painted 'Primrose Yellow', and the tables and chairs chosen in colours to complete the scheme.

Life as 'tea trolley lady' and canteen assistant

Phyllis Roberts was a canteen assistant around the time of the Duke of Edinburgh's visit. Her mother was already working there and had helped get her a job when she was 15. Originally, Phyllis was offered silver service waitressing, but it was as the 'tea trolley lady' that everyone remembered her. In the Coombes Croft project, she recounted her experiences:

> I mean I used to get lost in there, because one of the first jobs I had, I was on a tea trolley. This woman took me down, there was like a little station, room, down there where you made the tea. Big trolleys, huge,

Top: Meal preparation in the Harris Lebus canteen during the 1950s

(Reproduced with special permission from Waltham Forest Local History Archives, Vestry House Museum)

Above: Staff enjoying the canteen facilities

> I mean the urns was like this, they was massive – five feet tall? Well it seemed like it to me. And then, underneath the trolley you used to have all drawers, which they used to have made-up rolls in there, you know, for the factory workers. I mean I'm not sure about the actual rolls, I don't know if they baked them, I can't remember that, but I remember making up the rolls, like Spam, Spam and brown sauce, cheese and pickle. And then you'd have cakes as

well. We made the tea in the actual urns, you had two urns and the men used to come up with their cups, they used to have their own cups.

And you weren't allowed to have a ready-reckoner with you, used to have a little book, ready-reckoner used to have to conceal that somewhere, because we had to add it all up, and you'd have a roll, tuppence ha'penny and things like that… and you'd have all these men round you saying 'six teas, and I'll have three o' them' and you'd have to check it all up… which you could do after a little while, you know, it does come easy after a while. I think it was a drawer to put the money in, a small drawer at the front, if I remember right.

But if you didn't watch, the blokes used to get behind and pinch the rolls off you if they'd got a thin arm, they could get… so you had to have your eyes open. I used to feel a bit of a fool, you know, I used to blush quite a lot. I did the breakfast rolls, and then took the trolley round, and then I helped out with serving lunch.

I was getting in about half past seven but there were women there earlier than that… because you'd have these women… you know, the women who prepare the food… you did work Saturdays there, and used to… I think it was overtime if I remember right, you worked Saturday morning. I finished at about half past five (weekdays).

You had like a pecking order there, you know what I mean, so when I went, I was just a general… just picking up and clearing… I didn't stay there long, 'cos it was such a… funny atmosphere, like I say my mum could adjust to do that sort of thing, but I couldn't. And I'm afraid I had a couple of arguments with a few of the women, 'cos like I say, mum was easy-going, and one girl had a right go at her so she upset me… and I'd retaliate quite quickly… so I got reprimanded for that.

You're not in the kitchen, if you know what I mean, it's only like… the veg cook…

the chef and the pastry cook and all that sort of thing, and certain women would work in there, you know, you had like… you had a cook and then her assistant and all that kind of thing, and the people like me, we used to be on the counter serving up. We wore this overall and hat. A white wrap-over… short-sleeved and you know the chef's hats but a much smaller version, you know, flat. See we were all the Manager's staff; he used to be over the women, directly, Foreman or something and I think he used to be… like in charge of ordering all the stuff in for the chefs. So he'd be getting all the big stores in, he'd be ordering the flour and the eggs and the marge and all that sort of thing… he was more or less the women's supervisor, you know, if you needed anything… the Manageress, and the Under-Manageress.

So, I mean some of these canteen assistants done silver service, but my mum had always worked in service… she'd come… my mum's a Geordie, she'd come down from a mining village like, and… I wasn't going to be like that, I wasn't going to be a cleaner, and I wasn't going to be anybody's servant and I thought that's what silver service was… what an idiot! I mean look at the money you could make on that, I mean you could earn good money even now. But that was my philosophy at the time. What an idiot!

I think my mum used to go up to Maddox Street. Every year they used to have like a… I wonder if it was anything to do with showing off the furniture and that they'd done? You know, like a business thing? Because she used to go up there and do a bit of waitressing… getting the food prepared and that… so that was every now and again.

But I was only in the factory canteen. I think there was three canteens… well, I say one was a dining room, directors, then you had the Office Canteen, then you had the Factory one. A dining room that they had for the bosses, like Lebus and that, and you had the proper waitresses there and everything.

Mum used to go in at lunch time and wash the tables down and all that, and then she'd go back again about 5 or 6 'til half past nine, ten o'clock. So they had an evening shift, it was continuous work there.

And after you'd served them their dinner and all that, then you was clearing the counter and you'd have to do the washing up. I always remember, they had a man there washing up all the tins and that… he was displaced, what they called a 'displaced person', like might have been Polish or something, and he used to have to wash all the big, greasy meat tins and things like that, and the saucepans. They had washing-up machines, I think it was dishwashers… yes, they did, they had big dishwashers, but you used to have to get all the stuff out and check it over, see if it was clean. It was a long table, and you dished up, the people didn't help their-selves. They'd come by in a queue with a plate, and they'd tell you what they wanted. And then they'd carry on. At the end was a cashier, similar to, you know how British Home Stores used to be, that kind of thing, real cafeteria sort of style.

In the same 2008 oral history project, Ada Frost from the Wages Office said she used to go up to the canteen sometimes to give change:

They'd give me a ten shilling note perhaps, and I'd change it up so they could give the right money in the canteen, and this cut the queues down. I didn't like doing it, it was all men.

There was a quite varied menu I think, like I say it's a long time ago, but yes you used to get, like Fridays you'd have fish obviously, and I think they used to give them like a couple of dinners to choose from, meat and veg, sausage and mash, pie… think they used to do soup.

Ron Turton used the canteen:

Lovely meals. Saturday I may go along there, everybody mixed in then. You had other canteens, office staff, and shift-work you had meals at different times. Wasn't a lot of money in them days, 'reasonable', you'd say, prices. A 'meat and two veg' meal with pudding and tea or coffee worked out at just over a shilling. A cup of tea was 2d at May 1961 prices.

The canteen chef as at July 1959 was Paul Cunningham and the canteen manageress was Miss. Johnstone. In 1967, Dennis Osborne was general catering manager.

All crockery was white, and items such as the upper rim of plates were embossed with the overlapping initials 'H.L.' in blue; cups had 'H. Lebus, Canteen, Tottenham' on the sides.

Using the barber's shop

Hilda Hewitt recalled that her husband, Bill, 'used to go to the barber at Lebus, have his hair done.' One great advantage of being in H/J shop at Tottenham, said Peter Baker, was 'the Barber's Shop right next door – one only had to pop in for a haircut during work time!'

Harris Lebus barbers, located in the middle of the factory

(Reproduced with special permission from Waltham Forest Local History Archives, Vestry House Museum)

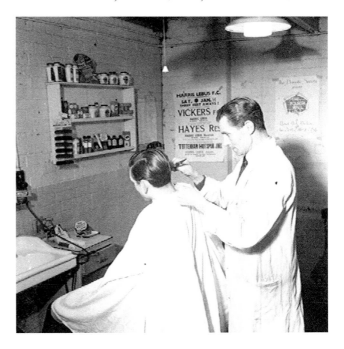

One of the perks of working for a furniture firm

'They had a sale of "rejects" or "seconds" now and again and you could put your name on it,' said Marion Cotton. 'Sometimes people would take your name off and put theirs on. I still own a "pie-crust" occasional table and a couple of fifties bedside cabinets.'

Ada Frost said: 'We had a Utility bedroom suite, a double and single wardrobe, a three-drawer chest with a mirror… and one without. Another room has a single wardrobe and a small chest (of drawers) same design. I think it's teak, and the first one was mahogany veneer.'

Working and singing to music

By the end of the 1930s the firm had wired up a radiogram with 60 loudspeakers playing music during working hours. Ron Turton remembered that during the 1950s and 1960s, the BBC's *Music While You Work* was on morning and afternoon. Similarly, Daphne Bradley recalled of the 1940s: 'Half an hour of popular tunes of the war years such as 'We'll Meet Again', 'Deep in the Heart of Texas', and many more. We all joined in the singing and we looked forward to it because it helped to break up the long hours of the day.' Meanwhile, a teenage Henry Jacobs, photography apprentice in the 1960s, recalled listening to the pirate station Radio Caroline on his portable radio, saying of that time 'the rest of my workmates were in their twenties'.

Post-war leisure use for war shelters

Gordon Shepherd remembered how the old air-raid shelters were put to leisure use in the 1950s: 'We used to have the breaks in the old air-raid shelter. It was right alongside the shop, we were near the Lea. The shelter was above ground, brick, held about 30 – 40 people, there was a bench in there, electric light, long benches both sides and a table down the middle.' Gordon also recalled how the old war shelters were used as cloakrooms as well as for leisure activities – allocated on different days for either men or women: 'One of the old shelters, it was big, racks all-round the walls with hooks for your jacket and that, no lockers,

Spaces created next to workshops as shelters from the war were later used by workers during their break times

(Reproduced with special permission from Waltham Forest Local History Archives, Vestry House Museum)

the women had lockers. Every Thursday you'd play bingo in the old shelter in the tea break. Women had the room on Friday.'

'Posh-do' – organised nights in town

Marian Cotton remembered paying a weekly amount to the section head and outings were arranged: 'I can remember the pleasure in going on one occasion to the Odeon cinema in Leicester Square and then having dinner in the restaurant. It was a very posh "do" with flowers on each table. We were brought back to our homes by taxi, which was an event in itself!'

Girls' night out in town

Daphne Bradley would sometimes go into town after work with her friend Ivy Eden:

> We were pretty well exhausted, but after we had clocked off… we would go to the ladies' washroom and change our clothes and get ready for a night out. We would get

on a bus outside the factory which would take us to Manor House tube station. From Manor House we would go to Covent Garden on the tube train. During the war, Covent Garden Opera House was a dance hall, so we used to dance all evening until 11 o'clock when the band played the last dance. We came back on the tube to Manor House and then got a bus home. By that time, it was almost midnight, so as we had to get up again the next morning to get to work by 7 o'clock, we had to get to bed pretty quickly. As you can see, it was quite a long day for us, but we had to have some leisure time after all of those long hours in a factory. We were, after all, quite young girls.

High days and holidays

Annual paid holidays were a feature of the 1950s and 1960s. Things had progressed from there being no paid holidays in early indentures through, in successive stages, to one week by the end of the 1930s. By the 1950s, Ron Turton explained, 'you got two weeks… [the factory] closed, paid holiday, all firms closed' (usually the last week in July and first in August). Many workers went away to the coast – often staying in digs furnished with Lebus-made furniture. Mr. J. H. Dashwood, Cornwall

sales representative, said: 'Some hotels have been buying Lebus furniture for many years and adding new wings until their bedrooms make quite a comprehensive exhibition of Lebus "period" pieces from pre-1914 days up to our latest designs.' And in-between, there appears to have been plenty of fun had at the firm, from organised clubs and societies to outings and evenings in town, and practical jokes and high jinks.

No prizes for guessing who used to dip an old copper half-penny in silver-nitrate developing fluid for a couple of hours until it went silver, attach an invisible black cotton and place it in the middle of the corridor to watch the girls bend over to pick it up as he peeked-out from hiding in his photographic studio; it was Henry Jacobs.

Harris Lebus clubs and societies

Many of the firm's clubs and societies were organised by the workers. There was anything from opera singing and concerts, amateur dramatics and plays, bowls and cricket, dancing and physical training, cycling and canoe-making, angling and darts, rambling and swimming, tennis and netball, boxing and camera club – and football (the team was called 'Pando' – Polishers and Offices). There

The Sir Herman Lebus Sports Pavilion, which housed leisure activities, pictured on the day of the Duke of Edinburgh's visit

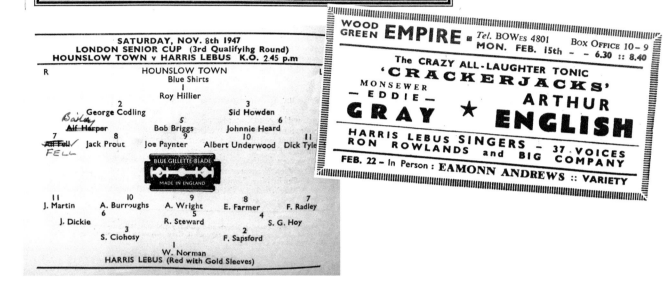

is a suggestion that what is now the Paddock nature field on Ferry Lane was once the firm's original sports ground, although no evidence could be found amongst the Lebus archives to substantiate this. However, it appears that when the firm acquired island B in 1937, the *Lebus Log* mentions a Lebus-owned sports facility in 1938 with changing facilities before the Sir Herman Lebus Sports Pavilion was opened in 1954.

A report on the sports page of the *Tottenham and Edmonton Weekly Herald*, 2 April 1945, records that the Harris Lebus first and second football teams had matches at Ferry Lane against the league leaders, winning 5:3 against Rayners Lane and 3:0 against Oxford House. When mass redundancies came in the 1960s, many of the clubs and societies folded. In the *Tottenham and Edmonton Weekly Herald*, 3 February 1967, there is an article on the sports page entitled 'Lebus bow out on a high note' – it was the end of the boxing club.

Pavilion parties

The Sir Herman Lebus Sports Pavilion, with licensed bar, provided a venue for many a retirement party, leaving 'do' and Christmas party. Phyllis Roberts also helped out there: 'I worked in the sports place… during the summer. I can't remember if they had a sports day or if they had cricket.'

Ron Turton remembered parties: 'I helped… it was for children of the workers there, we had a party for them every year, I think. Nice big dance floor, tables, chairs, a stage with curtains. My daughter had a party dress, green organza, frills, puff sleeves, she hated it! She didn't like dressing up! There was a piano there. The children had tea, games, dancing.'

Between mid-December 1955 and early February 1956, Miss. Johnstone organised 'shop' parties for some 2,000 children on nine successive Saturdays, either in the canteen or the sports pavilion (*Lebus Log*, No. 7, December 1955).

'Beanos' – organised coach outings

In the Coombes Croft project, Hilda Hewitt said that her husband Bill, a cabinet-maker, 'had what they called "Beanos"':

> The men in his section would have a day's outing. They'd have a coach and go to Clacton, and then from there they'd go to the restaurant, it was all booked, and then they'd have some music and a drink. Bill played a sort of washboard and he'd sing. And he'd come back and couldn't speak the next day because of the singing. They'd be out on the Saturday and back in the early hours of Sunday.

'Woodley Whispers' – 'A real family unit'

Some 250 people worked in the Woodley factory by the mid-1950s; about half were women. 'On the firm's outing, about 240 – just about the total strength went to Southsea in 1957,' reported the *Lebus Log*.

In recollections written for the author to use in this book, Shirley Hiscock said:

> It was a very good firm to work for... we all had moans every now and then, but generally the atmosphere was very good. It was a great place to work and everyone was so friendly; if anyone had a problem, we all sorted it for them. I think we worked about 35 hours a week.

Pictured in 1960, the entire Woodley upholstery workforce. The picture was requested by Adolphus Osigweh (first row seated, 10th from right) who was on management training from C. F. C. Lagos between autumn 1959 to spring 1960. Next to him, front right to left, Ken Nash and George Chaplin. Seated on the floor, right side, fourth is George Heath, in charge of the fabric store plus the cutters. Seated on the ground on the left side, fifth, is Paul Kellway, who kept all the sewing machines in working order. Shirley Hiscock (who kindly provided this photograph) is third from left, top row, and her best friend, Violet Brown, is on the second row, third from left.

The pay was very good, one of the best in the area; there were lots of families that worked there; brothers, sisters, aunts and uncles – a real family unit. The managers were lovely to us, always ready to help and have a laugh with us. But we respected them. We used to see Mr. Antony Lebus very often (we were told to call him 'Mr.'). He always came to see us the day we broke up for Christmas when we used to have some nibbles and a few drinks. Mr. Oliver Lebus came around sometimes, but not so often. In the later years we had a good social side. My friend Dianne and I used to organise Barn Dances and Discos. Also, we used to hold raffles each week from October, to collect money for a local orphanage. We used to have a party for them in our rest room, and Les Holdaway and Roger Dyke used to dress up and give them presents. Les was Father Christmas; Roger was a fairy – a good one at that!

'Woodley Whispers' – Lebus Lorries used for upholstery workers

Shirley Hiscock recalled an unusual public transport method in bad weather:

> [W]hen we used to have the smog come down – I think in the late fifties, we used to have a message from the bus company in Reading that they were taking the buses off because the driver couldn't see in the smog: so what would happen would be, the Transport Manager would bring a Lebus furniture lorry around the front of the factory and put bench seats in and take the workforce that travel normally by bus back in to Reading. Great fun for them; lucky I lived in Woodley so I could just walk home!

A Lebus lorry converted into a make-shift bus during a local bus strike

Local bus strike in May 1958 – Lebus vans used in Tottenham

During a strike in the 1950s, Lebus vans were also used as makeshift buses in Tottenham Hale; the local press heaped praise on the firm for the best improvised transport service. 'Bus strike – everybody helpful; local firms run their own services', was the headline article in the *Tottenham and Edmonton Weekly Herald*, 9 May 1958. The article commented: 'Among the best "pirate" service organised locally was that run by Harris Lebus Ltd., at Tottenham. Their "buses" were furniture vans fitted with seats and carrying route-boards indicating pick-up and setting down places. Route A was from the factory gates in Ferry Lane to Waltham Cross, via Bruce Grove, Angel Edmonton, Bounces Road, Southbury Road, and Bullsmoor Lane.'

Workers travelled afar

Ron Turton recalled his uncle's long journey to work:

> My uncle used to come in from Canvey Island, he worked in the Mill. Don't know what time he left home for a 7 o'clock start, and it was the old steam trains then. Some people lived in Harlow, Billericay. Bloke bought a transit van and brought them in from Harlow and charged so much a week; he was a polisher and he got this transit van. He brought people in from Harlow, Basildon, Hackney, they was really spread out, the wages was good. The Green Line bus was very unreliable. You could lose money, get the sack for bad timekeeping.
>
> Not many had cars then, they had bikes. Over the road [the other side of Ferry Lane in front of the new warehouse] used to have the bike racks, tin shelter, big hook, like butcher's hook, hang your front wheel on it. Had to remember where you put it, hundreds of bikes. Couldn't do it now – and the roads weren't so busy then for the bike riders.

'The Victoria line came just after I finished working there [opened on 7 March 1969] – it was 5d to Oxford Street,' recalled Henry Jacobs. Despite the proximity of Tottenham

TOTTENHAM HALE - LATE 1950'S

Tottenham Hale pictured during the 1950s

Hale underground station – the Ferry Lane underpass steps rose to virtually meet the factory's front entrance – it was too late to be of use to employees. 'You should have seen it on a Friday night', continued Ron Turton… all the factories finish at the same time; it was jammed! Lebus's, Keith Blackman's, Gestetner's… buses, cars, bikes, people walking…'.

As memories inevitably fade, it is the last thoughts of Henry Jacobs that seem now to conjure a ghostly image: 'Ferry Lane was packed at home time – a sea of people, lots had bikes; few had cars. It was a sea of humanity'.

CHAPTER SEVEN

Looking Back: Celebrating the Good Times

One last memory… that is of our foreign Travellers (Sales Representatives) with sun-tanned faces home on Christmas leave, walking round the workshops exchanging greetings and handing out cigars to our packers – boy-like, I would gaze at them in awe.

– Harry Thornton's memories of pre-World War One
(*Lebus Log*, No. 21, December 1961)

Drama: Armistice Day 1918, the Fitters' workshop

At the Finsbury Cabinet Works, in the Fitters' workshop (H/J), as many of the factory workers as it is physically possible to accommodate are stood together in anticipation. It is approaching the eleventh hour of the eleventh day of the eleventh month; all eyes want to be on a clock on the wall – some eyes are indeed on a clock on the wall.

The lighting is still reasonably dim – paint in various tones and shades of mud and cabbage green still camouflages the glass roof windows. Some, though not all, of the black-out window blinds have been raised, allowing light from the winter sun to filter through the dimness.

Many of the workers now are women, most of them employed while young men eligible and fit enough to fight a war are still far away on duty; the war is not yet over, at least for a few more minutes. They have waited a long, long time for this moment, and their wait is almost over.

All machines are switched off, and the room is silent and still. That is to say, relatively silent for a Monday morning approaching 11 a.m. in one of the noisiest, busiest parts of the largest furniture manufacturers in the world.

Some find it hard to contain their excitement; they are used to working in silence in a structured, relatively formal working environment, but are struggling not to let loose their emotions on this momentous occasion. Many are no more than teenage girls. Some of the women are holding hands, an expression of emotion, support, solidarity. Others are bobbing up and down as they stand on tiptoes for a few seconds at a time, straining to catch a glimpse of the time on one of the few clocks adorning the walls of this large workshop. A number of the women are wearing a customary white head cap and sit or stand together; many of the men wear a dark cloth cap and also sit or stand together. As heads move to the left and then to the right to see over those before them, it is as if a giant zebra walks the earth.

Some are looking at Louis sat in front of a piano wheeled in especially for the occasion, his fingers poised and ready; they know it is he that will give the signal for the performance to start. Dark-suited, bow-tied, white-shirted – a faint glimmer of light from one of the windows catches the shirt of Louis. He looks every inch the music-hall impresario.

And as if controlled to precision timing by a backstage hand, the glimmer of sunlight intensifies into a shard of spotlight; the signal is given, the time has arrived, the ivories tinkle, the showman bursts into song and the show begins!

Oh, we take him from the city or the plough…

As Louis plays piano and sings, most are surprised, delightfully so, at his vocal ability – some open their eyes wide in disbelief, some tap each other and nod simultaneously in approval, and some begin to jig in rhythm to the voice described as 'excellent' by LS.

> *Tommy, Tommy Atkins, you're a 'good 'un', heart and hand;*
>
> *You're a credit to your calling, and to all your native land;*
>
> *May your luck be never failing, may your love be ever true;*
>
> *God bless you, Tommy Atkins, here's your country's love to you.*

By the end of the second run of the chorus most of the workers who didn't know the song 'Private Tommy Atkins' before now can sing at least some of it and hum along with the rest. In the centre of the workshop delineated by makeshift ropes and stands, many are engaged in dance. The end of the song was met with tumultuous applause and, as Louis takes a bow to the assembled hall, he could pass for a music-hall star. The audience call for more; all formalities are waived for today; such is the magnitude of the celebration and Louis obliges with another rousing song.

And most of the assembled crowd are happy, joyous even. But for some the joy is all bittersweet. Some former colleagues have gone, never to return, and will not be forgotten. If not directly affected, most will know someone who has lost a relative: father, son, brother, uncle or nephew. One of those affected was architect Samuel Clifford Tee: just a few months ago, the end of the war nearing, his only son, 20-year-old Clifford Vernon Tee, was killed on active duty in France, on 11 August. He was a second lieutenant in the 153rd Siege Battery, Royal Garrison Artillery, and was buried in Terlincthun British Cemetery at Wimille on the northern outskirts of Boulogne. For some, life would never be the same again. But life did indeed go on, and the singing and dancing went on for a couple of hours more, playing out as a real-life opera before the curtain closed, the encore was made and the works closed for the rest of the day.

Workers gathered in celebration of the Armistice; a section in the centre of the workshop has been roped off and some are enjoying a dance

Workshop cleared, workers
and their families enjoy the
Queen's coronation party

Tradition for celebration

A tradition for celebration was well established at Harris Lebus whether the occasion be the end of a war (World War One or World War Two), the coronation of a new King or Queen (George V on Thursday 22 June 1911; George VI on Wednesday 12 May 1937; or Elizabeth II on Tuesday 2 June 1953) or the visit of a prince or princess (the Duke of Edinburgh on Thursday 10 November 1955; Princess Margaret on Wednesday 10 April 1968). There were annual dances between the two world wars, though these stopped during World War Two. The Royal, 415–419 High Road, Tottenham – a dance hall with big band, jazz and swing themed nights from the mid-1920s – was a favoured venue; LS had combined his wedding celebration with the annual dance of 1928.

Family Birthday Celebrations

'Coming of age' parties – Louis in 1904 and Herman in 1905

When Louis and Herman turned 21, Harris and Sarah organised lavish celebrations. Louis's party was combined with a wedding breakfast for his oldest sister, Lena, on Thursday 11 April 1904 at the Café Royal, Regent Street. The same venue was used the following year for Herman's birthday dinner on Saturday 3 June 1905.

Invitation cards to each party contained the words 'to the staff' – perhaps some 50 or so were invited. Since a distinction was made between salaried 'white collar' staff and hourly paid 'blue collar' manual workers, it was presumably the former who received invitations.

Sir Herman's 70th birthday celebrations in 1954

Sir Herman's 70th birthday party was held on Friday 4 June 1954 at the Connaught Rooms, Holborn, London and was attended by 750 employees with more than 21 years' service. Of these, 19 employees had 50 years or more service, four had 49, seven had 48, five had 47, six had 46, six had 45, 29 had service ranging between 44 and 40 years, and 225 had 30–39 years of service.

Ada Smith of the Laboratory stores was the company's longest-serving female employee at 44 years. Two married couples with each spouse having more than 21 years' service were invited: Sissy Lewis the spray polisher and her husband Tom of 22 shop attended; Mr. and Mrs. Arthur Burton of the Makers and Personnel, respectively, were unable to attend as a couple – Mrs. Burton was ill that day.

Only one employee, Carver Albert Church, equalled Sir Herman's 55 years; his privilege was to unveil the portrait of Sir Herman as a gift from the staff to their chairman and managing director.

'Harris Lebus was the first firm to introduce a five-day week, a week's holiday with pay, and payment for statutory holidays long before it had become an obligation,' he took pride in reminding his party.

LS took his programme around with him on the evening (it has his initials on the top-right of the outside back cover) and asked for the autographs of some of the 'good and the great' of the firm. Among these are the signatures of Robert Taylor, Monty Newman, G. A. Baldock (Zone Three), T. W. Hinton (Zone Two), W. Gibson (Stores), H. Trew, T. A. Rowland (Zone Two), Arthur Easter, Bill Thear, William O'Hare, H. I. Fisher, E. D. Petry, Frank Felce and Jock Boryer.

Factory-shaped Birthday Cake

A birthday cake for Sir Herman made specially to resemble the factory was presented to him at his party in the Connaught Rooms. Afterward, he decided that he would like to donate the cake to the children at the Furniture Trades Benevolent Association (FTBA) home in Apsley Guise, Bedfordshire. 'Miss. M. Currie, Matron,

was overjoyed and the children were able to have many helpings – tackling Zones One, Two and Three in that order ending up with the chimney,' explained the *Lebus Log*, No. 2, September 1954.

A Gift from the Staff to Sir Herman – Portrait by Simon Elwes

As mentioned above, when Sir Herman reached 70, a portrait in oil by the renowned society artist, Simon Elwes, was given to him as a birthday gift from the staff. It measures 36 by 26 inches and depicts Sir Herman proudly wearing his liveryman attire, his robe as master of the Furniture Makers' Guild, against a royal blue background. A report in the *Cabinet Maker and Complete House Furnisher* 12 June 1954 tells how each employee received a mounted black and white photograph of the painting as a souvenir. 'I hope you will have no regrets for having perpetuated the old man!' he joked at his party.

The portrait was shown at the Royal Academy Summer Exhibition 1955 at Burlington House, along with two portraits of the Queen – one also by Simon Elwes and one by Pietro Annigoni. Thereafter, it adorned the walls of the Sir Herman Lebus Sports Pavilion. The portrait remains in the family and is now owned by one of Sir Herman's grandchildren.

Sir Herman's 70th birthday cake in the shape of the factory

Portrait of Sir Herman Lebus C.B.E. J.P.
presented to him
by employees of Harris Lebus
on his 70th Birthday, 1st June 1954.

Painted by Simon Elwes

Sir Herman's portrait souvenir card presented to Harris Lebus workers; they had each contributed to the portrait in oils by Simon Elwes

A Gift from Sir Herman to the Staff – A Sports Pavilion

'It is Sir Herman's hope that the Pavilion will, in years to come, act as a real community centre for all members of the organisation,' stated the *Lebus Log*, No. 1 in June 1954, informing workers of the gift from Sir Herman. The facility was formally opened in a ceremony on 1 June 1954. Located in its own six-acre grounds north of Ferry Lane, the Sir Herman Lebus Sports Pavilion was presented to the employees by the chairman and managing director, Sir Herman Lebus, to mark his 70th birthday on the afternoon of 1 June 1954. 'It was a dull showery morning, but the experts assured us it would brighten up by midday. As usual they were completely correct, and we were able to go ahead promptly at 2 p.m. with the opening ceremony (*Lebus Log*, No. 2, September 1954). The Duke of Edinburgh sent a telegram of congratulations as president of the National Playing Fields Association. The Sir Herman Lebus Sports Pavilion measured 6,000 square feet and was made of laminated wood by Kingston Architectural Craftsmen

The official opening and presentation by Sir Herman Lebus of the sports pavilion bearing his name

Limited (coincidentally, a firm based in Hull, where Louis Lebus had arrived from Germany in the 1840s). Much of the groundwork on the site was carried out by local Tottenham firm, Messrs. Carpenter Brothers. An advertisement in *The Times* on 21 July 1954 proudly affirmed that 'from request to completion was just ten weeks'.

News of the Pavilion was recorded in the *Furniture Record*, 18 November 1955 and in the *Cabinet Maker and Complete House Furnisher*, 12 June 1954. The latter described the Pavilion thus:

> One of whose principal features were the large windows, it is in two sections connected by the entrance vestibule. Noteworthy are the almost Gothic-style laminated arches of timber construction, moulded and glued, which support the deep sloping roof of red cedar shingles. The outer walls are timber clad and painted green, reeded hardboard has been used for the interior timber walls where the flooring is of oak. Pastel colours were chosen for the colour scheme inside, red, blue and grey, reminiscent of the firm's corporate colour scheme, predominate in the furnishing. The lounge, or tearoom section is equipped with a licensed bar, and the other, in which there is a stage, has been designed for use as a hall.

Charity Football Match and Carnival

Celebrity charity football match

'The "stars" shine at Tottenham,' read an article in the *Lebus Log* as a crowd of 3,000 gathered on the sports field on Sunday 22 February 1959. They had come to watch a special celebrity charity football match in aid of the FTBA, between the 'laughter-makers' and the cabinet-makers. The match was refereed by Tommy Docherty. The 'All Stars Eleven' consisted of celebrities from television, stage and radio including Tommy Steele, Alfie Bass and Lonnie Donegan, and they won 4:3. There was just one injury – Maurice Kaufman collided with Stan Hall and had to have a stitch

A charity football match for the Furniture Trades Benevolent Association on Harris Lebus sports ground, Sunday 22 February 1959 – workers play against a team of celebrities of the day

above his eye. Mr. Anthony Lebus hosted an after-match tea in the Pavilion, along with an impromptu cabaret as the celebrities sang 'You Got to Have Heart' and were presented with a souvenir polyester tea tray.

Carnival time

Ben Judd led a committee to organise a carnival at the sports ground on Saturday 30 June 1962. The Mayor of Haringey, Alderman Mrs. L. R. Harrington J.P., welcomed 1,500 people who attended the carnival – and chance to see celebrity, Miss. Ann Cullen (Mrs.

Grenville of *The Archers* radio serial drama). There was a gymnastics display by the West Green School Association and competitions for carnival queen, children's fancy dress and a tug of war. There were also donkey rides, a refreshments bar, burger stall and beer tent with open-air dancing in the evening. The weather 'could have been kinder but the rain kept off' (*Lebus Log*, No. 22, September 1962). The event was to fundraise for the retired employees' annual holiday and party.

Long Service Awards and Annual Dance

'There were flowers in abundance to remind us of the summer days to come, and – alas; all of the summers that have passed! There was an atmosphere of cordiality and friendship which results from the long years of everybody knowing everybody else. There was a buzz of conversation – the annual stock-taking of the events of the past year – the weddings of sons and daughters and the latest score of grandchildren and their achievements.'

– Lebus Log, No. 20, September 1961

'To the 47 long-service employees, who were to receive service tokens, add those who have already received theirs in the last eight years (204), sprinkle generously with a high proportion of those who have retired, and you have the perfect ingredients for a wonderful party – the Annual Reunion.'

– Lebus Log, No. 28, December 1964

Sir Herman's 50 years' service party, 1949

All employees who had completed more than 25 years' service, regardless of their status as either office staff or manual worker, were invited to Sir Herman's party to celebrate his milestone 50 years at Harris Lebus. This took place on Saturday 9 April 1949 and, like Louis's coming of age party back in 1904, took place at the Café Royal.

Of the 270 employees with 25 or more years of service with the firm, ten were women. In an internal list, they were typed in red:

> Mrs. Ada Smith, Laboratory Stores with 38 years and one month's service
>
> Mrs. B. Russell, Stores, 34 years and seven months
>
> Mrs. L. Williams, also of Stores, 34 years and five months
>
> Miss. E. Petry, Purchase Department, 33 years and one month
>
> Miss. E. Middleton, personal assistant, 32 years and eight months
>
> Miss. Doris Middleton, personal assistant, 31 years and 11 months

> Miss. S. Gimber, Sales Department, 27 years and seven months
>
> Mrs. G. Mahoney, Canteen, 27 years and five months
>
> Miss. E. Fisher, Purchase Department, 27 years and four months
>
> Miss. V. Dunham, Purchase Department, 27 years and two months.

Only two employees exceeded Sir Herman's 50 years' service – A. J. Douse (known as 'Jimmie') with 53 years as a machinist in Zone One, and Ben Goddard, who had served 51 years in charge of the Stores – both of whom had recently retired.

One serving employee equalled Sir Herman's 50 years – Albert Church, the early morning gas-lamp lighter in Tabernacle Street, who went on to be an excellent carver and inspector of samples in T1.

Seated at the top table with Sir Herman and Lady Lebus were 40 of the longest-serving employees and their spouses – their service records ranged from 41 to 53 years and included those who had now retired. Jimmie Douse, Ben Goddard and Albert Church proudly took their prestigious seats, along with retired Jock Boryer and Frank Felce (the faces of Tabernacle Street), Bill Thear (who remembered locals bathing in the brook by the Tottenham factory in the early days), Joseph Clohosy (who set the 'piece-work' rates in the Makers), William O'Hare (who had recently retired after 46 years as a polisher during which time he witnessed the change from French to spray polishing), John Rollings (who had worked in timber purchasing since 1904), Arthur Easter (who worked the Railway department from 1906 and was latterly in Sales), 'Monty' Newman (who came to the General Office in Tottenham from Tabernacle Street in 1906 and worked in Sales) and Charlie Holland (who started as a crate-maker in 1908).

Apologies included Dickie Porch – the only draughtsman in the early days – and Charlie Oliver, the Maples runner.

SERVICE ROLL

NAME	YEARS	NAME	YEARS
Mr. A. E. WATTS	54	Mr. G. H. KNIGHT	40
Mr. C. OLIVER	54	Mr. W. D. CROSS	40
Mr. C. CLARK	53	Mr. A. F. THOMPSON	40
Mr. A. J. DOUSE	53	Mr. W. S. GIBSON	40
Mr. B. J. GODDARD	51	Mr. J. J. A. FLACK	40
Mr. W. A. UPTON	51	Mr. A. E. LOVEDAY	40
Sir HERMAN LEBUS	50	Mr. S. D. PORCH	39
Mr. W. J. WILD	50	Mr. A. E. MOUNTFORD	39
Mr. J. RIDER	50	Mr. E. C. PARFORD	39
Mr. A. G. CHURCH	50	Mr. P. G. IRISH	39
Mr. A. W. LONGLEY	50	Mr. H. H. D. COLES	39
Mr. A. E. NEWMAN	50	Mr. H. C. MADDEN	39
Mr. B. SMITHERS	49	Mr. E. A. KANARENS	39
Mr. E. E. FYSON	49	Mrs. A. SMITH	38
Mr. V. J. CLOHOSY	49	Mr. T. A. SANSUM	38
Mr. H. TREW	48	Mr. H. C. BAXTER	38
Mr. W. R. STUTTERS	48	Mr. F. H. DAVIS	38
Mr. H. R. KINSLEY	48	Mr. L. S. LEBUS	37
Mr. G. C. ROBINSON	48	Mr. C. F. SMITH	37
Mr. F. W. SAVAGE	47	Mr. F. G. BURGE	37
Mr. C. STOCKWELL	46	Mr. J. C. RAYNER	37
Mr. W. O'HARE	46	Mr. R. J. WALLEDGE	37
Mr. M. T. TOBICH	46	Mr. J. BALDOCK	37
Mr. F. C. FELCE	46	Mr. A. BAILEY	37
Mr. A. E. HICKFORD	46	Mr. G. ELLIOTT	37
Mr. J. S. DILWORTH	46	Mr. J. KNIGHT	36
Mr. W. S. CULLEN	46	Mr. E. G. STEWART	36
Mr. G. A. BALDOCK	46	Mr. A. J. TURNER	35
Mr. F. J. CULLEN	46	Mrs. B. RUSSELL	35
Mr. E. ZALA	46	Mrs. L. WILLIAMS	35
Mr. E. PROFAZE	46	Mr. A. C. J. NASH	35
Mr. J. GOLDINSKY	45	Mr. H. KANARENS	35
Mr. C. H. BORYER	45	Mr. W. T. SPENCER	34
Mr. H. LOWE	45	Mr. W. H. BALLS	34
Mr. T. ROWLAND	45	Mr. G. F. BENNETT	34
Mr. G. E. SAVAGE	45	Mr. W. WHALLEY	34
Mr. J. W. N. ROLLINGS	45	Mr. A. E. SINNING	34
Mr. J. W. HUNT	45	Mr. A. J. PRIOR	34
Mr. G. NORTH	45	Mrs. S. E. HUTCHINSON	34
Mr. A. CLUFF	44	Miss E. F. PETRY	33
Mr. B. SACK	44	Mr. W. F. WILLMOTT	33
Mr. A. BROWN	44	Miss E. G. MIDDLETON	33
Mr. T. W. HINTON	44	Mr. E. E. MONTGOMERY	33
Mr. T. K. BESSENT	43	Mr. A. O. RICH	33
Mr. G. H. BAKER	43	Mr. A. RACKHAM	32
Mr. A. J. EASTER	42	Mr. W. WILSON	32
Mr. E. O. PAYNE	42	Miss D. MIDDLETON	32
Mr. W. J. THEAR	42	Mr. T. H. HARRIS	32
Mr. W. J. COCKAYNE	42	Mr. H. S. THOMAS	32
Mr. A. J. F. HEDGER	41	Mr. A. H. BEAUMONT	32
Mr. C. W. HOLLAND	41	Mr. H. J. HARRISON	32
Mr. R. GUNNELL	40	Mr. C. F. MOORE	32

The first page of the invitees to Sir Herman's party celebrating his fifty years – the experiences of a number of these workers at Harris Lebus are featured in this book

A special, unique and personal token

Between 1955 and 1964, 251 employees received a unique and personal token of recognition of their commitment to Harris Lebus. The introduction of Long Service Awards – personally inscribed gold watches – was made at the Annual Dance on Friday 7 October 1955. With an attendance of over 200 (although the log reads, almost certainly erroneously, 2,000), the event was held at the Royal Dance Hall, Tottenham. The *Lebus Log*, No. 7, December 1955, lists 30 who received awards for 45 or more years' service.

The following year, the Annual Dance was on Friday 5 October 1956 once again at the Royal Dance Hall and seven employees were presented with their personally inscribed gold watches.

There are no records for awards in the years 1957 and 1958.

In 1959, the event on 1 May was described as the Second Annual Reunion, combined with the Annual Dance and Long Service Awards; 26 employees were recognised. The venue was moved to the Regal Rooms, Edmonton. More than 200 attended and many of these travelled long distances to be there. These included Willie Stark from Edinburgh, Bill Rowland from Paignton, Ted Kanarens from Norfolk, Bill Ferris from Gillingham, together with Miss. E. Middleton, Miss. E. Petrie, Miss. Jeff, Grace Mahoney and Beattie Russell.

The Regal Rooms were again the venue for the Third Annual Reunion on Friday 6 May 1960. 32 Long Service Awards were presented in front of a crowd of 270; 35 awardees had given more than 40 years' service and 54 were retired long-service employees.

The Fourth Annual Reunion, at the Regal Rooms, was on 5 May the following year. Again, the number of Long Service Awards presented was 32. Anthony and Oliver, who were on tour in Africa, sent a telegram of congratulations.

Friday 4 May 1962 saw another 32 Long Service Awards made at Edmonton's Regal Rooms for the Fifth Annual Reunion. On the eve of the football Cup Final, Tom Turpin was lucky enough to win a ticket for the next day's match. Coincidentally, the Cup Final was won by Lebus's local team: Tottenham Hotspur, who beat Burnley 3:1.

'The biggest and best' Annual Reunion, according to the *Lebus Log*, No. 25, in June 1963, took place in May 1963. The log reads: 'It is significant that five years ago, 260 attended the Annual Reunion of 1959, and now the party has grown to 450.' On 3 May at the Regal Rooms, 38 employees who had given more than 40 years' service to the firm were presented with their personally engraved gold watches.

'When the number reached 400, we did not dare continue to count…'

The last Annual Reunion recorded by the *Lebus Log*, No. 28, December 1964, was that of 18 September 1964, at the usual favoured venue: the Regal Rooms. 'Mr. Sid Bracken was again the capable "host" supported by the voices we know so well, led the singing of old and familiar songs – songs we have heard many times in the last 50 years'.

The same *Lebus Log* stated how LS and his wife made the presentations 'an occasion tinged with emotion and pride at perhaps his last official appearance after a lifetime with us prior to his retirement at the end of the year. Our last memories were the farewells – the handshakes, the back-slapping and the ladies with their flowers to remind them of a very happy evening'.

The Duke of Edinburgh's Visit – Thursday 10 November 1955

On his factory visit, the Duke met with 39 managers and foremen and had lunch with the board of directors – Bernard Humphrey, LS, Sir Herman, Anthony, Oliver, Sir Laurence Watkinson, Arthur Tunley, Raymond Lamb and Desmond Stratton.

Albert Church, who joined Harris Lebus in the same year as Sir Herman Lebus, is presented by him to the Duke of Edinburgh on his visit, 10 November 1955

After lunch with the board, the Duke, as president of the National Playing Fields Association, was taken by car to the new Sir Herman Lebus Sports Pavilion, past the site of the proposed new north warehouse and offices. The route to the Pavilion was lined by 1,000 wives, mothers and other relatives of the employees.

The Duke met eight employees with over 50 years' service

Inside the Pavilion, the Duke spoke to the men and women who had worked for Harris Lebus for 50 years or more (there were nearly 700 who had been with the company 21 years or more). These included:

- Albert Church, 44 Woodland Park Road, N15, carver

- Joseph Clohosy, 18 Rowdem Road, Chingford, E4, cabinet-maker

- J. Dilworth, 251 Sewardstone Road, Chingford, E4, inspector

- G. Baldock, 22 Westward Road, Chingford, E4, foreman

- Edmund Zala, 20 Albermarle Gardens, Ilford, manager

- G. E. North, 15, Bromley Road, N17, foreman

- T. W. Hinton, 53 Scales Road, N17, cabinet-maker

- W. S. Gibson, 103 Weir Gardens, Rayleigh, stores checker.

The Duke met ten employees of the third generation

The Duke also spoke with the ten representatives of families who had worked for the firm for three generations:

- Miss. Jean Bradley, a secretary in the Timber department, who lived in Marmion Avenue, South Chingford, and who had worked for the firm for 14 years; her father, Mr. Harry Bradley, was still there after 37 years' service and his father had been employed for 47 years

- Miss. V. K. Butville, clerk, Springfield Road, South Tottenham

- Mrs. E. Fuller, sprayer, Hertford Road, Edmonton

- J. M. Smith, improver, Veneer shop, Walthamstow

- M. Chadwick, improver, Cabinet-maker, Chingford

- Sid. Bracken, cabinet-maker, Walthamstow

- S. Trew, traveller, Hoppers Road, Winchmore Hill

- Alf Brown, manager, Mandeville Road, Southgate

- Dr. R. Hickford, engineer

- A. H. Humm, cabinet-maker, Eckington Road, Tottenham.

Newspaper coverage of the Duke's visit

'They Meet Again'

Evening News, 10 November 1955

'While serving in the navy during the war, the Duke of Edinburgh chatted with three Royal Air Force officers, in an officer's mess at Gibraltar. Today, he met one of those officers again… ex. Flight Lieutenant Frederick Forrest, now aged 48, is the firm's Transport Manager.'

Photos in the *Daily Star*

Photos of groups of female employees appeared in the *Daily Star*: Joyce Sutton, Edmonton; June Warren, Tottenham; Pauline Bird, Walthamstow; Ellen McCarthy, Tottenham; Sheila Saunders, Epping; Veronica Loughton, Tottenham; Maureen Clarabut, Walthamstow; Patricia Frindle, Edmonton; Josephine Peachey, Walthamstow; Sheila Greenhill, Edmonton; Rosina West, Tottenham.

The photo session was also covered in the *Evening Standard*, 10 November 1955:

'Smile Please', She Tells Prince Phillip

'I'm shaky,' she says as he poses for a special 'snap'

'This is the view of Mrs. Melanie Rogers' box camera that Prince Phillip got this afternoon, when he posed specially for her. "I was dared to do it by the other girls," she said. "Press photographers were asked not to use their cameras because of the danger of explosive flash bulbs. I was determined to get a picture, so I stepped out in front of the Duke in the polishing shop and asked if he would pose for me." Prince Phillip stood still and said, "Come closer; you

are not near enough for a picture". "Smile please" Melanie said just before she took her snap. The 25-year-old Addressograph Operator and mother of two who has been with the firm two years, was shaking. The Prince said, "don't shake it about so much", later he asked for a laugh "would you like a button for a souvenir?" "I think he's smashing; Johnnie Ray has got nothing on him" she told her workmates.'

A Doll's House for a Princess – From a Knight of the Realm

The story goes that when Prince Phillip visited the factory in November 1955, he was presented with tiny doll's-house-size versions of the Link furniture range currently being produced by the firm. When he said that his daughter, Princess Anne, did not have a doll's house, Sir Herman and the senior managers decided to make one for her.

The *Lebus Log*, No. 8, April 1956, informed workers:

The idea is that it should be a simple, modern two-storey house complete with garage and roof balcony – with outside walls that can be raised or lowered like an ordinary window. It will all be made to a

Workers prepare to transport the doll's house they have designed and made especially for the young Princess Anne after her father Prince Phillip was heard to say she does not have one

BUCKINGHAM PALACE.

From : Lieut.-General Sir Frederick A. M. Browning, K.C.V.O., K.B.E., C.B., D.S.O. ....16th July, 19 56.

Dear *Herman*

I am commanded by The Queen to write and thank you most sincerely for the beautifully designed and made Dolls House which you and your firm were kind enough to present to The Princess Anne. Her Majesty and The Duke of Edinburgh thought both the design and workmanship were quite first class, and naturally the children are delighted with it.

Perhaps you would be good enough to convey the gratitude of The Queen, The Duke of Edinburgh, and the children to all those concerned with this delightful present.

Yours very sincerely

[signature]

Sir Herman Lebus, C.B.E., J.P.,
    Finsbury Works,
        Tottenham,
            London, N.17.

scale of one inch to one foot which means that the house (which stands on a base two feet high) will measure 42 inches from floor to the top of balcony.

The *Cabinet Maker and Complete House Furnisher*, 21 July 1956 noted: '"Fit for a Princess" certainly describes this truly magnificent doll's house. It is based on an actual house which was built about two years ago at Accra, in the Gold Coast, to the design of James Cubitt and Partners Architects of 25 Gloucester Place W1. The firm acted as honorary architects for the model.'

The doll's house was of modern design and measured five feet six inches by two feet seven-and-a-half inches by two feet six inches, with a base six feet by three feet six inches. The table on which it stood was two-feet high and was fitted with rubber-tyre castors. Beneath this table were cupboards that contained the mechanical devices necessary to operate the lighting, the radio and the water circulation.

On the front of the table was a control panel with operating switches for such devices.

The house had two floors and a roof garden. The back wall supported a veranda that covered the entire length of the house. Both the wall and the veranda could be lowered to show the whole interior. The roof garden with pergola and lily pond was reached by the spiral staircase at the front.

The main floor consisted of a large entrance hall, a lounge dining room, a library and a kitchen. The kitchen had a stainless-steel sink with running water, sliding door fitments and wall cupboards, a cooker, a refrigerator and a washing machine. The colour scheme was white and pale blue. The lounge dining room was royal blue and white with beige curtains. The furniture for the dinning section was of light oak with red chair seats and backs. The lounge and library section was furnished with waxed walnut furniture upholstered in red, black and yellow.

The description of the Link furnishings and colour schemes chosen hint at the decadence of the day; interiors that many aspire to at a time of flair and design.

On the first floor there were two suites of rooms. One had a bedroom, bathroom and dressing room and the other had a bedroom and bathroom. The suites were separated by a gallery that looked down upon the main-floor lounge. The main bedroom was furnished in light oak and the colour scheme was in pale green with a canary carpet. The second bedroom was in yellow and white with pastel blue carpet and furniture of waxed walnut. The third bedroom was in primrose with a pastel grey carpet and furniture of waxed oak.

The bedrooms had bedside lamps, with wall lights and standard lamps, all of which were operated from the control panel. The roof garden was equipped with metal furniture and deck chairs. The doors to the house opened with tiny keys that worked and the cars in its tiny carport operated on a battery. The upholstered furniture was made at Woodley, with the project directed by Edmund Zala.

Ron Turton remembers the doll's house: 'it took one man months to make, it was perfect. The front came open. We were all allowed to go and look at it.'

When the presentation was made at Buckingham Palace, Sir Herman Lebus was accompanied by Edmund Zala and two employees of the firm who had been chosen to represent those members of the staff who contributed to its construction. Fanny Barret, 13, daughter of a cabinet-maker father who helped to make it, was pictured in a national newspaper.

The doll's house was presented in the afternoon of 13 July 1956 to the Princess who was with the Queen, the Duke of Edinburgh and Prince Charles, and a letter of thanks was received from Sir Frederick Browning, the Duke's treasurer, who accompanied him to the factory visit. The *Lebus Log* ended with this line: 'it is interesting to note the reference (in the letter of thanks) to 'the children', and it is, no doubt, in the mechanical details that Prince Charles finds most pleasure' (*Lebus Log*, No. 9, July 1956).

Celebrating a Life – Sir Herman Lebus, 1884–1957

Sir Herman Andrew Harris Lebus died at home (18 Grosvenor Square, Westminster) on Sunday 15 December 1957, aged 73. 'It is no easy task to sum up in a few brief lines my father's many varied achievements spread over a long and active life,' wrote Anthony in the *Lebus Log*, No. 12, July 1958. He continued:

> Maybe the finest tribute one can pay to him – and one that he would have valued beyond all others – is the simple fact that we all of us miss him so much, whether we happen to be one of his family, or one who worked with him, or whether we just used to say 'Good Morning' to him when we saw him around the factory.
>
> His heart and soul were centred here. It was in fact his world – not always an easy world but one that was always full of interest and more than full of jobs to do. He will be remembered too, in years to come for all the work he did for the industry as a whole, for employers and workers alike – for his good advice and help in guiding to success the Utility scheme – for his help to the new, the Furniture Makers Guild, and for many, many other things. And now we are all trying hard, not so much to fill his place, but to forge ahead in the direction in which he led us for so many years. He was, and remains, an inspiration to all who knew him.

Sir Herman's will – Harris Lebus Limited to continue to prosper

An article in the *Tottenham and Edmonton Weekly Herald*, 4 April 1958, reported that Sir Herman Lebus left £165,325 gross, £118,425 net value (duty paid £60,469).

He declared in his will 'that he made no provision for charities as he had contributed according to his means during his lifetime'. He left £100 each to friends, Douglas Clarke, Walter Parker and George Watkinson, also to his cousin LS, and the remainder on trust to his wife. He was clearly concerned to maintain the family's shareholding in the business, as evidenced by the following:

> Whereas I anticipate that under the terms of policies of insurance moneys will become payable on my death to one or more of my children and whereas I am chairman and managing director of Harris Lebus Ltd., and a large part of my estate consists of stock in Harris Lebus Ltd., and I am apprehensive that when I die it may be necessary for my executors to realise a great part of such stock in order to meet death duties and other liabilities of my estate, and that such realisations may result in my family's interests in that company being much decreased and in the price of the stock (which at any case is likely to fall as a result of my death) being unduly lowered by forced sales… to avoid these results I desire that my children should, if my trustees so require, use the proceeds of the policies in purchasing from my estate stock in Harris Lebus Ltd.

Obituary

Sir Herman's obituary in *The Times* reminded the reader that, in addition to running Harris Lebus, during his lifetime he had been: chairman of the Furniture Industry Post-War Reconstruction Committee in 1943; a member of the Board of Trade Utility Furniture Advisory Committee, 1942–1949; an adviser to the president of the Board of Trade on Utility Furniture, 1942–1945; a member of the Board of Trade Furniture Production Committee, 1944–1949; president of the British Furniture Trade Confederation, 1944–1950; employer member of the Board of Trade Working Party, 1945–1946; a member of the committee on Long Term Requirements and Supplies of Timber, 1947–1948; and employer member of the Furniture Development Council, 1949–1957. In addition, he was a past master of the

Furniture Makers' Guild, a liveryman of the Worshipful Company of Coopers since 1910 and was a justice of the peace for the County of London.

For his contribution to the two world wars, he was appointed a CBE in 1920 and received his knighthood in 1946. He left a widow, Ethel Hart (the daughter of Charles Hart of Chicago, whom he married in 1912), and a daughter, Barbara, as well as Anthony and Oliver.

His funeral took place at Golders Green Crematorium, Thursday 19 December 1957.

A Mace as Memorial to Sir Herman at the Furniture Makers' Guild

In the *Lebus Log*, No. 15, December 1959, Oliver Lebus wrote: 'My father was Master of the Guild for the year 1953–1954. On his death my brother (Anthony) and I felt that we would like to have some permanent memorial to him at the Furniture Makers Guild.'

Sir Herman had been one of a group of leading men in the industry to campaign to establish the Furniture Makers' Guild alongside the ancient City Livery companies such as the Goldsmiths and the Merchant Taylors. The Livery was granted on 6 March 1963. Its objective was 'fostering the ancient craft of furniture making in the United Kingdom in such manner as is calculated to advance the standard of technical design and knowledge of those in the craft and generally to direct the design of furniture to the benefit of the community'.

'It seemed fitting wood should play an important part in the design,' commented Oliver in the article. The main part of the head and shaft was made from turned and polished yew. Mounted on opposite sides of the head of the mace were the arms of the Furniture Makers' Guild and the arms of the late Sir Herman Lebus, CBE, JP in parcel-gilt and enamelled silver.

The presentation was made at the Annual Guild Dinner held on 13 April 1959 in the presence of the Lord Mayor of London and the sheriffs.

Anthony Lebus Elected Master of Livery Company, 1967

Anthony Lebus was elected master of the Worshipful Company of Furniture Makers in May 1967. To mark his election, Anthony, then aged 53 and deputy chairman of the firm, presented the Livery Company with 'a modern silver loving cup and cover,' reported the *Tottenham and Edmonton Weekly Herald*, 26 May 1967. 'The cup, which has three handles and a cone-shaped stem, bears an engraved decoration in the form of dovetails and the arms of the Company,' continued the article. The Livery Company was the 83rd to be granted since the reign of Queen Anne, who first granted Livery status, and it was indeed another fitting tribute to Sir Herman for Anthony to be elected, just six years after Herman's death, to the role of master to the company he helped to establish.

Lebus Cake for the Prince of Wales General Hospital in its Centenary Year

On Monday 20 February 1967, Oliver Lebus presented a cake made by Dennis Osborne, chief catering manager at the firm's canteen, to the children of the Prince of Wales General Hospital at Tottenham. Originally made for the firm's furniture exhibition the previous week at Maddox Street, the cake (24 lbs of Madeira sponge) was decorated with five pieces of iced Capitol furniture (the firm's then-current line of products). The firm had supplied all the furniture for the nurses' home and Oliver was an active member of the Tottenham Group of Hospitals' Management Committee.

Princess Margaret's Visit – Wednesday 10 April 1968

'Princess Margaret in spring outfit visits Lebus factory' was the headline in the *Tottenham and Edmonton Weekly Herald*, 12 April 1968. The author took great delight in describing her outfit: 'A two-piece in chunky knit brown and pink tweed with knee length skirt, a large matching hat trimmed with a broad brim of brown velvet, and brown leather accessories and a shocking pink jumper!' Although not of such high profile as the Duke of Edinburgh's visit 13 years before, it was another of those special occasions to celebrate in the history of the firm. 'The Princess was received by Alderman Vic. Gellay, Mayor of Tottenham, who was wearing his chain of office. After a short chat he went off to change and she later met him again at work in the Laboratory as a physicist specialising on furniture finishing developments,' read the article.

Oliver Lebus presents a cake, complete with iced furniture shapes, to children at the Prince of Wales Hospital, High Road Tottenham, Monday 20 February 1967. The cake was made by the company's chief catering manager for the Harris Lebus furniture exhibition in Maddox Street the previous week

This was the last celebration at the firm at a time when the future still looked good. Within two short years, in February 1970, the firm announced that it was closing down at Tottenham. Despite overwhelming sadness, it was a time for employees to celebrate the good times of the past. Sissy Lewis takes up the story (*Furnishing the World*):

> The shop stewards were called into the office and we were told that we would go in groups according to how long we'd worked there. Those who had worked there the least would go first and then down the line. I was one of the last to go with a number of other girls. The oldest Lebus son (Anthony) had us in his office and said how sorry he was. We all talked about the old times. He cried. He thanked us all for the years we had worked there. Oh dear, it was sad. Part of my life had gone. Fortunately, we got full pay from January and being made redundant in May, plus I got a thousand pounds.

> We walked out and went over to the Pavilion and had our own little parties.

Oliver Lebus with Princess Margaret on her visit to Harris Lebus, 10 April 1968

Postscript:
Tottenham after Lebus –
Lebus after Tottenham

Tuesday 5 March 2013, Victoria Road, W8

I was sitting in Oliver's study with Peter (LS's son) and Tim (Oliver's son). Piles of archived material weighed down a fold-away table. We had chosen this day at random – it was convenient for all. Tim, who had just finished gathering together the last of Oliver's Lebus archives, had invited me to meet with him and Peter, to see if I wanted to pick out any useful information for this book. As we were chatting, I casually asked Tim for the date Oliver had passed away – I knew it was around this time of year. Tim confirmed in response: 'It's coming up to the anniversary of my father's death any time now'. Then, as he looked in his diary to check, he said 'It was four years ago today!' Just another of those curious coincidences…

Tottenham Hale's Changing Landscape

Tottenham Hale industries collectively employed thousands

Just as the migration of Harris Lebus from the city to Tottenham Hale had set a precedent for other furniture manufacturers, the closure of what had been the largest furniture factory in the world – and by implication, the largest in the vicinity – would set another. The decline and withdrawal of industry from Tottenham Hale was slow at first. Ron Turton recalled how

for a while Merchandise Transport continued and 'went to the Standard at Walthamstow: Lebus had a unit there. Lebus had their own lorries, and they'd contract off at Wades, a bit further up the road (40 Ferry Lane)'. Ron believed some employees went to work at Gestetner. With social housing planned, other industries gradually left: Bamberger's at Ferry Lane Wharf, which handled timber and employed many in the 1950s, came and went; Millington's stationery factory also closed in 1970; Eagle Pencils (now Berol Limited) undertook a gradual move to Kings Lynn from 1978 onwards and the works closed fully in 1992; the Gestetner company was sold to a Japanese firm in 1996 and closed down soon after.

Hale Village

In June 2008, almost 40 years after Lebus left Tottenham Hale, *Village News*, produced by the developers, Lee Valley Estates, commented: 'Passers-by in Ferry Lane can see three tall cranes in place with heavy earth-moving plant in constant action. Work forges ahead to transform the former… industrial site into Hale Village, a sustainable urban community that will push forward the long-term regeneration of Tottenham Hale.'

Some of the names in Hale Village reflect the area's heritage and pay tribute to the

INTERNAL TELEPHONE LIST

COMBINED NORTH AND SOUTH - IN CASE OF FIRE DIAL 222

From: P.J. Brignell.
O.&.M. Dept.
January 1970.

DIRECTORS

213	Bennett, K.P. Mr.	257	Evans, D. Mr.	282	Parfitt, N. Miss.
207	Brown, A.F. Mr.	319	Everson, E. Mr.	348	Parford, E. Mr.
201	Dean, K.J. Mr.		**F**	283	Personnel Dept.
202	Grosbard, L.A. Mr.	257	Factored Dept.	284	Pidduck, L. Mr.
203	Lebus, A.H.H. Mr.	240	Factored G.I.	341	Pipefitters.
204	Lebus, O.H.H. Mr.	251	Field, P. Mr.	290	Pitcher, G. Mr.
205	Mahlich, R.J. Mr.	221	Foot, B. Miss.	346	Power House.
200	Boardroom.	219	Forrest, F.E. Mr.	311	Print Polishers.
	A	339	Franklin, A. Mr.	318	Production Control.
241	Accounts Department.	316	Furguson, D. Mr.	353	Production Eng.
337	Allen, S. Mr.		**G**	279	Purchase Department.
242	Assembly F'Man.	352	Garage.	327	Q.&.R. Control.
	B	251	Gaw, E. Mrs.		**R**
350	B.Shop Table Sect.	250	Gettleston, J. Mr.	287	Rainbird, H. Mr.
331	Boiler House.	260	Gibbins, W. Mr.	239	Rawlinson, R. Mr.
215	Brown, A.F. Secretary.	254	Goodfellow, D. Mr.	288	Reception.
244	Brignell, P.J. Mr.	264	Goods Inwards.	275	Robshaw, S. Mr.
206	Brimmer, K. Mr.	265	G.P.O. Operators.	227	Rollings, D.H.B. Mr.
216	Bruce, S.H. Mr.	266	Greening, F. Miss.	313	Rose, W. Mr.
332	Bull, Mr.	231	Griffin, R. Mr.	233	Rostgaard, C. Mr.
333	Burton, A. Mr.		**H**		**S**
317	Burton, R.F. Mr.	330	Hairdresser.	292	S/A's. Page, F. Mr.
	C	268	Hammond, J. Mr.	293	S/A's Ledwith & Harris.
208	Canteen W/H.Kitc.	243	Hatton, D. Mr.	294	S/A's. Matthews & McCarthy
321	Canteen Kitchen.	269	Higgins, W. Mr.	347	Saws.
324	Canteen Snack 1.	270	Hilsdon, R. Mr. (Kent)	280	Silk, D. Miss.
323	Canteen Snack 2.	312	Hughes, P. Miss.	228	Simmance, H. Mr.
334	Carrington, A. Mr.		**I.J. & L.**	279	Solari, R.A. Mr.
246	Cash Office.	356	Imber, W. Mr.	357	South Gate.
322	Catering Manager.	250	Jackson, A. Mr.	273	Spires, M. Mrs.
298	Chazalon, R. Mr.	342	Jigmakers.	295	Sports Pavillion.
273	Clarke, E. Mr.	224	Jewell, A. Mr.	342	Squires, D. Mr.
329	Crampton, D. Mrs.	343	Laboratory.	315	Stokes, J. Mr.
248	Creasey, E. Mrs.	272	Lenton, J. Mr.	351	Surgery.
283	Crump, G. Mr.	355	Levett, L. Mr.		**T**
249	Cullington, D. Mr.	320	Loading Floor Office.	345	T. Shop Repairs.
218	Curran, J. Mr.	345	Loveday, R. Mr.	215	Thatcher, S. Mr.
	D		**M**	299	Thomas, J. Mr.
335	Daniels, J. Mr.	212	Maclean, A.H. Mr.	353	Thornton, A. Mr.
230	Davies, D. Mr.	310	Mail Order, C.S.D.	332	Timber Inwards Plng.
336	Design Development.	325	M/C. Shop Engineer.	296	Time Study.
337	Devon, R. Mr.	274	M/C. Shop Foreman.	297	Time Study.
252	Dickie, J. Mr.	252	Merchandise Transport.	298	Transport Gate.
253	Dorling, P.M. Mrs.	277	Milan, D. Mr.	263	Traylen, N. Mr.
338	Drawing Office.	337	Mill.	256	Trew, E. Mr.
211	Dunne, C. Mr.	279	Mote, F.C. Mr.		**U. & W.**
	E		**N**	225	Uff, J. Mrs.
349	Eagle, C. Mr.	346	Nash, W. Mr.	278	Wages.
217	Edwards, P. Mr.	281	North Gate.	289	Waring, T. Mr.
340	Electricians.		**O.P. & Q.**	279	Wilkins, N,O. Mr.
255	Embling, F. Mr.	322	Osborne, D. Mr.	247	Williams, S. Mr.
259	Engineers Stores.	358	P. Shop.	354	Wilson, F. Mr.
				344	Wise, R. Mr.
				245	Wyatt, R. Mr.

The last internal telephone extension list, found amongst Oliver's personal archives; I imagine he unpinned this from his noticeboard on the last day at Tottenham

Lebus has left the building

Lebus family and its contribution, not just to the community's local history but to the furniture industry as a whole and to that of the twentieth century's two world wars. The main thoroughfare has been named Lebus Street and, on Waterside Way, there is a building named Albermarle Court, after one of the types of war aircraft produced by the firm. (I can see why they didn't opt for a Mosquito Close.)

At one stage, just before the last leg of building work, I was allowed into the site and I am convinced I found the clay tiles forming part of the foundations that once supported the Sir Herman Lebus Sports Pavilion; the distinct shape was evident in the footprint. The building work is now finished and the transformation from industrial to residential use complete.

The Lebus Business

Lebus Upholstery – Silver anniversary in Woodley, 23 July 1975

On 23 July 1975 the *Reading Post* had a double-page spread to celebrate 25 years of Lebus Upholstery in Woodley ('Lebus Silver Anniversary: Celebrating 25 Years of Upholstery Production at Woodley'). At that point, 465 people were employed in Lebus Upholstery and Anthony and Oliver were heading the firm. Turnover was around £15 million and the future looked rosy. Frank Woolliams, who was part of the team in 1954, was now assistant managing director. Ken Jury, who had joined 23 years ago, was now foreman. Besides Frank, the team in 1975 comprised Ken Barrett (managing director), Ian Fraser (marketing director), David Copeland (development manager), Alan Thorngate (production director), Richard Willmott and Rex Butters. And when Tottenham closed and cabinet-making ceased, 'Mac' Maclean and Cyril Rostgaard stayed on as sales director and design director respectively. In the *Reading Post* article, Rostgaard said:

Lebus Upholstery silver-anniversary pull-out, *Reading Evening Post*, July 1975, left to right: Ian Fraser, Frank Woolliams, Ken Bennett, 'Mac' Maclean, Oliver Lebus, Cyril Rostgaard, Alan Thorngate, Richard Willmott, Rex Butters

The Tudor 3-piece suite in traditional style covered in rayon and cotton tapestry.
Recommended retail price with 2-seater settee £169. With 3-seater settee £189 (including VAT)

NEW DESIGNS IN COMFORT

The Milan 3-piece suite in the voluptuous Italian style covered in easy-care Boccara.
Recommended retail price £379.00 (including VAT)

Advertisement for three-piece suites, *Reading Evening Post*, July 1975

Scandinavia has always been responsible for influencing fabric designs… in recent years Italy has been a tremendous influence on designs… Germany has always been a major influence in furniture design. Ninety percent of all cabinet-making equipment is made in Germany. They were responsible for inventing chipboard. We don't attempt to be 'avant-garde' we just attempt to interpret design trends.

Inevitably, the article looked back nostalgically; in 1950 there had been just two delivery trucks and by 1975 there was a modern fleet of 50. During the early 1950s, a young couple could have furnished their home for £350; now it would cost more in the region of £1,500. The article quoted Ian Fraser, marketing director: 'Today the lounge is used by the kids, dad, mum, friends at all times and the furniture has to take a lot more wear'. In 1975, a white melamine and teak finished suite comprising of the latest four-drawer, knee-hole dressing table and 'his' and 'hers' wardrobes with mirror cost £193 with VAT.

However, by the end of the decade the company was in trouble. Former employee Shirley Hiscock said:

> I was there until 1981 – when we were bought out. I've been in contact with a couple of friends recently. We all had the opportunity to buy our machines, which I did! And a few more girls did. I think I paid £125 for it – which was a lot of money then – but it has done well and is still going. I use it to make scatter cushion covers for our local cancer charity shop. The factory still stands to this day – it is now a 'Go-Cart park' – I think the carts go around the old machine shop!

Another former employee, Dave Lewis, said:

> The reason it went under was because most of its products would be for catalogues… and the cost of sending it to someone's home, and then having to collect it if they did not like it, was too much. At the time furniture was being imported – much cheaper than we could make it, so we were all out of a job. I went on to work in London for some of the top designers in the furniture world and even today I still have an upholstery background – I design VIP aircraft seats.

By the late 1970s, the firm's finances were under increasing pressure and in July 1979 it

was sold to PMA Holdings, a company owned
by Malcolm Meredith. He had built up a group
of furniture businesses including Gower
Furniture and Bridgecraft Upholstery. However,
Meredith may not have appreciated just how
difficult trading had become. When there was
a further drop in demand for furniture in the
1980–1981 recession, PMA itself went into
receivership in 1981. Some 120 years after
Harris Lebus started trading in Tabernacle
Street, the company ceased trading and was
finally wound up in 1982.

The Lebus name did not disappear from
the furniture industry. The receiver sold
the trade name to the Christie-Tyler Group,
which like PMA owned a number of furniture
manufacturers. However, Christie-Tyler also
became a victim of the changing shape of
furniture retailing. Following the demise
of two of its major retail customers, Allders
and Courts, Christie-Tyler also went into
receivership in 2005. Lebus Upholstery was
bought out by its management and makes sofas
and recliners at its plant in Scunthorpe. In a
way, the name had come back to its origins.
Scunthorpe is only 25 miles south of where
Louis Lebus arrived in Britain from Wroclaw in
the 1840s and had started his cabinet-making
business.

Once a Lebus boy, always a Lebus boy: appreciation from Peter Baker

'To announce that you were a "Lebus boy" was
almost a guarantee of employment,' said Peter
Baker in a reminiscence piece written for the
author. He continued:

> It was also the 'management training
> ground' for the industry. In later life and
> at other factories, I met many others who
> were extremely proud of the fact that
> they were also 'Lebus boys'. In fact, it was
> purely because of my Lebus training that
> I was equipped to work as a management
> consultant for some twenty years. I shall
> always be proud to claim that I am a Lebus
> boy. My training there has always enabled
> me to earn a good living, whether 'at the
> bench' or as a management consultant.
> [Writing in 2013] I am currently a director
> of a small furniture company in the East
> Midlands which has an unwritten motto
> of 'Only the best is good enough'. I have
> completed the circle in the most beautiful
> business with the most beautiful product
> ever, and all because 'I had decided to
> go into industry' after National Service.
> Thank you, Sir Herman and Harris Lebus.'

The Lebus Family

Sol's line of descendants:

Sol and Esther

Sol and Esther had two boys and one girl: LS (born 1894), Bob (born 1897) and Helene Pearl (born 1898).

Bob Lebus

Bob retired when the partnership was dissolved in 1947. Oliver mentioned to me in conversation that Bob had a restaurant in Brighton afterwards. He never married and died in 1959.

LS Lebus

LS married Edith Anne Mannheim and had one girl and two boys: Pat (born 1929), John (born 1932) and Peter (born 1934). LS was 89 when he died on 27 October 1983.

John Lebus

John joined Harris Lebus in September 1956 with a degree in economics from Cambridge, studied at High Wycombe Technical College and gained industrial experience in a factory in the United States, at Venesta, the Metal Box Company, and Furniture Industries Ltd.

Peter Lebus

Peter joined the company in November 1958 with a degree in engineering, also from Cambridge, a year's experience in the USA, mainly in Chicago (at Ecko, a light engineering firm), a course on operational research and a stint with a furniture retailer.

Harris's line of descendants:

Louis Lebus – A tribute

Tucked in a drawer amongst Oliver's archives was a rather special book. It had a hardbound red-leather cover and was about 18 inches high and 12 inches wide. The pages are 'nice jotting paper' style; to describe it as a rather classy scrap book would not do it justice. The first page informs the reader what it is: a

Family group, November 1959; Louis makes a rare visit since his retirement twelve years earlier. He is pictured with his nephews, Anthony and Oliver (left to right), in the front row; LS is in the middle of the back row with his sons, John and Peter (left to right).

presentation book from the Furniture Trades Benevolent Association to thank Louis Lebus for his contribution and work to steer the association as chairman from 1941 to 1947. It was all done with hand calligraphy in black and red ink, and with various illustrations taken from annual reports over the years, depicting the various institutions established to support those in need. The middle pages contain original signatures of all the members of the board; each person has signed the page using their favourite pen and ink – all in different shades of blue and black. It is a stunning artefact, both visually and in terms of its historical merit.

The Annual Report 1974 of the Furniture Trades Benevolent Association paid this tribute to Louis:

On 13 January 1974, the Association suffered the sad loss of its Treasurer – Louis Harris Lebus. He had served as treasurer for nearly 30 years. His interest in the Association, his kindness and humanity made Louis Lebus many friends and, although in committee he could be firm when the situation demanded firmness, his conclusions were always accepted as being wise and humane and commanded the respect of his fellow committee members.

Among other things, he was architect of the division of the company into areas. He devised this scheme during his term as national president and introduced it after the Second World War.

A 'Lebus' had held the post of treasurer since its inception in 1903 – Harris was the first. Oliver has consented to carry on the tradition.

Louis had retired when the partnership was dissolved in 1947. He lived in an apartment at the Savoy Hotel, London with his wife, Elizabeth, known as Claire. They had no children. Claire died in 1968 several years before Louis. The *London Evening News* reported: '17 February 1969, Latest Wills, £1 million estate left by woman: Mrs. Elizabeth Lebus, of the Savoy Hotel, London, wife of Mr. Louis Lebus, retired manufacturer, left £1,077,052 net (duty paid £830,587)'. After personal bequests amounting to £2,500, she left the residue on trust to her husband for life and then to the grandchildren of the late Sarah Harris Lebus.

In late 1959 Louis had made one (perhaps his only) visit to the factory following his retirement – he was photographed flanked by his nephews, Anthony and Oliver, and with his cousin LS and LS's two sons, Peter and John.

Sir Herman Lebus

Louis's brother, Sir Herman Lebus, as we know, died still holding tightly onto the reigns. He married Ethel Hart, who was born in 1887 and who died in 1976. They had two boys and one girl: Anthony Hart Herman Lebus (1914–1983), Barbara (Barbie) (1916–1993) and Oliver Hart Herman Lebus (1918–2009).

Anthony Lebus

Anthony married Barbara (Bunty) Hedley and had two girls and a boy: Rosemary (born 1946), Philippa (born 1948) and Richard (born 1950). Following Oxford, he served in the Royal Marines during World War Two. He had been a justice of the peace for Essex, president of the British Furniture Manufacturers' Federated Association and served as master of the Worshipful Company of Furniture Makers in 1967–1968. Anthony died on 4 September 1983 at the age of 69.

Oliver Lebus

Oliver was born in the last year of World War One and went to Cambridge in 1937. He joined the Royal Signals in World War Two. He married Barbara (Squawck) Selz and had one girl and two boys: Miranda (born 1948), Timothy (born 1951) and William (born 1953).

Oliver took the Ministry of Labour Course in Business Administration and joined Harris Lebus just as it became a public company in 1947. Oliver was sales director for 13 years, becoming chairman in December 1960. He devoted his entire working career to the business.

He was master of the Furniture Makers in 1979–1980 and was a member of the management committee of the Tottenham Group of Hospitals and on the House Committee of the Prince of Wales General Hospital, Tottenham. He had been on the council of the Royal College of Art and a member of the National Advisory Council on Art Education. Oliver was on the executive board of the Furniture Trades Benevolent Association and was London area president for three years – he was still a management committee member when he died on 5 March 2009.

Last Words

'In virtually two generations the business had grown from the smallest beginnings and become by far the largest furniture production unit in the country with 30 acres on the south side of Ferry Lane with a covered floor space of a million square feet and ten acres of land on the north side of Ferry Lane'. This was the last sentence written by LS. His last words left the history of the business frozen in the year 1947. Now, supplemented with newly researched information providing an account of the public company years – which spanned a further thirty years, all told – this rich and fascinating history is, for the very first time, complete.

Have I done justice to LS's wish to see the history of Harris Lebus preserved and made accessible to those who want to delve into this prodigious story? Have I answered questions for some, stirred thoughts and conjured memories for others? I hope so.

To think 'Harris Lebus' is to evoke many thoughts: factory and furniture, manufacture and enterprise, workshops and employees, local history and world-wide influence, 'the largest furniture factory in the world'… and the romance of bygone days. Depending on individual perspective, interest, insight, knowledge, taste even, it may be to revel in the notion of 'the gentle art of cabinet-making', with images of hand-carved,

individually crafted, vintage styles – dressers and sideboards, tables and chairs, wardrobes, chests of drawers, dressing tables, all with heavily stained and French-polished finishes. Alternatively, perhaps, it may conjure images of mass-produced, plywood-backed, dark-cellulose-finished 'utility' and functional pieces that seem somewhat dated. For some, Harris Lebus means Handley Page, Vickers Vimy and Mosquito aircraft, and Hotspur and Horsa gliders, all engineered in wood. And for some, maybe the Link and Europa furniture ranges of the 1950s and 1960s. I wonder now what other chapters may have followed had the restructured company's fortunes fared differently, in a new-town site, with robot-made Europa furniture pieces – ironically, the style of furniture in this branding, just like that of Gomme's G-Plan range, is now back in vogue in retro interiors.

I have dedicated this book to Oliver Lebus, with whom I had a special bond during the initial research stage. His son, Tim, has continued that which his father gave to me – support and practical help – as have LS's sons, Peter and John, who have been of huge support to me throughout and have provided me with encouragement through my good days, and exercised patience through my not-so-good days. This is for their father.

List of Main Sources

History of Harris Lebus 1840–1947 (unpublished), Louis Sol Lebus, 1965, Ashmele family online

The Cabinet Maker and Complete House Furnisher (various dates)

The Development and Structure of the Furniture Industry, J. L. Oliver

Furnishing the World: The East London Furniture Trade 1830–1980, Pat Kirkham, Rodney Mace and Julia Porter, 1987

The History of the Ancient Parish of Tottenham, Fred Fisk, 1923

'How Lebus Turned Round', in *Management Today*, July 1968

How Things Were: Growing-up in Tottenham 1890–1920, Tottenham History Workshop, 1982

Immigrant Furniture Workers in London 1881–1939 & the Jewish Contribution to the Furniture Trade – A Supplement, William I. Massil, 1997

The *Jewish Chronicle* online archives

Lebus furniture catalogues

The *Lebus Log* in-house magazines

National census records online

Reminiscences gathered by Deborah Hedgecock and Hazel Whitehouse, Bruce Castle Museum (Haringey Archive and Museum Service) with Coombes Croft Library Reminiscence Group, 2007

The Times online archives

Tottenham and Edmonton Weekly Herald

'Tottenham: Public Services', *A History of the County of Middlesex: Volume 5*, A. P. Baggs et al., 1976